JACK
NORTHROP
AND THE
FLYING
WING

JACK
NORTHROP
AND THE
FLYING
WING

THE STORY BEHIND
THE STEALTH BOMBER

TED COLEMAN
with Robert Wenkam

PARAGON HOUSE
New York

First edition, 1988

Published in the United States by

Paragon House Publishers
90 Fifth Avenue
New York, NY 10011

Design by Stanley S. Drate/Folio Graphics Co. Inc.

Manufactured in the United States of America

Library of Congress Cataloging-in-Publication Data

Coleman, Theodore, 1903–
  Jack Northrop and the Flying Wing / by Theodore Coleman. —— 1st ed.
    p. cm.
  Bibliography: p.
  ISBN 1-55778-079-X
  1. Northrop, John Knudsen, 1895–1981. 2. Aeronautical engineers——United States——Biography. I. title.
TL540.N595C65 1988
338.7'62913'0092——dc19
[B]   87-37198
                                                                                  CIP

For Jack and his family

CONTENTS

FOREWORD

I was closely associated with Jack Northrop for a period of almost fifty years. I first knew him while I served as a Director of the Douglas Aircraft Company and Jack was the Chief Engineer of their important El Segundo Division, which he founded. I became very close to him while serving as Chairman of the Northrop Aircraft Inc. Board of Directors following World War II, after I resigned my position as President of the Vultee Aircraft Company. I continued on the Northrop board long after he retired, and was instrumental in having him return to the Northrop Corporation as Director Emeritus. Our association continued until he passed away in 1981 at the age of 86.

Without question, Jack Northrop was the most talented, and at the same time, the most sincere and gracious person I have ever met. Like all of us, he did have his faults, but in spite of them he had the outstanding ability to look far into the future, and to persevere in spite of the many serious obstacles placed in his path by those who lacked his vision.

Jack was not only a fine aeronautical engineer, in spite of a lack of formal education in the field, but he had the wisdom to surround himself with those with great ability, and encourage them to work together as a team. He was as well regarded for his progressive industrial relations policies as he was as a designer of superb airplanes. As a result, the Northrop Corporation became known as a very good place to work.

I shared one very sad experience with Jack Northrop. I refer to the various conferences we had with high government officials and with Floyd Odlum, Chairman of the Board of Convair, in 1949, leading to a decision to discontinue the financial support of work by the Air Force for the spectacular YB–49 flying wing Bomber. This unhappy occurrence was indirectly responsible for Jack's premature retirement from the company in 1953.

With due respect for the very able management team, which since Jack Northrop's retirement in 1953, has rebuilt the company into one of the country's leading aerospace firms, I can truthfully say that it was a real tragedy, and a loss to the country when the Northrop flying wing that Jack Northrop so diligently pioneered was dropped for lack of governmental financial support. Let us hope that a new flying wing will be resurrected again, and that Jack Northrop will receive the credit for it he so richly deserves.

RICHARD W. MILLAR
Pasadena, California

PREFACE

I t is impossible to imagine, unless you were there, how a highly
successful designer and builder of lethal military weapons could
have emerged from a soft and delicate embryo, the product of an
idealistic engineering genius who was born to create, not to destroy.

Like the eagle soaring gracefully from its nest, high on a cliff, a
modern corporate giant does have a heart.

This is the story of Jack Northrop and his early associates who
shared his dream of a Flying Wing, who created and led this giant—a
corporation whose principal products and services came from a demand for the most effective and deadly military weapons systems its
engineers and scientists could devise.

In no way was Jack Northrop responsible for this demand, nor
could he be criticized for the role his company played in a modern
world gone berserk, seemingly with an insane desire to destroy itself.
These men, and the Northrop Corporation, have often been the vic-
tims as well as the beneficiaries of the politics of military procurement.

I knew the men who created this giant intimately. I was one of
them.

TED COLEMAN
Pasadena, California

ACKNOWLEDGMENTS

I am most grateful for the valuable assistance and encouragement I have received from innumerable friends and associates while gathering the facts and writing this history of Jack Northrop and his flying wing.

Dr. Ira Chart, retired Northrop historian, and his associate, Jack Manion, 45-year Northrop employee and a retired Vice President, were of particular help in making documents and valuable pictures taken by veteran company photographer, Roy Wolford, available to me.

I also appreciate the encouragement and help I received from Welko Gasich, a senior Northrop corporate vice president, and from veterans Darrell McNeil, and Irving Ashkenas, aerodynamicist. Arthur Phelan, the original chief engineer for Northrop's innovative Tyrbodyne gas turbine engine project, was most generous in supplying me with authentic information about this ill-fated Northrop project.

Valuable suggestions were made to me by Dr. John Rae, aviation historian and Professor Emeritus, Harvey Mudd College. Reviews by Dr. Robert Middlekoff, former Director of Pasadena's Huntington Library, and by Dr. Lance Davis, Professor of economic history at Caltech, were most helpful.

Max Stanley, chief engineering test pilot on the flying wing bomber projects, who spent more time piloting Northrop flying wings than any other person, has been most cooperative, and he voluntarily contributed his extensive knowledge to this story. I have also received valuable comments from former test pilot John Myers, who took my place as Vice President-Sales when I left Northrop in 1946, and from Gil Nettleton, who worked directly with John at the time the flying wing projects were dropped by the Air Force.

My friend, Carlos Wood, retired Vice President and Chief Engineer of the Sikorsky Division, United Aircraft, and one of Dr. Theodore Von Karman's early students at the Guggenheim Aeronautical Laboratory of Caltech, was most helpful in supplying personal information about this famous scientist who became Jack Northrop's principal consultant during World War II. Von Karman's former pupil, Dr. William Sears, a Caltech graduate student who became chief of aerodynamics for Jack Northrop in 1941 and was closely involved in the flying wing developments, has contributed to my story. Dr. Sears was later nationally recognized as Director of Cornell University's aeronautics department and continues to be active as a professor at the University of Arizona.

My friends, John Northrop, Jr. and his sister, Bette Johansing, son and daughter of Jack Northrop, have been most helpful in supplying me with personal anecdotes and recollections about their father. John also supplied me with innumerable family pictures, heretofore unpublished.

Richard Millar, a Northrop business associate and friend for over half a century, who as Chairman of the Board in 1949 participated with Jack in vital conferences with Air Force officials and Floyd Odlum at that time, graciously volunteered to write a foreword for this book. There is no one living today who is better qualified to tell the true story of exactly why Northrop lost government financial support for the big YB–49 flying wing bomber, and I feel privileged to have him participate in this project.

I am also grateful to Arthur Neff, for introducing me to Robert Wenkam. Bob's great writing ability and his enthusiastic support has made this book possible.

Harvey Christen, a friend and old time Lockheed pioneer, who was associated with Jack Northrop in 1927, volunteered valuable information about their early days together at Lockheed.

I particularly wish to thank my former private secretaries, P. J.

Everett, who encouraged me to undertake the project, and Dorothy Lasher, who greatly assisted me by typing the original manuscript.

Above all, I am grateful for the continuous encouragement I received from my loving wife, Anne, who laboriously proofread my text and put up with my repetitive narrative of events as I recalled them from memory, or found them recorded in my ancient diaries.

CHRONOLOGY

Chronology of aircraft designed by Jack Northrop, aircraft and aerospace equipment manufactured by the Northrop companies, and major events in the Northrop companies.

Year	Aircraft	Company
1916	Participated in design of Loughead S.1.A seaplane.	Loughead, Santa Barbara
1920	Designed Loughead S-1 *Sportsplane.*	Loughead, Santa Barbara
1923	Participated in design of Douglas *Cloudster* "Around the World Cruisers."	Douglas, Santa Monica
1926	Participated in design of Charles Lindbergh's "Spirit of St. Louis."	Ryan, San Diego
1927	Designed Lockheed *Vega.*	Lockheed, Burbank
1928	Designed first prototype flying wing. Developed all-metal, multicellular, stressed skin design.	Avion, Burbank
1930	Designed Northrop *Alpha*, first all-metal aircraft designed by Northrop.	Northrop subsidiary of United Aircraft, Burbank
1931	Designed Northrop *Beta.*	Northrop, Burbank
1933	Designed Northrop *Gamma.*	Northrop subsidiary of Douglas, El Segundo
1934	Designed Northrop XFT-1, first low-wing, all-metal U.S. Navy fighter.	Northrop, E. Segundo

Year	Aircraft	Company
1935	Designed Northrop *Delta*. Designed Northrop 3-A, first low-wing, all-metal U.S. Army Air Corps pursuit.	Northrop, E. Segundo
1936	Designed Northrop BT-1 dive bomber for the U.S. Navy, the Douglas *Dauntless*.	Northrop, El Segundo
1937	Designed Northrop A-17 attack aircraft for U.S. Army Air Corps.	Northrop, E. Segundo
1940	Designed the first true flying wing, N-1M *Jeep*. Designed the Northrop N-3PB patrol bomber. Subcontract for Consolidated PBY *Catalina* tail surfaces. Awarded production contract for Vultee *Vengeance* aircraft. Subcontract for Boeing B-17 *Flying Fortress* engine nacelles and cowlings.	Northrop, Hawthorne
1941	Designed Northrop P-61 *Black Widow* night fighter, first with radar. Awarded U.S. Navy contract for development of first gas turbine aircraft engine, the *Turbodyne*. Awarded contract for design of first flying wing bomber, the Northrop XB-35.	Northrop, Hawthorne
1942	Designed Northrop XP-56, all-welded, magnesium, tail-less fighter. Contract for conversion of V-72 *Vengeance* dive bomber into A-31 attack aircraft for U.S. Army Air Corps. Began delivery of P-61.	Northrop, Hawthorne
1943	Designed MX-334 rocket-powered, flying wing military interceptor. Designed JB-1 pilotless flying wing *Buzz Bomb*. Designed XB-79 *Flying Ram*. Armor-plated flying wing interceptor for ramming.	Northrop, Hawthorne
1944	Designed J-10 pilot-less *Jet Bomb*.	Northrop, Hawthorne
1945	Designed X-4 *Skylancer*. Northrop, Hawthorne	
1946	First flight of XB-35 flying wing bomber. Designed *Snark*, first jet-powered cruise missile guided by onboard computer. La Motte Cohu, Gage Irvine, and Ted Coleman resign.	Northrop, Hawthorne
1947	Designed Northrop *Pioneer* transport and U.S. Army assault aircraft C-125 *Raider*. Designed jet-powered version of flying wing bomber, YB-49.	Northrop, Hawthorne

Year	Aircraft	Company
1948	Last aircraft designed under direct supervision of Jack Northrop, the F–89 *Scorpion*. Work begun on conversion of piston engine powered XB-35 into jet-powered YB-49. Transcontinental non-stop speed records established by YB-49 flying wing bomber. YB-49 crashes at Muroc with Captain Glenn Edwards aboard. Plans made to subcontract YB-49 work to Consolidated Vultee. All flying wing Air Force contracts cancelled. Eleven scrapped. Consolidated Vultee receives contract for strategic B-36 bomber.	Northrop, Hawthorne
1950	Air Force cancels *Turbodyne* jet engine development contract. Production begins for *Snark* missile with MEDIDA guidance system.	Northrop, Hawthorne
1952	Jack Northrop resigns. Replaced by Ed Schmued.	Northrop, Hawthorne
1955	General Echols retires. Replaced by Whitney Collins. Tom Jones joins Northrop as Director of Engineering Planning.	Northrop, Hawthorne
1956	Northrop N-156 fighter designed at company expense. Later to become the F-5 *Freedom Fighter.*	Northrop, Hawthorne
1958	Northrop T-38 *Talon,* advanced supersonic trainer developed.	Northrop, Hawthorne
1959	Whitney Collins dies. Tom Jones becomes President and General Manager. Company name is changed to Northrop Corporation. Overseas aircraft service company organized. Northrop T-38 *Talon* becomes standard Air Force supersonic trainer. Last of F–89s and *Snarks* delivered.	Northrop, Hawthorne
1960	Northrop F-5 first flown.	Northrop, Hawthorne
1962	Northrop F-5 goes into large-scale production. Modified versions of the F-5 still being manufactured and sold. Tom Jones becomes Chairman and CEO. Northrop diversifies with new electronics division and new east coast avionics subsidiaries.	Northrop, Hawthorne
1970	Northrop P-553 *Cobra* advanced fighter first flown.	Northrop, Hawthorne

Year	Aircraft	Company
1974	Northrop YF-17 prototype becomes U.S. Navy carrier fighter as Douglas F/A-18. Subcontracts for manufacture of Boeing 747 transport fuselage.	Northrop, Hawthorne
1981	Northrop awarded contract to develop ATB Stealth bomber.	Northrop, Hawthorne
1982	Northrop develops F-20 *Tigershark* fighter at company expense.	Northrop, Hawthorne
1983	Northrop awarded U.S. Air Force contract for IMU guidance system for MX missile.	Northrop, Hawthorne
1985	Two F-20 *Tigershark* fighters crash and test pilots killed.	Northrop, Hawthorne
1986	U.S. Air Force puts F-20 in direct competition with General Dynamics Convair F-16. Northrop receives no contract for F-20. Political pressure mounts to continue production of Rockwell B-1B bomber and cut funds for Northrop ATB Stealth.	Northrop, Hawthorne
1987	Northrop awarded ATF development contract with McDonnell Douglas. Northrop awarded first production contract for ATB Stealth B-2 bomber. Northrop F-20 program cancelled.	Northrop, Hawthorne
1988	First Northrop ATB Stealth B-2 bomber completed.	Northrop, Hawthorne

JACK
NORTHROP
AND THE
FLYING
WING

1

THE DREAM COMES TRUE

It took off by itself. Northrop test pilot Vance Breeze was making a high-speed taxi run on Baker Dry Lake near the Nevada border when Jack Northrop's small scale flying wing hit a rough spot on the hard sand, bounced into the air about ten feet above the dry lake surface, and flew several hundred feet without difficulty before Vance brought the aircraft back down for a safe landing.

Observers compared the accidental first flight of the flying wing to the Wright Brothers first hundred feet at Kitty Hawk and were reminded of Howard Hughes taking his giant flying boat, the Spruce Goose, into the air three feet above Santa Monica Bay when he had only intended a taxi run. It was the only time the Spruce Goose flew, but for the engineers watching the Northrop N–1M flying wing prototype actually take to the air, the flight was an inspiring recall of the Wright Brothers experience almost forty years earlier. On that California day, they saw the reality of Northrop's dream of flying wings come true, and the beginning of a new era of advanced aircraft design they were confident would influence aviation for decades to come. It was July 3, 1941.

There were still doubters in the aviation fraternity. Northrop's fellow aircraft engineers at Lockheed and Douglas, while admiring Jack as a designing genius, were quite skeptical of his flying wing ideas and had often suggested that Jack not "waste his time" on such a radical approach to flying. Northrop persisted.

Many years earlier, at the very beginning of his career in designing aircraft, Jack had become convinced of the fundamental aerodynamic principle realized in the flying wing design—that an all-wing aircraft would be substantially more efficient than conventional airplanes with encumbering fuselage and tail surfaces sticking out at the rear. These unnecessary surfaces only created friction and drag, without substantially contributing to the lift or the plane's ability to fly. Drag reduces airspeed. Overcoming the drag with additional horsepower only made the flying machine less efficient and reduced its load carrying capacity. A plane's efficiency is measured by comparing its lift to the drag—known as the lift-to-drag ratio. If the lifting forces are high compared to drag forces, the plane will fly faster and further with the same payload. What is ordinary in aircraft today, Jack had invented many years earlier for use in his record breaking *Vega* and *Alpha* airplanes, the first truly streamlined planes of their era. He discovered in the process that there was a limit beyond which drag could not be further reduced in conventional designs.

Jack needed a new approach to flight. Remembering the birds of his youth, gliding and diving in the air over Santa Barbara beaches, retracting their legs up against the body in flight, twisting their wings to turn and bank in the sky and then float effortlessly back onto the beach, he thought of an airplane with only wings. The gulls, as he recollected, were mostly all-wing. This appeared to be the natural way of flying. He demonstrated to his friends the flying skills of birds by folding pieces of paper into the shape of a flying wing. Launching the paper glider, he admired its graceful flight for some distance until it glided smoothly back to earth.

Dr. Theodore Von Karman, one of the world's leading authorities on aerodynamics, and his Caltech protege, Dr. William Sears, agreed that Northrop's flying wing concept was practical, and would be a necessary evolutionary breakthrough in aircraft design. At the time Jack designed the little N–1M, his competitors were convinced that a pure flying wing could not be adequately controlled in flight—there was no way a pilot of any skill or experience could safely fly such an aircraft. Jack was seemingly unaware of this problem, preferring to approach designing aircraft as an art, not as a dry and complicated science. Perhaps because he did not possess an aeronautical engineering degree, he was not discouraged by what conventional thought decided was impractical.

He was quite impatient with younger colleagues who wanted to solve engineering problems the easy way, which meant a conventional design contributing little to improved methods of engineering. Jack had no respect for an engineer whose solution to a design problem was "to invent rubber gloves to use with leaky fountain pens," as he said more than once. His staff soon learned they should not go to the boss with a problem unless they were also bringing a proposal for a solution.

Jack's designs, and his detailed engineering solutions, were characterized by ingenuity, engineering efficiency, and incredibly effective use of space. Nothing was wasted—everything included was part of the system. He never hesitated to employ new materials and processes that would further his search for the most compact and effective solution. Jack firmly believed that if something is efficient and beautiful it is right, a principle that guided Northrop throughout his professional career. The prototype flying wing N–1M was beautiful, like a bird.

After his first freehand sketches were completed, actually nothing more than thoughts with a pencil, Jack prepared a detailed drawing for his aerodynamicists to check out, although his staff had already informed him that since no flying wings had been flown before, there was little to check out as to potential performance and stability analysis. In 1939 computation of dynamic stability was beyond the knowledge of aeronautical engineers, and even if useful equations had been available, the calculations would have been impossible to do in a practical time frame using the mechanical calculators and slide rules of the day. His staff did their best to check out the obvious, and were satisfied that the flying wing would fly with the predicted weights. The center of gravity was located in the proper position. The downturn of the wingtips as in Jack's original sketch would help prevent the aircraft from stalling in a spin, and they fully expected the plane to spin, since every aircraft designed in those days fell into a spin with the slightest provocation. Their work was done in the old Hawthorne Hotel building before new Northrop engineering offices had been built, using tables and chairs available in the unused hotel lobby.

There was no mention that Jack's flying wing concept might have followed earlier efforts in Germany. No one knew that at the time. His engineers' analyses were not based upon anything previously designed because there was no aeronautical literature existing on how to design a flying wing or calculate its performance. They did not think of comparing the seed pods spinning down from elm trees in autumn as possible prototype aerodynamic characteristics for a flying wing. Jack's airplane was a totally new airplane.

"All calculations were done with slide rules," recalls early aerodynamicist Herb DeCenzo. "We only had two small manual calculators in engineering. We got our numbers off to two decimal points or three percent, which was as good as our theories. We made calculations the hard way, and it would take us three or four days to figure out the consequences of a particular angle of attack for the wing, with the span-wise load calculated so we would not get into anything like a wing tip stall, which would be a serious problem in a spin.

"We worked out some equations on our own. Von Karman worked on equations on a black board with no notes or anything, writing up difficult equations just out of his head, picking up his cigar every so often, muttering to himself, ashes falling on his vest. He would walk up and down, study it and look at it and study it some more and make a few changes and work out a procedure that took only an hour and a half, as compared to the two or three days we were taking. And Von Karman's method was more accurate. Differences between the quicker Von Karman method was zero, a little bit more than the width of a pencil line on my desk."

Northrop's engineers constructed a small scale model out of balsa wood, with a wing span of about 15 inches, carefully balanced, which they took to the Pasadena Civic Auditorium to fly. Jack launched the flying wing model from an upper balcony to the engineers below so they could observe the plane spinning. It wouldn't spin. Jack tried to make the model spin by putting it into a hard spiral when he threw it into the air, trying his best to spin the craft by launching it at higher and higher angles of attack, but the flying wing model refused to spin and always recovered normal flight before landing on the floor. Jack threw it over and over again many times into the still auditorium air, before everyone was satisfied that the model would not spin.

The Northrop wood shop made another small model out of white pine for tests to be conducted at the Pasadena Junior College wind tunnel, because the Caltech tunnel was not available. Their wind tunnel was not much bigger than the tunnel the Wright Brothers had, but tests were successfully completed in two weeks by a junior college professor, with Von Karman driving over from nearby Caltech from time to time, looking in on the procedure. At the conclusion of these tests, another model was made with flight controls that could be moved to overcome or neutralize any spin, for testing in the more sophisticated vertical NACA spin test wind tunnel. Nor could NACA get the flying wing model to spin more than a quarter turn. The engineers were convinced, even without calculations to prove it, that Northrop's airplane would be safe to fly. The flying wing would not spin in, a common problem with planes of those days, making the flying wing N–1M perhaps the safest plane of its time to fly.

Actually, the first flight of the N–1M was observed with some trepidation by the engineers assembled on the dry lake at Muroc. After the first taxi tests it was discovered by test pilot Vance Breeze that the plane could hardly get off the ground. It was overweight, as later calculated, by some 200 pounds. None of the engineers seemed to have learned that fact during designing and building. Weight and balance was all right, but it was overweight. The N–1M would get off the ground and fly straight ahead several feet up, but in no way could the pilot lower the nose or climb or do anything else. Adjustable pitch propellers didn't help. Full throttle did nothing. Changing the original four-cylinder Franklin engine to a six-cylinder engine with more horsepower finally got the plane off the ground and into full flight. The propeller was also changed from two blades to three. With the exception of these mechanical substitutions, no changes were made in the original configuration of the flying wing as drawn by Jack. The center of gravity never changed from the calculations by Von Karman.

The little 30-foot miniature flying wing was incredibly sleek in flight with its tricycle landing gear retracted, disappearing completely inside the wing. The twin 65-horsepower, air-cooled Monasco engines, each connected by a drive shaft to three-bladed pusher propellers at the rear, were buried in the wings. The pilot also sat within the wing, with only his head appearing above the airfoil surface inside protective streamlined Plexiglas. It was made of plywood so changes in shape and moving parts could be easily made and the plane could again be tested in flight. As the pilot's safety was always a concern of his, Jack provided each propeller with a spring-loaded brake operated from the cockpit, to stop the propeller from windmilling should the pilot be required to bail out over the wing's trailing edge during an in-flight emergency.

Six months later, on December 6, 1941, while aircraft carriers of the Imperial Japanese Navy prepared to launch dive bombers and torpedo planes for an attack on Pearl Harbor, a demonstration flight of the N–1M flying wing was arranged for newsreel cameramen and the southern California press, again at Baker Dry Lake.

Newsmen and Northrop were anxious to tell the world about the graceful little aircraft without any body—only a streamlined wing that photographed like a sharp knife cutting through the air. The all-wing aircraft flew well that day in the hands of veteran pilot Moye Stephens, chief test pilot for Northrop. Those present for the first scheduled flight were impressed by the demonstration and predicted a favorable future for the efficient, radically new design. The small group of observers were visibly excited as the aircraft took off smoothly and flew close to the newsreel cameramen and reporters.

Jack Northrop was obviously very pleased, as his dream of so many years flew gracefully in the skies overhead. He stood alongside Dr. Von Karman, hands folded together across his waist, confident and pleased. Von Karman consulted often with Jack, helping him solve design problems unique to his flying wing. Von Karman worked closely with his former star pupil at Caltech, Dr. William Sears, who had been hired by Jack as the Northrop Chief of Aerodynamics. It was Von Karman who suggested that the wing tips be bent down at a shallow angle from the horizontal main structure, after wind tunnel tests indicated this design would make for a more stable aircraft. As a result the N–1M presented a decided bat-like appearance and was quite photogenic.

The N–1M, standing for "Northrop's model 1," had been designed and built at company expense. It was a private aircraft not subject to national security restrictions. While high-ranking officers of the Army Air Corps had already seen the spectacular little plane, they had not indicated much interest in placing purchase orders. The Assistant Secretary of War, Chief of the Army Air Corps, and Commander of the Air Material Command, all visited the Hawthorne plant during 1941 to see the new airplane and confer with the designer, Jack Northrop. Staff planners at the War Department were unable to think of any military application for the experimental N–1M at the time, and the one-of-a-kind aircraft was not considered a secret by the military. As news photographers packed their equipment away for the long drive back to processing laboratories in Los Angeles, they were sure their dramatic newsreel pictures would create a sensation in movie theaters across the nation, where films of the flying wing were already scheduled to be shown.

The next day, December 7, 1941, the world changed. Pearl Harbor was bombed and war news crowded everything else from the front pages and newsreels. Before the day was over, the United States had declared war against Japan and the Axis powers. The still photographs and movies of Northrop's flying wing never appeared in the newspapers or on the theater screen. Not a word was printed. The military, belatedly remembering Jack's little flying wing out in the desert, quickly classified the aircraft and his flying wing designs top secret. The public was told nothing about Northrop's experimental work on all-wing airplane projects that were thereafter financed by the Army Air Corps and kept secret until long after World War II.

Jack Northrop and his engineers had been working on the flying wing since the first day his new company began manufacturing operations in 1939. For the first time in twenty-two years of designing airplanes for others, he was his own boss, and his dream of the world's most efficient airplane—a true flying wing—had come true, in spite of the skepticism of most of his earlier associates in aviation.

With war clouds gathering over the Pacific and Atlantic Oceans, the military brass were now expressing considerable interest in Jack's flying wing creation. General Henry "Hap" Arnold, Chief of the Army Air Corps, had been a friend and admirer since the days immediately following World War I when, as an enthusiastic young Army Air Service pilot, he had flown the first airplane Jack had designed, the Loughead S–1 sports biplane. During a 1920 sales demonstration, the S–1 was an honored visitor in the Bay area. On several flights it flew directly from the paved plaza in front of the San Francisco city hall.

General "Hap" Arnold later flew the Northrop designed Lockheed *Vega*. Like all pilots, such as Amelia Earhart and Roscoe Turner, who had the opportunity to fly the record breaking *Vega*, he expressed the opinion that the high-wing *Vega* monoplane was years ahead of any other aircraft built and flown, at a time when wood and fabric biplanes were still commonplace.

In search of a long-range bomber capable of striking Germany from the continental United States, the generals returned to the Northrop plant at Hawthorne. The Battle of Britain was at its peak and Nazi armies were poised across the English Channel, ready to invade. Military planners in the United States were deeply concerned with the potential problems facing America if Great Britain should fall to Hitler's Nazi Germany. It was a worse-case scenario that involved waging intercontinental war from bases in the western hemisphere. Jack's unique N–1M flying wing design might finally have a practical application.

General Arnold had recently flown many hours in the Air Corp's A–17 attack bomber, designed by Jack Northrop when he worked as chief engineer for the Douglas Northrop Division and was a great admirer of Jack. He now saw in the prototype flying wing, so successfully demonstrated in the desert, a possible future long-range bomber. With other top brass he met with the four principal Northrop Aircraft company executives, Jack Northrop, chairman LaMotte Cohu, vice president Gage Irving, and myself, to discuss such a possibility.

The group agreed that a large, long-range, fast bomber with a flying wing configuration like the N–1M, would be an ideal solution to the problem facing them. London was being bombed and the Royal Air Force was having a difficult time against superior German forces. Should it become necessary for the United States to carry on the fight against Germany alone, these same officers would have the awesome task of carrying on the war in Europe from bases in the United States. It would be necessary to bomb Europe directly, flying nonstop from the East Coast. No airplane then existing had a range sufficiently long to make such a trip and return.

Secretary of War Robert Lovett and the generals decided that a large flying wing bomber should be designed, built, and tested by Northrop. Because this might take more time than designing and testing a conventional bomber, another manufacturer should be invited to meet the same long-range, load-carrying specifications. It was anticipated that the conventional bomber would be ready for production at an earlier date, but if the flying wing bomber proved to be the superior performer, it would replace the more conventional bomber at a later date.

The Northrop bomber would be called the XB–35, X for experimental, and the conventional bomber designated the XB–36. Specifications for both were identical: an aircraft that could carry 10,000 pounds of bombs for a distance of 10,000 miles (the equivalent of flying from the United States to Germany and back) without refueling. The cruising speed was to be in excess of 240 miles per hour.

Throughout aeronautical history, the classic way to achieve longer range has been to build a bigger airplane. It was easily seen that a conventional aircraft like the XB–36 would probably meet the Air Corps' requirements, but it would need to be a very large and expensive aircraft. This was not Northrop's way of doing things, so the Army Air Corps' listened carefully when Jack explained to them how he would actually exceed the 10,000 miles–10,000 pounds specification with a much smaller, four-engined flying wing.

In early 1942, Northrop received War Department contracts to design and build two XB–35 flying wing bombers and four one-third scale flying prototypes of the big wing, designated N–9M. The smaller models were to fly first to obtain useful flight data, before the two larger XB–35 aircraft were flown. Northrop later received a contract for an additional thirteen YB–35 operational aircraft.

The several flying wing contracts that were awarded to Northrop by the U.S. Army Air Corps during World War II were classified secret. The public had no opportunity to learn of the progress being made in developing the Northrop XB–35 bomber and its record breaking jet-powered successor, the YB–49, an advanced aircraft that in 1947 broke every aeronautical record in its class.

Consolidated Aircraft of San Diego, predecessor to General Dynamics Convair Division, was awarded the contract to construct a conventional XB–36 bomber, beginning the competition for military contracts between Northrop and General Dynamics that continues to the present day.

The unfavorable outcome of the flying wing bomber contracts, following government and corporate collusion, eventually resulted in destruction, by order of the Air Force, of the eleven Northrop built flying wing YB–49 bombers awaiting final assembly on the ramp at Hawthorne. This greatly influenced Jack Northrop's early retirement from aviation. The wanton destruction of his flying wings, by order of the government, undoubtedly contributed to his death.

During the six year period, 1983–88, it is estimated that the United States government will have paid over $12 billion dollars to Northrop to start all over again—to design and build the first Northrop ATB Stealth bomber, an advanced technological flying wing strategic bomber based on the same aerodynamic principles developed by Jack Northrop in his flying wing bombers destroyed by the Air Force 45 years earlier.

2

AN ENGINEERING GENIUS CALLED JACK

From the very early days of the infant aircraft industry, Jack Northrop, then a young man in his teens, was recognized as an airplane design genius. His skills were first revealed when he was working for the two Loughead brothers, Allan and Malcolm, who, in 1916, opened a small shop near Northrop's home, at the foot of State Street near the beach in Santa Barbara.

They were building by hand, in the manner of the day, a small flying boat to take paying passengers on sightseeing trips over the bay and town. The small shop was named Loughead Aircraft Manufacturing Company. The brothers had moved to southern California from San Francisco, where they ran a successful business taking visitors to the 1915 World's Fair on flights over the fair grounds and San Francisco Bay in the first seaplane they had built. They now intended to build a larger flying boat to take tourists for their first airplane rides in southern California.

The outbreak of World War I in Europe, where flying was used by the military primarily for reconnaissance, had sparked the public's imagination. Barnstorming pilots, flying in their wood and fabric biplanes (some resembling the Wright Brothers original machines), were doing a thriving business. The Loughead brothers would launch their new seaplane from the beach and use the ocean as an airport. The tourists were waiting.

A local architect friend of his father hired Jack Northrop fresh out of Santa Barbara High School when he graduated in 1913, bringing with him considerable skill in math and drafting. Jack had earned his way through school working at an automobile repair shop in the same building housing Loughead's fledgling aircraft organization. Jack was a frequent visitor in the shop, fascinated by the airplane slowly taking shape, curious about everything going on, watching with keen interest the construction underway. When Jack realized the two Lougheads were building their airplane without any engineering drawings, actually attempting to solve structural problems as they were encountered, he offered to help, telling them his current work as an architectural draftsman was somewhat boring and pointing out how he would be able to save them time and money by making stress analysis of the various aircraft components before they were fabricated. He would be able to prepare complete engineering drawings for their seaplane.

Jack later recollected,

I had a little experience as a garage mechanic and I worked a year as a draftsman for an architect and I worked for my father who was in the building business and this sort of qualified me to design airplanes, you can understand . . . The Loughead's plane was just being built sort of by guess and by golly. When I got there I was given the job of designing the wing struts. I hardly feel I was qualified, but at least the wings didn't come off.

Jack was hired immediately. Allen was the pilot and promoter, and his brother Malcolm a highly skilled mechanic. Working as construction foreman for the brothers was Anthony Stadlman, a Czechoslovakian immigrant, whose skills were all-important to the enterprise. Jack joined the team as a very enthusiastic employee, determined to learn how to build airplanes. In 1916 there were few college degrees offered in aeronautical design. A high school diploma, some inventive skills, and ambition was all that was necessary. These attributes were present at the age of 16 when Jack watched a French pilot assemble his small airplane in a grassy field near town.

The pilot took off and, after flying around to the delight of everyone watching, this French birdman landed safely on the lawn in front of the Potter Hotel in downtown Santa Barbara. Jack thought he could improve on the flimsy looking flying machine constructed of wood and fabric held together by a maze of wires, and resolved to do so. The high school drafting board and automobile repairing were but preparatory steps in expanding Jack's early aptitude for inventive concepts. He loved to experiment with mechanical devices, and in his mind he was already improving what others had designed.

The Wright Brothers had made their historic first flight at Kitty Hawk a year before Jack Northrop arrived in Santa Barbara in 1904, when he was nine years old. Jack was born in Newark, New Jersey in 1895, the only child of Charles Wheeler Northrop and Helen Knudsen Northrop. Charles was a down east Yankee, and Helen was born of a Norwegian father and American mother. It was her second marriage. As a widow with two sons, Roy and Donald Lippincott, she had married Charles Northrop, and Jack grew up with two slightly older half brothers. Their father had bequeathed some money for the education of his own sons and they both went on to college. Jack's father was less prosperous so Jack decided to seek work after graduating from high school and not depend on his father for support. The lack of an academic education was no deterrent to Jack Northrop, as his eventual sketches for futuristic aircraft were not to be inhibited by knowledge of what could not be. As a young man his visions of flight were to be inspired not by engineering theory, but by observing soaring birds in the sky overhead.

The Charles Northrop family left Newark when Jack was very young, and moved out west in stages, first to Chicago, and then on to Lincoln, Nebraska, where Jack's father secured work as head of the book and picture department in Lincoln's leading department store. But they enjoyed the outdoors, and the flat, uninviting farm country around Lincoln proved unsuitable for their favorite pastime of hiking and camping. When the Northrop family learned that California offered considerably better opportunities to be at the beach or in the mountains, they planned to move on. Santa Barbara had gained a reputation as being the ideal place to live. Charles took the chance that he could find a job in the distant city. Using the small savings he had been able to accumulate, the family moved to California, where Charles found work as a carpenter.

Jack said,

I have really only one clear memory of Nebraska, outside of the fact that it was a pretty dreary place to live—at least we all felt it was at the time—flat country, either too cold or too hot and very little to see . . . . The family heard of a stream that was called the Big Blue, which was fifteen miles out of town, and so after a great deal of saving and planning, my Dad hired a surrey and a couple of horses. Lunch was packed and we all, with great expectations, went out to have a picnic on the Big Blue River. When we got there the Big Blue was about four feet wide and three feet deep and was a muddy creek. So, that's the way Nebraska affected all of us.

Jack's father built a two room tent-house with wood floor and stud frame covered with canvas, in a canyon close to the beach that offered enjoyable recreation, and yet was not far from town. Soon after the family's arrival, young Jack joined a local Boy Scout troop, where he furthered his interest in hiking, camping, swimming, and canoeing, remaining an active scout for many years. He was particularly fond of fishing and boating. The family rode bicycles until Charles was able to buy a five-passenger Overland touring car in 1912. Within a few years Charles Northrop was a contractor with his own building business in the growing southern California economy.

Jack was always more relaxed with close friends and family, seldom being involved in team sports or social activities where large numbers of people were involved. He had a fine sense of humor and conversation was easy with close friends. Developing a love of music at an early age, he learned to play the ukulele and accordion, enjoying the fun of accompanying the family in frequent evening songfests.

Jack enjoyed high school.

In those days there was only one Santa Barbara High School. I feel now that we worked a lot harder in high school than they do these days. I believe that the high school training I received was the sort of thing you would expect in a junior college at this time. Of course, my grammar and high school education, outside of the school of hard knocks, was the only education I ever had. I didn't go to college. I didn't have any correspondence courses, or anything of this sort. But at Santa Barbara High School they had good courses in math, physics, chemistry, mechanical drawing, all of the scientific subjects which were of great interest to me and later proved of value. I owe that school a great deal for the job that they were doing for their students in those days. Math, of course, was absolutely essential. Physics was very good. Geometry was almost essential. Chemistry was useful in many, many ways in later years. They had an excellent course in algebra. And I was good in this kind of thing. I wasn't particularly good in English, languages or any of the other so-called advanced intellectual courses.

*   *   *

An exciting present awaited Jack upon his graduation from high school. Augustus Knudsen, a cousin of Jack's mother, lived in Hawaii, where he owned a large cattle ranch on the south shore of Kauai island. He invited Jack Northrop to join his family on the island for three months. Jack's interest in the outdoors made the vacation an outstanding experience. At the time, Kauai was relatively undeveloped with only large cattle ranches and sugar plantations, and Jack spent considerable time exploring the island, staying in Knudsen's cabin high in the Kokee mountains and hiking on trails overlooking Kalalau Valley. He hunted wild feral goat and pig, went thrownet fishing with the natives, and learned how to surf on the long boards provided by his newly found Hawaiian friends.
Jack recalled,

They had a huge cattle ranch there and a home near the beach at Waimea; also a mountain home near Kokee. I was given the opportunity of going there directly out of high school and spending three months as a member of the family. It was an unique, character-building and body-building experience that I feel favorably affected the rest of my life in many ways. The island of Kauai, as most people know now, was probably the least developed and at that time there were very few people living there except native Hawaiians. . . . The area I was active in included the Waimea Canyon and the Kalalau Cliffs, which provided the most gorgeous scenery and the most wonderful hiking, hunting, and fishing you could possibly imagine . . . There were also wild cattle, which had developed from strays and could be hunted; and there were many wild goats. In fact, there were so many wild goats that they were denuding the foliage on the more rugged parts of the island. Before my vacation ended I was offered the job of official wild goat hunter if I cared to stay on, because I was pretty good with a rifle. I didn't stay, but you can imagine the pleasure of hiking, of horseback riding, of exploring this type of country and having an opportunity to hunt when the hunting—using a new word—was *ecologically* advantageous. It was something that needed to be done and you didn't feel that you were destroying animals that should be left alive. They were not an endangered species. They endangered the island of Kauai.

His new job with the Loughead brothers had stimulated his earlier interest in airplanes and flight but, unlike so many other young men,

Jack showed little interest in becoming an aviator. He preferred to tinker with the family automobile, make his own boat, and be involved with the mechanical end of the activity, whatever it was. He liked to work with his hands and particularly enjoyed mechanical drawing and sketching. He kept a drawing board at home where he would sketch new ideas for airplanes that excited his imagination. The habit continued for the rest of his professional life, and some of Northrop's most famous planes were first conceived as a sketch on his personal drawing board. After becoming an executive with his own large company, Jack continued to keep a drawing board in his private office: paper, pencils, and slide rule at the ready. The practice became a Northrop trademark.

On his own, Jack studied all he could learn about stress, structures, and strength of materials, acquiring an ability to quickly find the answer in a handy book when his own knowledge proved insufficient. Problems encountered on the job made for a rapid learning experience, and he soon became a valuable employee. With Jack computing possible damaging stresses, the Loughead seaplane could be dragged over the beach and into the water without damage, then flown and landed safely. Up to the time Jack introduced his engineering skills to the firm, very little thought had been given to the large amount of stress imposed on the fragile airplane structure during a severe storm, or in sudden aerial maneuvers. After Jack designed the wings they were sure to stay on, and Jack stayed on the job as the Loughead's only engineer, proving his worth in spite of an absence of previous aeronautical experience.

The Loughead's next project was a larger, ten passenger, twin-engine biplane, called the Loughead F.1.A., finished about the time the United States entered World War I. This larger airplane attracted many celebrities to Santa Barbara to fly over the bay and circle the nearby mountains on flights with Allen Loughead at the controls. Among these passengers were the King and Queen of Belgium, whom Jack met after their flight. With the United States at war and needing warplanes, the now well-known Loughead Aircraft Manufacturing Company was awarded a contract to build two Curtiss HS2L flying boats.

With World War I continuing, Jack was drafted into the Army, taking his basic training at Camp Lewis in Washington. When the military learned of his aeronautical experience, he was transferred to the Army Signal Corps, which at the time was the aviation branch of the army. Before long it was realized that Jack's special engineering skills were more importantly used in building warplanes, and Jack was furloughed back to his employer at Loughead in Santa Barbara to help with construction of Curtiss flying boats for the Navy.

After the war ended in 1918, Jack continued working with the Loughead brothers. He designed his first airplane for them with the help of Anthony Stadlman, the Loughead's construction foreman who had become a Loughead partner. It was a small civilian sport biplane called the Loughead S-1 sportplane, incorporating several innovative Northrop features in its design.

Tony Stadlman had seen one of the best German fighter planes, the Albatros D.Va, when the plane was brought to San Francisco for exhibition after the war. The Albatros was the plane flown most often by the famed German ace, Manfried Von Richtofen, and, as an outstanding fighting plane, was largely responsible for Germany's domination of the air during World War I. The Albatros design, which incorporated perhaps the first fully streamlined, wood molded fuselage, aroused Jack's curiosity. With the help of Stadlman, Jack adopted the same feature when designing the Loughead S-1. Similar in appearance to the Albatros, the Loughead sportplane was constructed with the smooth monocoque fuselage carrying all stresses and loads in the molded plywood skin. The mold into which the smooth streamlined plywood fuselage was placed during construction was made of concrete. The plywood skin was shaped against the concrete mold by inflating a balloon inside the mold while the plywood was still wet. Each of the plywood sheets making up the completed fuselage was glued together while firmly held in the mold in order to retain the semicircular shape. The two upper and lower halves of the fuselage were then glued together. It was a most ingenious process, one worked out by Stadlman after studying the original Albatros.

The biplane wings were constructed of wood ribs on spars in the conventional manner, and covered with fabric. Only a minimum of struts and wires were used, for even at this early date Jack recognized that clean, smooth lines were essential for an airplane to fly efficiently. One noteworthy feature not on the Albatros was a narrow lower wing that could be rotated by the pilot while in flight, slowing the plane down for landing, perhaps the first "flaps" on any airplane. The S-1 cruised at 75 miles per hour, but could be landed safely at a speed as low as 30 miles per hour. Landing into the wind the sportplane would roll to a stop within a few feet. Northrop had remembered the sea gulls landing at Santa Barbara, watching them twist their wings almost to a vertical position in order to slow their flight for landing on the water. He reasoned that his airplane could also do the same if he designed the wing accordingly. In doing so, he invented wing flaps. Jack also designed the wings so they could be folded alongside the fuselage, making it possible for the plane to be stored in a garage or towed down the highway to the airport.

The Northrop designed Loughead model S–1 was the first of over fifty airplanes designed by Northrop with innovative features far ahead of their time, features that within a few years were to become standard design elements on every aircraft built. Jack's competitors affirmed twenty years later that, "Every airplane which flies today has some of Jack Northrop in it."

Unfortunately for the Loughead brothers and Northrop, the S–1 was designed and built a decade too soon. It was ill-timed. At a sale price of $2,500 the sportplane could not compete on the market with hundreds of surplus military JN4 Jenny trainers, available new in original shipping cases as war surplus for as little as $400. Not a single S–1 was ever sold.

The Loughead aircraft manufacturing business in Santa Barbara closed its doors in 1920. Malcolm took the train to Detroit where he was successful in manufacturing hydraulic brakes for the new automobiles then appearing in large numbers on the road. Allan, the pilot and promoter, became a Los Angeles real estate developer and salesman. There was little money to be made in aviation in the early 1920s. Even barnstorming around the country in the surplus Jennys never paid well, and Allan was not going to fly any Jennys. Jack went back into architectural drafting and helped his father design and build homes, working with his father for the next three years. When even the building business experienced financial trouble in 1923, both Jack and his father left to seek work elsewhere.

Three years after leaving the Lougheads at Santa Barbara, Jack found work with Donald Douglas in Santa Monica. The ambition as a young man out of high school remained, however. He wanted his own aircraft factory where he would be able to design and build his own airplanes. Many of the unique features in the Loughead S–1 sportplane, with its streamlined monocoque fuselage, later formed the basis of the Lockheed *Vega* high wing monoplane, which Northrop designed on his own time, using the drafting board he kept at home. He showed the design to Lockheed in 1926 while working for Douglas, explaining that he was looking for an aircraft company to manufacture his new airplane.

Jack had met and fallen in love with an attractive girl, Inez Harmer, while they were in high school together. She was the daughter of a well-known artist, Alexander F. Harmer and Felicidad Abadie, a descendant of one of the early California Spanish families. They waited until Jack was self-supporting before being married in 1918, after he had been discharged from the Army and was working full-time for the Lougheads. They were married in a Catholic ceremony performed in the historic Riverside Inn, in Riverside, California.

The Northrops had three children: a son John, and two daughters, Bette and Ynez. Jack was close to his children and enjoyed reading them stories at bedtime. The children have fond memories of the pleasant evening hours spent at home, after homework was completed, listening to their father read his favorite children's stories: Tarzan of the Apes, The Wizard of Oz, and almost all of the magazine serials by popular author, Clarence Buddington Kelland.

The children developed a fondness for classical music as a result of listening with their father and mother to Sunday symphony concerts on the radio. Jack always helped Inez in the kitchen, insisting on cooking breakfast Sunday morning, refusing to eat himself until everyone in the family had finished. He cooked the entire meal, which always ended with hot syrup on pancakes or waffles.

While the children were growing up, the family enjoyed vacations together in a mountain cabin they built at Lake Arrowhead in 1931. Jack was an enthusiastic fisherman, and spent many relaxing hours trolling for lake trout and bass, perhaps marveling at their streamlined bodies all the while. He also taught the children how to water ski. His son, John, recalls that he made an 8mm home movie with the help of his dad, giving it the title, "How to Water Ski in Six Easy Dunks." Jack was an avid movie fan, and on weekends he took the entire family to previews of new movies in Hollywood. Providing for recreation at home, he built a miniature bowling alley in their Baldwin Hills residence. In 1966 the close-knit family was shattered by a tragic automobile accident that claimed the life of daughter Ynez, her husband, and their two children.

The older daughter, Bette, was a very attractive young lady. Whenever she visited her father at the Hawthorne Northrop plant, there was much commotion as workers stopped to stare. Bette later married a successful insurance broker, Paul Johansing. They have eight children and twenty-eight grandchildren.

Son John married Mary Bohmner, and they also have a large family. One son is a Catholic priest. John did not follow in his father's footsteps and join his company as an aeronautical engineer, although he undoubtedly would have enjoyed the work. Both father and son decided he would be at a disadvantage if he joined his well-known dad at the Northrop company. Neither did he wish to work for any other organization and compete against his father in designing airplanes. Later, while working for the Matell Company, he developed many toy construction kits and flyable model airplanes, including a small flying wing that flew as well as his father's famous aircraft.

3

THE GOLDEN AGE OF AVIATION

Aviation in the United States came of age after World War I. In its mid-adolescence only 15 years after Kitty Hawk, aviation emerged from the war ready for adventure. Having fought duels in the sky in flimsy fabric and wood warplanes, and winning a war in the process, aviators would never be content with the ordinary again. There was a fascination with flight that seemingly had no limits in a land searching the sky for the newest hero to fly overhead, looking for aerial records to be broken—records never before imagined.

Then came the dramatic solo flight by Charles Lindbergh, across the Atlantic to Paris in a single engine Ryan monoplane. The country turned airminded with a vengeance. The beginning of airmail routes across the country, barnstormers flying war surplus military trainers out of farmers' fields, primitive airshows at state fairs with airplanes racing automobiles, all contributed to an enthusiasm for aviation that gave every visionary a chance to dream.

In the 1920s, commercial aviation, long a crawling child in the United States, grew up quickly, as investors and the government together began to realize its potential. The rumblings of distant war, already being heard in the 1930s, led to new interest in military aircraft. Combined with civilian uses, a peacetime aircraft industry slowly emerged as flying for sport and business changed a pygmy enterprise into a growing industrial giant.

America invented aviation, but was slow in its commercial application. Within a year after the Armistice was signed in Europe, air passenger service was already underway in Germany. Twelve months later the British were flying passengers between London and Paris. It took several years for American post office officials to determine the best way to fly airmail. Airplane designers and aircraft manufacturers who managed to stay in business after war contracts were cancelled were finally rewarded by congressional legislation designed expressly to encourage the growth of commercial aviation.

It all began with General Billy Mitchell sinking the surrendered German battleships with a 1920s Martin bomber and a report inspired by Secretary of Commerce Herbert Hoover. The result was the Air Commerce and Air Corps Act, both of 1926. Combined with the Kelly Airmail Act of the year before, these laws provided the legal and economic basis for an aviation industry, setting up a Bureau of Aeronautics (predecessor of the Civil Aeronautics Administration) for commercial aviation and providing for renewable military contracts by initiating 5-year purchase programs. The government prepared the foundation for rapid technological advance in aviation to be implemented by young aircraft designers with little more than dreams, small change in their pockets, and the desire to build an airplane in the garage next door.

The first aeronautical engineer in the United States, Grover Loening, graduated in 1911, but times were still favorable for the visionary with hunches and gut feelings. It was not for a couple of decades that mathematical calculation and exhaustive testing replaced the young airplane designer with intuitive breakthroughs. Jack Northrop in his early years presided over an engineer's kitchen. He was the chef devising new dishes by taste out of traditional meat and potato combinations.

Many of the new visionaries did not remain in the chancy occupation for long. Business obstacles and personality clashes caused Northrop himself to become frustrated and walk out on several occasions and start all over again. But the thrill of flight itself, and the new discoveries to be made, was always enthralling. The opportunities for changes came so rapidly and the needed improvements were so obvious, that the academically trained engineer working slowly by the book, would for many years still be the person who only confirmed what the visionary invented.

Before 1925 the post office was still flying airmail in antiquated planes designed during the war. With new laws on the books, the postmaster was now able to contract for commercial aviation to carry airmail through a program of indirect subsidies to private operators.

Private industry would design and build the airplanes and develop a national air route system, while the government provided the incentive and necessary regulation.

The process began when bids were opened for smaller "feeder" airmail routes, and ended with transfer of the main transcontinental route from New York to San Francisco in 1927. Juan Trippe's New York to Boston Colonial Air Transport (CAT) was awarded the first contract mail route. Shortly afterward all twelve of the post office feeder routes were being flown by private operators. The transcontinental route was doled out in two slices, National Air Transport receiving the eastern half, and United Aircraft and Transport (later United Airlines), the western portion. Although CAT began carrying passengers with the mail, their planes were generally too small, noisy, slow, and generally inadequate. Lindbergh commented upon his return from Paris, "All Europe looks to our airmail service with reverence . . . but, whereas we have air lines, they have passenger lines."

Lindbergh perhaps did more for the popular cause of aviation than any other flyer in history, stimulating a series of daring aerial stunts by barnstormers, air races, and endurance flying from just about anywhere to somewhere else. There were uncounted cross-country flights, most begun and never completed, and thirty-one crossings of the Atlantic by air in the year after Lindbergh's flight. Ten were successful in reaching the other side, but twenty people died.

Chamberlin and Levine in a Bellanca reached Berlin nonstop from New York. Admiral Byrd's Fokker tri-moter *America* demonstrated that large aircraft could fly the ocean in bad weather. Kingsford-Smith's Fokker *Southern Cross* flight to Australia via Hawaii and the Fiji Islands was a significant navigational feat. Smith and Bronte took off from Oakland for Honolulu and ended up in a Kiawe treetop on Molokai Island when they ran out of gas. The two adventurers flew a newly developed air line radio beam part of the way from California. As pilots began viewing the entire world as a challenge, Wiley Post, with only one good eye, circled the globe in a single engine Lockheed *Vega* designed by Jack Northrop. Women also took part in these early aerial adventures, particularly Amelia Earhart, whose solo hops, many in Northrop-designed airplanes, caught the public imagination.

The aerial exploits, many valuable, some foolhardy and unnecessary, came to a frightening climax when in 1927, Dole Pineapple Company sponsored a 2,400 mile air race from California to Hawaii that ended in disaster. There were sixteen entries. Out of the eight heavily loaded airplanes that were finally able to become airborne at the Oakland Airport, beginning their takeoff roll from a specially prepared inclined ramp, only two arrived in Honolulu. The winner was Art Goebel, in his plane *Woolaroc*. Second was *Aloha*, but ten lives were lost in the six planes that never arrived. The first *Vega* off the Lockheed production line, designed by Northrop and named *The Golden Eagle*, disappeared over the Pacific and was never seen again.

Public opinion changed, but the interest of investment bankers did not. Aware of the aviation growth stimulated by private airmail routes in the era of Coolidge prosperity, business was in a mood to speculate and the first aviation stocks appeared on Wall Street exchanges. Their value began to climb and soon topped all others. By late 1928 there were forty-eight airways in the United States with a combined length of 20,000 miles. By 1929, aircraft manufacturers were delivering an incredible 7,000 planes a year. Individual aircraft designers began to achieve fame as their airplanes, like the Lockheed *Vega*, broke every record in the books, plus several more not previously thought of.

In the Hoover administration, Postmaster General Walter Brown urged merger of small aviation firms into large corporations, believing that, otherwise, expensive national passenger-carrying airlines would never be established. Brown sponsored the McNary-Watres Act, which authorized direct subsidies. Eighteen new airmail contracts were awarded to airlines dominated by North American, United Aircraft, and the new Aviation Corporation that was eventually to become part of General Dynamics, a move that effectively excluded most of the smaller, independent operators. Aviation Corporation soon had control of almost half the airmail routes, including more than 20,000 airline miles and several manufacturing subsidiaries. In 1930 it centralized its airline holdings under American Airways (later American Airlines), flying the new all-metal Ford trimotors.

The depression following the Wall Street crash of 1929, brought on radical changes. President Roosevelt replaced Postmaster Brown with James Farley, who lent an ear to the small airmail contractors who had been previously excluded. There was a Senate investigation and in 1934 Roosevelt cancelled all airmail contracts, asking the Air Corps to fly the mails pending reorganization of the routes. The result was disaster. By the end of the first week, five Air Corps pilots, flying unfamiliar routes in winter, had been killed, six injured, and eight planes destroyed. Inexperienced military pilots suffered so many crashes and accidents that the government was forced within a few months to return contracts to waiting private operators. With larger planes carrying passengers and mail, the nation's airline system became a thriving business and service.

Private buyers of personal aircraft entered the marketplace after war surplus Curtiss JN4 *Jennys* outlived their usefulness. Flamboyant pilots and wealthy businessmen recognized the advantages of newly designed aircraft becoming available; the Lockheed *Vega*, Stinson *Reliant*, and even biplanes for those who still felt more secure with two wings, the Pitcairn *Sport Mailwing*. Stearman Aircraft of Wichita, advertised its single engine biplane to reflect the excitement of flying your own aircraft, telling how a Texas oil operator reached his hunting club from home, "in five and one-half hours. By train or automobile the trip would take two nights and a day." A 1930 advertisement tells of how private plane customers, "Mr. Wakefield and Mr. Elkins flew off for hunting and bagged a mountain sheep a half hour after landing." Convenience was touted in a country still without many improved airports, saying, "Mr. R. F. Garland . . . made a landing within 200 feet of the clubhouse . . . rolled not over 75 feet."

Publishers discovered the private planes to be very useful, not only in reporting fast-breaking news, but in delivering their papers to widely scattered rural areas. To fly an airplane was to be progressive, important, and it provided good public relations, as well. Gilmore Oil Company sponsored an airplane and a pilot: an all-white Lockheed *Air Express* model with open cockpit and a pilot, Roscoe Turner, dressed in a pale blue military style uniform that he designed himself, flying with a mascot lioness complete with her own parachute. Roscoe Turner regularly carried celebrities to various destinations in his sleek, white airplane, everyone reveling in the publicity at every landing. As a Sunday drive in the country was becoming traditional in the family car, so was a picnic by air. Travel Air of Wichita advertised their sport biplane as excellent for a picnicking couple, complete with red wine toasts in long-stemmed glassware. An important yearly event was the National Air Races in Cleveland, where modified military planes routinely won the races until 1929, when the civilian built Travel Air Model R *Mystery Ship*, the first landplane to exceed 200 miles per hour with a radial engine, beat all contenders. The Wright Whirlwind radial engine became an international standard.

With commendable foresight or sheer luck, considering the stock market crash of 1929 was only months away, the Lockheed brothers sold out to an ambitious Detroit Aircraft Company early in the year. Detroit was trying to become the "General Motors of the Air." Jack Northrop, Lockheed's chief engineer, had left a year earlier to form Avion with Ken Jay. Gerald Vultee, who had been assistant to Jack, continued with the new management as chief engineer.

Designed for Hubert Wilkins and named in his honor, the *Explorer*, a version of the *Vega* and Lockheed's first low-wing aircraft, had been laid out two years earlier by Jack as a single float seaplane with outriggers, but engineering was never completed. The airplane was redesigned by Vultee to have much longer range in an attempt to win a $25,000 prize for the first nonstop flight between Japan and America. The wingspan was substantially increased over the *Vega* in order to lift the nearly 1,000 gallons of fuel required for the 4,500 mile distance. On one test flight, Explorer did lift off with a load of 8,500 pounds after a takeoff roll of nearly a mile.

Redesigned again with twin floats, the *Explorer* was plagued with bad luck and never succeeded in flying anywhere very far. Although problems could be expected with an aircraft designed to lift three times its own weight, the first three models built crashed for different reasons. Vultee continued to experiment with several variations of vertical rudders, including an unsuccessful overhung counterbalanced affair, in this era of "cut and try" engineering methods. The fourth and last version, built to carry a slightly reduced fuel load, made the first nonstop flight to the Panama Canal Zone, before crashing four days later. In a tragic postscript to an ill-fated aircraft, the wings from the damaged airplane, without approval of Lockheed, were mated in 1935 to an *Orion* fuselage and non-standard floats added to create the *Orion-Explorer*. It was this hybrid that crashed on takeoff in Alaska, killing Wiley Post and his flying companion, Will Rogers.

Lessons learned in developing the *Explorer* were applied very successfully to several low-wing models of similar wing span and area with a larger rounded fin and rudder. The new design was called *Sirius*, the first model incorporating many modifications specified by its famous owners, Charles and Anne Lindbergh. Dual controls were installed in tandem cockpits, which at the suggestion of Anne were enclosed under a sliding canopy, probably the first application of this device. Originally fitted with a fixed landing gear, at Lindbergh's request a retractable landing gear was installed in a new wing. Upon taking delivery of their *Sirius*, the Lindberghs almost casually broke the transcontinental speed record, flying to New York in under 15 hours, including a fuel stop. By 1930 this particular speed mark had been held successively by the *Vega*, *Air Express*, and *Sirius*. In 1931, the Lindberghs flew their *Sirius*, further modified with twin floats and a larger Wright Cyclone engine, on survey flights around the world for Pan American Airways, covering 30,000 miles over four continents, pioneering future international air routes still flown today.

A noted innovation of the 1930s was the trimotor airliner that gave the United States world dominance in civil aviation. With powerful radial engines, stronger all-metal airframes, new controllable pitch propellers, and NACA engine cowling, the modern transport came of age. William Stout's dependable all-metal Ford tri-motor, the "tin goose," led the field, Fokker's plywood and fabric trimotor having quickly lost favor after a crash in 1931 killed football coach Knute Rockne.

The first truly modern transport was Boeing's twin-engine 247 of 1933. After United Airlines had optioned all of Boeing's 247 production, preventing competing airlines from replacing their suddenly obsolete aircraft, Douglas was approached to design and build an airliner that was able to "support itself in the air financially as well as mechanically." The DC-2 and DC-3 (originally designed as a sleeper aircraft for American Airlines, replacing their fabric covered Curtiss *Condor* biplanes), first flew in 1936, the most successful airliners flying prior to World War II. Both the Boeing and Douglas airliners incorporated all-metal monocoque construction devised by Northrop and first used in his Northrop *Gamma*.

Among the pioneering aircraft designers in the early years, was Gerald Vultee, almost morbidly shy, educated as an aeronautical engineer, and, like Jack Northrop, a considerable contrast to most of the happy-go-lucky barnstormers and dashing pilots of the day. From 1926 to 1932, Vultee was with Douglas and Lockheed, where he worked with Jack Northrop on the *Vega*, completing design work on the *Sirius* after Northrop left. Early in 1932 he set up the Airplane Development Corporation in Glendale, California, where he designed a single-engine transport, the Vultee V-1, almost a copy of Northrop's *Delta*. American Airways bought ten of the planes. He redesigned the V-1 as the V-11 attack bomber, which began selling in quantity to foreign governments. The Vultee V-1A *Lady Peace* was flown round trip from New York to England in 1936 by Dick Merrill and entertainer Harry

Richman, who had the wings of their Vultee packed with 40,000 Ping-pong balls so the plane would float if forced down in the Atlantic. Vultee and his young wife died in an airplane crash in 1938. He was 38 years old.

The Stinson company, launched in Detroit in the 1930s, was the largest producer of commercial cabin planes. When Eddie Stinson and his friend, Bill Mara, decided to build airplanes, Eddie was already known as a popular pilot and his designs were looked forward to by ready buyers in the private market. Warm and likeable, he had been taught to fly by his sister, becoming a highly paid barnstormer and professional pilot after the war. His first design, the Stinson *Detroiter*, was built in a city loft one winter, the beginning of a line of versatile cabin planes that became very popular with private flyers and businessmen. A Stinson was the first to fly from New York to Bermuda and the first aircraft to explore the Greenland route to Europe. After several lives were lost in the increasing numbers of ocean-crossing attempts, Eddie refused to sell any more planes to would-be heroes. Stinson himself died in one of his own planes in 1932. Like Vultee, he was also only 38. Thousands attended his funeral, including many of the greatest flyers of the day. His company was acquired by United Aircraft and Transport.

The pioneers of the golden age of aviation were a mixed lot of designers, salesmen, builders, and fund raisers, all contributing their skills to the era. Glenn L. Martin started in aviation as a young man without a formal education in aeronautics, who built his own seaplane in a garage near his home in Orange County, California, successfully flying it himself the 30 miles across the ocean from Balboa to Catalina Island, on what may have been the first over water flight in the United States.

Initially, Martin built gliders, in 1909 completing construction of his first powered aircraft, using a Ford Model "T" engine. In 1912 he opened his own small factory in Santa Ana, where he did exhibition flying for small change and delivered newspapers as a publicity stunt in a Curtiss pusher biplane. Glenn was soon dubbed "the flying dude" for his neat dress while flying and daring low altitude exploits. Martin's career spanned the entire era of aviation's "golden age." He later became one of the nation's top manufacturers of military bombers and large flying boats.

Martin did not have the usual inventive bent of his contemporaries, but proved to be an accomplished businessman. He decided to move to the East Coast where he opened an aircraft factory in Baltimore with the help of a large investment by Aviation Corporation. At the time, in the early 1930s, Curtiss Wright in Buffalo was the only other large airplane manufacturer. The Loughead brothers had closed down their Santa Barbara factory and Bill Boeing in Seattle had not yet begun his. Sikorsky had only recently arrived in Hartford from Russia and Army Major Reuben Fleet was still to demonstrate his mettle as a super salesman. Martin hired several bright young engineers to work with him in Baltimore, including Donald Douglas, a graduate of the U.S. Naval Academy and MIT; Dutch Kindelberger, who later left with Douglas to return to California as his chief engineer; and Lawrence Bell, who joined Major Fleet and Consolidated at a new factory in Buffalo, New York.

In the early 1930s the concept of strategic bombing was not part of conventional military planning. Airplanes were considered primarily a tactical weapon, for use in close support of ground troops and observation. President Roosevelt's appointment of General Henry "Hap" Arnold, the Army's leading exponent of Billy Mitchell's strategic air theories, as Chief of the Air Corps brought into the military an entirely new official philosophy of air power. The first aircraft to satisfy this new concept, was the twin engine, mid-wing, Martin B–10 bomber, with a ceiling of 28,000 feet and speed of over 200 mph. Successful performance of the Martin B–10 led to development of Boeing's B–17 *Flying Fortress* and Consolidated's B–24 *Liberator* of World War II fame.

Glenn Martin's company built the famous China Clipper to Pan American Airways' specifications. His company won the contract as the low bidder, but then lost money building the giant flying boat. Apparently low bidding was a difficult to learn lesson, as Martin had previously lost money as the low bidder on an earlier Navy contract. During prewar years when the giant four engine flying clipper ship routinely carried airmail and passengers across the Pacific, visitors to Martin's office in Baltimore could not help noticing the large map of southern California on the wall behind his desk, showing where he had taken off from Balboa so many years before in his home-built seaplane on the over ocean flight to Catalina. The map even located his first "aircraft factory" in Santa Ana, the garage near his home. Martin was quite aware that engineering ability and financial acumen were seldom, if ever, found in the same person, saying on one of my visits with him on Northrop business, "These engineering types are not very good businessmen. They can use your help and I wish you luck."

In the beginning there were literally hundreds of small aircraft builders. Mostly begun by visionary pilots and ambitious designers with too few practical ideas beyond a desire to fly, with little hope of financial backing, only a few survived to become major aircraft manufacturers. Investors soon learned that the new companies must quickly adapt to building fully engineered aircraft capable of achieving increasingly higher levels of speed, range, and altitude, or suffer bankruptcy. Genius alone was not enough to meet demands for better airplanes. Nor would having yesterday's best plane keep a company from going out of business. Some, like once giant Curtiss-Wright, apparently concentrated on the financial aspects of the business, neglecting engineering, and found themselves unable to compete in the area of high performance pursuits they once dominated. Others, like Aviation Corporation, appeared to successfully walk a fine line, balancing engineering skills with financial shrewdness. A few of the early names remain—Loughead (as Lockheed), Douglas, Cessna, Northrop, Boeing, Grumman, Fleet, Bell, and Vultee. Many names disappeared as smaller firms merged into larger corporations—Vultee became part of Consolidated; Stinson merged with Vultee; Stearman merged with Boeing; Douglas joined with McDonnell after World War II; and Fleet moved west to become Consolidated Aircraft of San Diego before in turn becoming Convair. Bell stayed in Buffalo. North American became Rockwell International. Other names like Keystone, Berliner-Joyce, Great Lakes, Loening, Ballanca, Waco, and Thomas-Morse were never seen again. They simply could not cope or merged into oblivion.

Donald Douglas and his manufacturing company in Santa Monica first became well-known as a result of the 1924 around-the-world flight by Army pilots flying single engine Douglas-designed biplanes. Later, the company prospered with their successful design of twin engine airliners, the famous Douglas DC–2 and DC–3, aircraft that were eventually flown by virtually every airline in the world—the first airliner that could make money by carrying only passengers. In postwar years the company continued as a pre-eminent builder of commercial aircraft with the four-engine DC–4, DC–6, and DC–7, followed by the jet powered DC–8 and DC–9. It may well be that everyone who has flown, at one time or another has flown in a Douglas-designed airliner.

More of a businessman than an imaginative designer, Donald Douglas associated himself with able executives such as Harry Wetzel, Dutch Kindelberger, and Cliff Garrett. Garrett later headed another aircraft organization in southern California, the Garrett Corporation. Jack Northrop was chief engineer in the El Segundo Division of Douglas. One of Donald's favorite associates was Ted Conant, who became a yachting companion. As soon as Douglas could afford it, he bought a yacht named the Cloudster, and Conant became a frequent skipper on the sheltered waters between Santa Monica and Catalina Island. Douglas was a handsome man of medium build, tanned, and physically fit. He possessed a delightful sense of humor, was modest in manner, and not gregarious, preferring the company of a few close friends.

William Boeing started up his company in a red barn near Seattle in 1916, calling his firm the Boeing Commercial Airplane Company. Boeing is the only company from pioneering days still calling itself by the original name. Beginning with a single-float seaplane like the Loughead brothers, Boeing was fortunate in being awarded an Air Corps contract for 200 Thomas-Morse designed MB–3 pursuit aircraft, the Army's chief pursuit during the 1920s. The contract made Boeing prosperous, but killed Thomas-Morse as a competitor. Boeing soon developed its own, superior fighter, the Army's Boeing P–12 and the Navy's twin, the F4B–4, by any measure one of the best looking biplane fighters ever made in any country. Boeing followed with the P–26A *Peashooter*, the nation's first line of air defense in the 1930s. Looking like a speedy, but traditional wood and fabric airplane with fixed landing gear and externally braced wings, the *Peashooter* was the first all-metal fighter in the Air Corps, and the last to have an open cockpit.

In partnership with the future United Airlines, Boeing built conventional trimotor passenger biplanes of steel tubing and fabric. An association with Jack Northrop, who was chief engineer for Avion, which had become a subsidiary of the then United Aircraft and Transport, gave Boeing access to Northrop developed engineering of all-metal monocoque construction. Boeing used these new technics for design of the single engine, all-metal *Monomail* and the first modern twin engine transport, the Boeing 247. A few years later, in 1939, the Boeing pressurized *Stratoliner* appeared, too late to be a civilian carrier before war began, but the age of four engine transport had arrived. Thousands of the Boeing B–17 *Flying Fortress* and B–29 *Superfortresses* would fly before their jet powered successor, the Boeing 707, revolutionized worldwide air transportation.

Major Reuben Fleet, founder of the Consolidated Aircraft Company of Buffalo, New York, was in charge of Army Air Service pilots when U.S. airmail service began in 1918. The inaugural flight by a Curtis *Jenny* was from Washington to New York. All did not go well from the very beginning. As President Wilson stood by to observe the takeoff, there was difficulty in starting the engine, until it was discovered the gas tank was nearly empty. Some of the first airmail stamps printed for the occasion showed the *Jenny* aircraft upside down, immediately becoming collector's items. Lt. Boyle, piloting the first flight, lost his way, and crash-landed in a Maryland cow pasture. The mail went on to New York by train.

Major Fleet was only thirty-six when, as president of Consolidated Aircraft in 1923, he received contracts for fifty rugged PT–1 primary trainers from the Army, placing company ledgers firmly in the black. Both military services eventually bought 470 trainers, in addition to planes sold to twenty-two foreign governments. In 1924 Major Fleet drove to his Buffalo plant in a Model T Ford coupe. Thanks to the PT–1, he was soon driving a Stutz *Bearcat*.

The Consolidated single engine, 8-place *Fleetster* was designed in 1929, but like Northrop's *Gamma* saw little passenger service after the newly formed government agencies decided that single engine passenger aircraft were unsafe. I. M. "Mac" Laddon, chief designer for Consolidated, designed the company's first flying boat, the twin engine XPY–1 *Admiral*, which was completed just after the 1929 stock market crash. As the company was tooling up for production, Glenn Martin won the production contract with a lower bid. To keep his company in the flying boat business, Fleet redesigned the *Admiral* into a luxurious passenger boat called the *Commodore*, and helped organize an overseas airline known as Nyrba (New York-Rio-Buenos Aires) to fly the boat. He sold fourteen *Commodores* and ten pontoon version *Fleetsters* to Nyrba. Nyrba later became Pan American and Consolidated became famous for flying boats. The third of Laddon's flying boat designs was the PBY *Catalina*, ordered by the hundreds by the Navy and foreign governments for operation in all theaters of World War II. The first *Catalina* was manufactured in Buffalo, and flew to San Diego via the Canal Zone to be present at the dedication of the new San Diego Consolidated factory in 1935.

Consolidated moved from Buffalo, New York, to San Diego after being awarded a large contract for flying boats. Their vice president, Lawrence Bell, resigned to set up Bell Aircraft Corporation in the Buffalo plant. Fleet wanted a factory site with better climate, closer to the ocean. Together with Claude Ryan, builder of Lindbergh's *Spirit of St. Louis,* they were the only aircraft plants of any size in San Diego. Both Ryan and Consolidated grew rapidly. While Fleet had been an Army officer, he was a very capable salesman and succeeded in lining up major naval aircraft contracts after moving to the West Coast and establishing his new plant adjacent to the naval docks and shipyard facilities on San Diego bay.

Reuben Fleet was also skilled at dealing with persistent West Coast union leaders, with whom he insisted on negotiating personally. On one occasion when labor representatives sat down in his office to present their case, the Major immediately began to talk about his company and the fine labor relations they were enjoying, without providing an opportunity for the labor representatives to interrupt and return to the new labor contract they had come to discuss. As noon approached he invited the union leaders to share lunch with him in the company's private dining room, suggesting they resume their business discussion afterward. They returned to his office, somewhat refreshed, and he continued his long-winded dissertation about Consolidated for another couple of hours. When the union men finally appeared tired of his conversation, he suddenly brought out a contract from his desk, saying, "Well, gentlemen, that should answer all your questions. Here is the new contract. You can sign it now." It is reported that the union representatives were so exhausted they did sign the contract, with the same terms called for in the previous year, and were glad to be able to leave.

The Lockheed saga began in 1913 with the first flight of Allan and Malcolm Loughead's hydro-aeroplane, as the single-float seaplane was described. They called their plane the Model G, to give the impression it was not the brothers' first airplane. The third brother, Victor, who didn't stay long with the young company, was an engineer with an impressive knowledge of aerodynamic theory, publishing many scholarly books that did much to popularize aviation. One of his books that revealed the wonderful excitement of the time when no license was required to do anything was titled *Aeroplane Designing for Amateurs.*

Allan taught himself to fly, working as a mechanic as well as a pilot. He became a flying instructor and exhibition flyer when he gained enough experience. He made three successful appearances at county fairs in Illinois before a fourth flight in a water-soaked and underpowered Curtiss did not gain sufficient altitude to clear some wires. He ended up hanging from the crossarm of a telegraph pole, ending his career of daredevil barnstorming. He had learned a lot about airplanes, and knew he could build a better one. He convinced his brother Malcolm to join him in designing and building the Model G, which they assembled at nights and on weekends in a frame garage at Pacific and Polk Streets in San Francisco.

Their beginning was typical of the era. The Loughead brothers' Model G, as did so many other pioneering aircraft, featured innovative details that were the forerunners of designs many years in the future. The entire tail assembly swung in pitch and yaw directions on a universal joint taken from an R. E. Olds transmission. The Model G was the first Lockheed airplane and first Lockheed transport with a "flying tail," predating the F–104 *Starfighter* and the L–1011 *TriStar* airliner by about a half century. The Lougheads later changed their name to Lockheed, because no one could pronounce Loughead properly and they were tired of being called "loafhead."

The modern Lockheed company, which Jack Northrop helped start with the design of the very successful Lockheed *Vega*, was facing bankruptcy after the 1929 crash. Robert and Cortland Gross, East Coast investment bankers, bought control with financing arranged by the California Bank (now First Interstate). Allan Loughead retired. The new management obtained a contract to build the Lockheed *Hudson* light bomber for the British. Modified as a small transport, named the *Lodestar*, a number were sold to smaller airlines and private buyers for executive use.

Many notable designers worked for Lockheed in the early years, including Jack Northrop and Gerald Vultee. Together they designed the Lockheed *Orion*, the first airliner with fully retractable landing gear, after building the Lockheed *Sirius*, designed at the request of Lindbergh with a retractable gear. This same plane was later redesigned into the YP–24 fighter with metal fuselage and cantilever wooden wing borrowed from the *Vega*. Powered by the new 600 hp Curtiss *Conqueror* liquid cooled engine, the revolutionary fighter reached a top speed of 235 mph, the fastest fighter of the 1930s. This Lockheed fighter, incorporating many features originated by Jack Northrop, became the basic configuration that would be followed many years later by the classic single engine fighters of all nations in World War II.

James Howard "Dutch" Kindelberger joined the Douglas company in the mid-1920s, at the same time Jack Northrop was at the firm working on the around-the-world Army planes. He had known Donald Douglas when they both worked for Martin in Baltimore. Like so many of the early aircraft designers, he, too, wanted his own company. With Lee Atwood, another Douglas engineer, he approached General Motors for capital to start North American Aviation in Inglewood. The new company was shortly awarded contracts for an advanced military training plane, the North American AT–6, an aircraft soon to be a familiar sight across the country. Another design, the P–51 *Mustang* became perhaps the most famous fighter plane of World War II. After the war North American became Rockwell International, builder of the B–1B bomber.

Kindelberger was a talented executive with a reputation for being a strict disciplinarian and the man in charge. On one occasion he was a passenger on a transcontinental flight where berths had been improvised for sleeping during the 18 hour trip. Dutch was already asleep, when sudden turbulence tossed him out of bed into the aisle. He was completely nude, which was his custom while sleeping. Ignoring the fact, and without embarrassment, he paced up and down the aisle cursing the airline and the pilot who had awakened him so rudely. Kindelberger, as was the case with most of the flamboyant individuals in the aviation industry, lived up to his reputation.

Of the many close individual relationships in the aircraft industry, perhaps few illustrate the situation better than the shifting employment of designers and executives at Douglas, Northrop, and Vultee. When Jack Northrop decided to affiliate with Douglas after United Aircraft and Transport merged his Northrop subsidiary with Stearman in Wichita (a not uncommon shifting of ownership and allegiances in the years when individual egos designed airplanes rather than corporations), it was Dick Millar who assisted Jack in arranging for him to work for Douglas. Later, after Gerry Vultee started Vultee aircraft, Millar joined Vultee. After Gerry died, Millar became president of the firm. Vultee had been an engineering associate of Jack's while they both were at Lockheed. Vultee, with the help of Dick Palmer, a Caltech graduate who had designed planes for Howard Hughes, designed a basic trainer that was adopted by the Air Force and the Navy. A young production man, Charles "Chuck" Parelle, manufactured the BT–13 trainer on the first powered production line similar to those used to assemble automobiles in Detroit. Parelle later became general manager for Hughes aircraft, while Hughes was building the famed *Spruce Goose*, but resigned within a year. Chuck couldn't stand being called to the telephone at three o'clock in the morning by eccentric Howard Hughes.

Soon after the first Northrop aircraft company was formed, a competing company, Major Reuben Fleet's Consolidated aircraft in San Diego, subcontracted the manufacture of vertical and horizontal tail surfaces for their new PBY flying boats to the fledgling Northrop company. It was the first order Northrop received and it kept their production line busy until Jack completed design of his first plane. The decision by Fleet was typical of early aviation pioneers—now a major part of an important industry—who still shared business among themselves, working together more as friends rather than competitors. They knew each other from the old days, and the close relationships and freely exchanged ideas for both airplanes and production technics were undoubtedly a reason for the superior aircraft designed in the United States, as well as the rapid increase in aircraft production realized at the beginning of America's entry into the war. President Roosevelt announced production goals to provide 10,000 planes a year with a capacity to produce twice that amount, goals considered astronomical at the time, and perhaps impossible of achievement. Within the first year of war they were exceeded, a magnificent testimonial to the American aircraft industry of the time, an industrial relationship based on personal friendship and collaboration.

4

SEARCHING FOR A PLACE TO DREAM

When Jack Northrop learned in 1923 that Donald Douglas had been awarded a contract to build four Around-the-World Cruisers for the Army Air Service, he applied for work at the Santa Monica Douglas plant. Allan Lockheed put in a good word for him and Jack was soon on the job assembling airplane wing ribs, repetitious labor that was far from what he actually wanted, but he was back in aviation, and they were exciting days. The airplane wings he was making were for large land planes with a single 400 horsepower engine, with fittings to exchange the wheeled landing gear with alternative floats when flying over water. The Around-the-World-Cruisers had sufficient range to enable Army pilots to fly around the world in a series of short hops between refueling stops—a considerable feat to be planning for and to be building special aircraft to accomplish, long before Lindbergh flew solo across the Atlantic in 1927. A flight around the world was, in 1923, just a dream.

Jack remembered what he thought was one of the worst times in his life when reporting to Douglas for the first time in the Engineering Department.

I was told to design the fuselage fairing on the Around the World Cruisers. Now, the fairing was simply a form and support for the fabric, which in those days surrounded a welded steel tube fuselage, which was basically rectangular. It made the fuselage a reasonably good streamlined shape to reduce wind resistance. It so happened that my work with Lockheed had never included designing fairing for any kind of a steel tube fuselage. I had no idea how to go about it, or what it was all about. I fussed and fiddled and stalled around all morning, getting more frightened all the time. I ate a bag lunch, which naturally didn't digest very well, became quite ill and hiked home, which was about a mile and a half from the office. I didn't know whether I had a job the following morning, or not. I was tremendously worried because of family obligations, and a very stringent financial situation. Fortunately for me, however, the next morning when I came back somebody else had been given the fairing job and I was asked to design the welded aluminum fuel tanks and this I knew all about and was perfectly at home with. From there on I got along quite well with the various jobs that were assigned to me.

Don Douglas worked as an engineer only occasionally and I simply don't recollect where the initial aircraft layouts came from. There was a Douglas observation plane for the Army. I believe the designation was the 0–2. I'm sure I had nothing to do with them and I don't remember that Doug had much to do with them. He was a master salesman and a fine engineer, but his primary job during the operation of the company at that time was to contact the military or other potential customers and try to get additional work for the company. . . . One such time is seared into my memory. There were about five or six engineers working at this time, and the group remained about the same throughout this particular period. Doug went east to try to get an order which was necessary to keep the gang going and to keep the house from falling in. We were all holding our breath. One morning we got a telegram from Doug which said, "Let all engineers go except Mankey and Northrop." Art Mankey was the chief draftsman, and I was the one remaining engineer for a period of several weeks, after which things began to pick up. But, I was one of only two members of the Engineering Department of Douglas Aircraft sometime around 1924 or 1925. So you can see how things went in those days. Before I left, however, the place had grown considerably in size. Dutch Kindelberger had come. He was the chief engineer. Lee Atwood was, I believe, the head of the stress department. Then there was a total of about 55 or 60 people in the Engineering Department; the place had grown that much between the time when there was just two of us and the time that I left at the end of 1926.

It did not take Douglas long to recognize Northrop's talent, and ten days after he first entered the shop, Jack was no longer assembling wing ribs. He was promoted to engineer and given the responsibility for designing the Cruiser wing tanks, a critical component of the aircraft design if the nonstop flying time between refueling was to be flown successfully. During the long hours aloft, across the Atlantic and the Pacific, the tanks performed perfectly. The first circumnavigation of the world was completed, although one plane was lost in Alaska, and another went down in the North Atlantic. The daring flight brought national attention to Douglas. When the first of the two remaining planes returned to southern California, somewhat the worse for wear, having been repaired repeatedly enroute, Jack was among the roaring crowd of spectators who welcomed the plane back home at Clover Field.

All engineering work at Douglas was performed by two engineers crowded together with executives in the same small office. Everyone in the company worked in the room: founder and chief executive Donald Douglas, Harry Wetzel, his general manager, and Chief Engineer Ed Doak. In the engineering department corner of the Douglas office, design work was largely confined to military airplanes. Jack did his preferred work at home, continuing to invent the future over his drawing board sketching civilian airplanes. He delineated in considerable detail an innovative high wing monoplane, with a cantilever wing that eliminated all external struts and braces. It even provided for a Plexiglas-covered cockpit forward of the wing, a feature quite daring in the early 1920s when aviators were convinced that successful flying of an airplane required the pilot to have his helmet-covered head exposed in the wind, the better to know if the airplane was functioning properly. Jack's imaginative airplane was to become the famous Lockheed *Vega*.

Jack went to work under James Howard Kindelberger, known to everyone as "Dutch," who came out west in 1926 from Glenn L. Martin's aircraft company in Baltimore. Kindelberger was hired by Douglas as Chief Engineer, and Lee Atwood was made head of the stress department. Working under the two more experienced men, Jack designed various parts and performed elementary engineering calculations as the Douglas engineering department gradually expanded from two to about fifty employees.

As a restless and ambitious engineer who wanted to design rather than just calculate, Jack soon began to lose interest in the work. It had become routine, and in his view, not very creative. Jack wanted to head a project of his own. He wanted to design airplanes, not parts.

Jack was still dreaming, while Douglas was a practical, conventional aircraft builder who did not encourage the use of company time for speculating about the future or experimenting with new aircraft fabrication methods. He felt his young company was doing just fine the way it was, and could not afford to be designing new aircraft and new ways of making them.

Northrop left Douglas the year before Lindbergh flew the Atlantic, after having worked at the plant in Santa Monica for three and a half years. He wanted to offer his high wing monoplane design to a company who would build it. His thoughts of who that might be included his friends from Santa Barbara days, the Lockheed brothers. He called Allan, who immediately expressed interest in the project and began soliciting capital to organize an aircraft manufacturing company for the purpose. Allan brought in Ken Jay to be the first general manager of the new firm to be called the Lockheed Aircraft Company. Allan was the president, nominal head of the operation, and promoter. Jack's old friend, Tony Stadlman, was located and hired as the shop superintendent to do the same work he did on the ill-fated *Sportsplane* S–1. Jack was back where he wanted to be, as chief designing engineer. He was to relate in later years, "with the exception of Ken Jay, it was the gathering together of the old clan."

The Lockheed company was founded in mid-1926. The first Lockheed *Vega* flew on July 4, 1927. In only six months the project moved from Jack's original drawings to a completed airplane. As Jack recollected these first tumultuous months at Lockheed, bringing to fruition his midnight work at home and wanting to keep intact the integrity of his personal design, "Allan kept insisting that we must put some braces under the wings, even if they were not necessary, because he felt that nobody would buy the airplane unless there was something to be seen to hold them up. I remember the arguments we had, but I won out."

From the time the beautiful red bird was rolled out of the factory and made its first flight from the unpaved airfield adjacent to Lockheed's Burbank plant, the *Vega* was celebrated as an aircraft a generation ahead of Douglas airplanes Jack had been working on in Santa Monica. His *Vega* was the first airplane to cruise over 140 miles per hour, having a top speed of 190 and a cruising speed of 150. The first *Vega* off the production line was purchased by aviation enthusiast Blanche Wilbur King, the young wife of George Randolph Hearst, who persuaded her wealthy father-in-law to buy her the *Vega* she named the *Golden Eagle*, beginning a long relationship with Jack Northrop which later enabled Ken Jay and Northrop to induce Hearst to put up part of the money needed to organize their own aircraft company in 1928.

The radically different design incorporated the same, sleek, monocoque fuselage pioneered on the S–1, mounting a cantilever high wing directly to the fuselage. This wing arrangement did not require the old-fashioned maze of struts, wires, and fabric. Although the airplane carried the Lockheed name, the *Vega* firmly established Jack Northrop as a design genius. Powered by the new Wright *Whirlwind* air-cooled radial engine, the *Vega* quickly established thirty-four new world records for speed and endurance. Expecting an easy win, the *Golden Eagle* was entered in the well-publicized Dole race from California to Hawaii. After taking off from Oakland with a full load of fuel for the 2,400 mile flight to Honolulu, the first *Vega* built was never heard from again.

Despite the tragic loss of the first *Vega* sold, Lockheed continued assembling the second *Vega* as orders for Jack's new plane poured into the Lockheed front office. The most famous fliers of the day praised the design as the best. In the National Air Races later that year, it took another *Vega* to beat a *Vega*. Wiley Post, Amelia Earhart, Art Goebel, and Sir Hubert Wilkins, the Arctic and Antarctic explorer, all flew Lockheed *Vegas*. Wilkins flew the second *Vega* constructed over the North Pole. Jimmy Mattern and Ruth Nichols flew their *Vegas* to new records on virtually every flight.

Wiley Post named his *Vega* the *Winnie Mae* and flew solo around the world in 1933 in a record of 7 days and 19 hours. Flying the same *Vega*, Post had won the National Air Race from Los Angeles to Chicago in 1928. He had already established a new high altitude record of 55,000 feet in the *Winnie Mae*, wearing a futuristic space suit in the cramped forward cockpit. The *Winnie Mae* was presented to the Smithsonian Institution in the same year Wiley Post and his passenger, Will Rogers, were killed in Alaska. They were on the first leg of what was to have been Wiley Post's third around-the-world flight.

Lockheed built 128 *Vegas* between 1927 and 1934, the best selling private aircraft of its time. Apart from its glamorous and dramatic record-breaking achievements, *Vegas* formed the foundation for a number of newly formed passenger and airmail carriers, being flown by no fewer than forty-seven airlines.

Amelia Earhart flew her Lockheed *Vega* across the Atlantic many years before she was lost crossing the Pacific in a twin-engine Lockheed Electra. Her time of only 15 hours from Newfoundland to Northern Ireland in a Lockheed *Vega* was another new record in 1932. Her *Vega* was given to the Franklin Institute in Philadelphia before eventually being moved to the Smithsonian Institution, where it is on display today, next to the *Winnie Mae*.

Commenting on the last flight of Earhart, around-the-world with her navigator Noonan, Northrop later said, "I think Amelia probably just ran out of fuel or encountered weather she wasn't able to handle during her Pacific flight when she was lost. I don't think there was any question that she was lost at sea. She was a very good pilot. I always enjoyed the business dealings I had with her."

A modification of the *Vega* design resulted in the Lockheed *Air Express*, a faster, parasol-wing version of the original *Vega* that bowed to the prejudices of pilots who insisted on an open cockpit so they could fly "by the seat of the pants" with the wind in their face. The plane was another record-breaker. Flown by Frank Hawks and Roscoe Turner, it broke every speed record in the books at air race meets around the country in the 1930s.

Personalized versions of the *Vega* rolled off the production line in increasing numbers, customized for idiosyncratic pilots flying in their own, personalized uniforms, breaking altitude records, and flying over both South and North Poles. The company began to concentrate on production of what was basically the same *Vega*, and sales were excellent. The desire to develop new products and use funds to research and design new airplanes was nowhere evident in a management quite contented with the profitable airplane Northrop had designed for them. After 18 months working in a company he made world famous, Northrop was again restless, with new designs churning in his head and sketched out in detail on his personal drawing board. The *Vega*, an advanced design, was still manufactured of wood. It was time to design an all-metal airplane. Newly formed airlines wanted larger airplanes with greater passenger carrying capacity. Jack was aware of airlines still carrying airmail and passengers in slow, cumbersome Boeing 40B fabric covered biplanes. Jack had ideas for improving the state-of-the-art.

Allan Lockheed wanted his company to concentrate on *Vega* production and expanded the original 50 employees to over 100, most of them working on the production line. As had occurred at the Douglas factory 18 months before, Jack was not encouraged to develop anything new as long as the money from *Vega* sales continued to roll in. Ray Acker, who had known Allan Lockheed years earlier, joined the company. According to Jack, Acker "began telling everybody in the place, particularly me, how airplanes should be designed. He said, in effect, oh, there's no use building anymore of these—you can't sell any. You've got to widen the cockpit for pilot and copilot and you've got to widen the fuselage enough to seat three or four abreast. He became rather obnoxious and it developed into a rather unhappy situation." Within a few weeks, Jack resigned from Lockheed.

"But before leaving," Jack affirmed,

I had laid out the original low-wing model, the *Air Express* and the *Sirus* models, in both parasol-wing and low-wing designs. All of these were mine so far as the basic layouts and the details of the configurations were concerned, as well as the basic concept on the *Vega*. Jerry Vultee was hired as an assistant engineer in the spring of 1928. His name soon became famous in the aircraft business. He was a fine gentleman, an exceedingly able engineer, a graduate of Cal Tech, I believe. He had an excellent technical education without losing a good feeling for the practical, too. And at the time that I left the company in mid-'28, he carried on as chief engineer and from that time on the development of the low-wing models and variations of them were his responsibility.

With Allan's consent, Jack had already been doing some moonlighting for Claude Ryan in San Diego. Ryan was building an airplane commissioned by Charles Lindbergh to fly the Atlantic solo. Lindbergh wanted to maximize the plane's fuel-carrying ability. He felt that reducing unnecessary structural weight and enhancing aerodynamic efficiency would do the trick. The airplane was modified in many ways after early calculations indicated that the basic Ryan M-2 could not make the 3,600 mile flight between New York and Paris.

Jack Northrop's work involved making major changes to improve the airplane's anticipated performance, by increasing the wing span from 36 to 46 feet without changing the wing chord, lightening the wing structure by careful engineering of new parts. (His changes were so extensive that it was not possible to use any of the original M-2 wing parts.) Northrop's suggestions included placing unusual emphasis on streamlining, changing the spacing of wing ribs from the conventional 14 to 15 inches to only 11 inches apart to provide a smoother fabric wing surface, and applying plywood completely covering the wing's leading edge back to the main spar. Lindbergh's NYP, as redesigned, proved to be 10 miles faster in test flights. Called *The Spirit of St. Louis* by the flight's sponsors, the silver plane flew on to fame and glory, another airplane with a little Northrop in it. It, too, is displayed in the Smithsonian.

Ken Jay also left Lockheed in mid-1928. He agreed to raise the capital for a new aircraft manufacturing company that would permit Jack to devote his time developing new airplanes, with Jay handling finance and general administration. The new firm, called Avion, located in Burbank, began operations in 1929. America was experiencing a tremendous wave of enthusiasm for commercial flying. Lindbergh was a national hero and flying a national pastime with air shows held everywhere a field was available. The new airlines, mostly flying noisy and uncomfortable airplanes while catering to the rich, were entering upon a new era of route expansion and modernization.

Shortly after returning from Paris, Lindbergh was retained as a consultant by Transworld Airlines, to assist them in planning routes for transcontinental airmail and passenger service. A veteran airmail pilot, Eddie Bellande, was assigned as Lindbergh's copilot. They began flying across the country determining the best transcontinental route for TWA, conferring with aircraft manufacturers on the East and West Coasts to select the best new airliner for TWA to fly.

With Blanche Hearst on the Avion board, representing her father-in-law, things were never dull. The Hearsts were divorced in 1932, and within two years she married Cortland Hill, the grandson of the Chicago railroad empire-builder, James J. Hill. She learned to fly, obtained a pilot's license, and became an enthusiastic supporter of Jack's many projects. Her new marriage to Cortland Hill led to the organization of Northill, with Jack Northrop as a partner. The new company built no airplanes, but concentrated on the development and sale of products like the small boat anchor invented by Jack. Northill later merged with the Garrett Corporation.

Never satisfied with his own designs, Jack Northrop was well aware that improvements could be made in the type of structure used in contemporary aircraft. Even his own *Vega* utilized conventional wood materials, plywood and glue, albeit in an advanced skin-stressed monocoque fuselage. Jack became convinced that a light metal alloy would be the ideal material for construction of the entire fuselage and wings. Visionary as well as practical, he proved amazingly resourceful in his ability to overcome the engineering and manufacturing problems inherent in his proposed use of the new material. Jack always proceeded as if the problem was part of the solution. He seemed to enjoy the challenge of solving complex fabrication and aerodynamic questions evolving from his own designs sketched out on the drawing board. He had no patience with contemporaries who cautioned him, "It couldn't be done." As far as Jack was concerned, that's when the fun of designing airplanes began.

It was obvious to Jack that traditional wood was not the aircraft manufacturing material of the future. He researched long and hard on the question of what material is lighter and stronger? Which material could be duplicated and fabricated on production line jigs and easily assembled, like Ford put together his new Model A automobile. Aluminum, of course. Jack experimented with aluminum that met his requirements. He then applied its very workable characteristics—strength and lightness—to the design of a unique all-metal, multicellular stressed skin fuselage and wings.

Jack used new-improved aluminum alloys, the famous 24ST specification, to design monocoque and cantilever structures in metal instead of wood. Jack's first all-metal aircraft, the Northrop *Alpha*, which first flew in 1930, essentially was a refined extension of earlier designs by Junkers and Rohrback in Germany, who were using metal merely as a substitution for wood and fabric. Northrop abandoned the slabsided corregated appearance of Junker's boxes and transformed aluminum into beautiful streamlined aircraft, making the skin itself a major structural component. A milestone achievement, Jack's *Alpha* pioneered all the principal structural features to be found in modern all-metal stressed-skin aircraft.

At Avion, Jack truly became his own boss for the first time, rarely required to perform routine engineering tasks that had been his eventual undoing at both Douglas and Lockheed. He launched himself enthusiastically into the task of designing his most complex airplane so far. For the first time an aircraft would have his own name designation. The first plane off the Avion production line was a high performance, single engine transport, capable of carrying seven passengers and mail, constructed wholly of stressed aluminum skin with multicellular wing and monocoque fuselage. He named his plane the Northrop *Alpha*. The new company immediately sold several to TWA for their new transcontinental routes, flying from coast-to-coast in more comfort and at twice the speed of competing American Airlines, still flying old Curtiss *Condor* wood and fabric biplanes.

According to Jack,

The first aerodynamically conventional airplane we built in this new company in early 1930 was called the Northrop *Alpha*. And it was built completely—wing, fuselage, and tail surfaces—of this monocoque sheet metal, or nested channel, structure. These airplanes were used to pioneer all-weather and night flying. Prior to this time, the mail had been carried in the daytime and when the weather was good, but it hadn't been carried under adverse weather conditions or at night. TWA used a number of these airplanes in carrying the mail on its segment of the airmail routes, which as I remember was from Kansas City to Los Angeles. It seems that a pilot got into weather trouble one day and had to make a landing in a small cow pasture. In order not to run into any rocks or trees at the end of the pasture, he made a very hard ground loop and ended with the right wing bent up at an angle of about 35 or 40 degrees. As you can imagine, the airplane didn't look very flyable at that stage of the game, but the pilot wasn't hurt and the airplane was otherwise undamaged . . . TWA mechanics came out from Kansas City with block and tackle and jacks and bent the wing down and the airplane was flown back to Kansas City. It's a rather wild story, but I believe that type of structure is capable of that kind of performance because it not only has an unexpectedly large reserve strength, but it maintains a high proportion of that strength over a wide range of structural damage . . . And that type of structure was used by us consistently for a number of years in all of our airplanes, as well as by others. Douglas Aircraft used it on the DC–3 and I just can't tell you the number of airplanes in which it served. It was a major development in aircraft structural methods.

Another interesting thing that was developed in connection with the *Alpha* was our discovery that the low-wing airplanes had a very unfortunate stall characteristic, in that the divergence of surfaces between the inner part of the wing and the rounded portion of the fuselage caused a slowing down of the airflow at that point. This would cause a localized stall which would shake the airplane and cause turbulence over the tail surfaces. So, we pioneered in the development of the wing-fuselage filleting, which is standard design in all airplanes today.

With his second successful airplane selling as fast as they could be made, and no one over him in the corporate establishment to complain of his dreaming, Northrop found time to renew his early interest in the concept of a flying wing. Jack designed and built his first, almost all-wing airplane, in 1929, and persuaded his friend from TWA, Eddie Bellande, to fly it. The plane wasn't quite all-wing—the vertical and horizontal tail surfaces were still in evidence, extending out the rear from the wing on two outrigger-type booms. Jack felt that additional flight testing of his "wing" would be prudent to determine if a pure all-wing airplane could be adequately controlled and flown.

The little monoplane, with an all-metal, stressed skin wing like the *Alpha*, had a wing span of only 30 feet 6 inches, deep and wide enough for the pilot and a 90 horsepower Monasco four-cylinder air-cooled engine buried within the wing near the center. Making its first flight off Muroc Dry Lake in late 1929, the small aircraft, even with its limited power, clearly demonstrated the greater efficiency of the flying wing. It performed with an improved rate of climb over any other aircraft with the same horsepower and proved capable of easy handling in takeoff and landing attitudes. Eddie Bellande loved to fly it. Jack was convinced he was on the right track, even though, as Jack remarked, "The design when completed, turned out to be about as queer a looking machine as one could wish to be seen. Those who had been associated with it for a year and a half have begun to get used to the appearance, but the newcomer is generally at a loss for words of comparison, and it is suspected that we very rarely heard the true opinion of those who saw the machine, as it was generally muttered under their breath."

Between stints at the drawing board working on his flying wing, Jack found time to design a two-place racing airplane, which he called the Northrop *Beta*. The plane was later modified into a single-place racer, and became the first airplane of 300 horsepower to exceed a speed of 200 miles per hour—another Northrop first.

Poor economic conditions then enveloping the country began to affect the Avion Corporation in 1930. The company lacked sufficient working capital. As initial sales of the *Alpha* and *Beta* airplanes began to wane, and then cease altogether, cash flow came to a sudden halt. Bill Boeing, the Seattle aviation pioneer who had closely followed Jack's career, had read enviously of Jack's success with the new *Alpha* transport. Upon learning of Avion's financial difficulties, Boeing flew down to California to personally assess the situation. After returning from a meeting with Ken Jay and Jack, he persuaded Boeing's large parent company, United Aircraft and Transport, to acquire Avion as a subsidiary.

United Aircraft, a large corporate monopoly, consisted of a number of widely scattered companies, including Pratt & Whitney, manufacturing aircraft engines in Hartford, Connecticut; Boeing Airplane Company in Seattle; Stearman Aircraft in Wichita; and United Airlines based in Chicago. Boeing engineers were still designing airplanes covered with fabric over welded steel tube fuselages. It was apparent that what Boeing may have wanted to acquire in buying Avion was Northrop's solution to design problems of all-metal aircraft fabrication and production. A deal was struck in 1931 and the company name was changed from Avion to Northrop Aircraft Company, to make sure Jack stayed with the new organization. The company would have been worth very little without Jack.

Within the year, Boeing announced their new all-metal plane, the first ever manufactured by the Seattle firm, called the *Monomail*. If Jack recognized some of his ideas in the plane, he never mentioned it, but observers at the time were convinced that what was labeled a Boeing design did resemble many Northrop ideas already incorporated in his *Alpha*.

A small number of the Northrop *Alpha* transports were sold to the Department of Commerce and the Army Air Corps by the new company, but aircraft sales continued to decline. In 1932, at the very bottom of the Great Depression, Boeing parent United Aircraft decided that the fledgling Northrop company was too much of a financial drain. It decided to merge the firm into Stearman Aircraft and combine the entire operation at the Stearman plant in Wichita, Kansas.

Jack Northrop had no desire whatsoever to live in the Midwest, remembering his unhappy childhood in flat Nebraska. He objected strongly to the move. United insisted that the California facility be closed. Northrop resigned as chief engineer of the United Aircraft subsidiary to stay in California. Ken Jay left with him, continuing the tradition of loyalty to Jack that continued throughout the many changes in his association with various companies. Shortly after, the United Aircraft conglomerate itself was forced to divest itself of the airline business by a ruling of the U.S. Justice Department, following airmail scandals of the early 1930s.

Jack had already completed preliminary design work on a new low wing, all metal, long range monoplane that would incorporate the first full-span split trailing edge flaps for use in low speed landing. Power was to be the new Wright *Cyclone* or Pratt & Whitney *Hornet* radial engines that had been developed recently. Northrop already had a name for the new plane, even if he didn't have a factory to make it in. He called his new plane the Northrop *Gamma*.

Hat in hand again, Jack and Jay approached his previous employer, Donald Douglas. With two very successful airplanes, the *Vega* and *Alpha*, having already secured his reputation in advance, few pleas were needed to form another Northrop Aircraft Company, this time in association with Douglas. The new company was located in the empty Moreland Aircraft building in Inglewood, with Douglas Aircraft holding 51 percent of the stock. The new company was in essence a subsidiary of Douglas. As a result of the acquisition, Douglas engineers obtained the benefit of Jack's pioneering work in all-metal fabrication technics and stressed skin design proven in the Northrop *Alpha*. There is no doubt that the famous Douglas DC–2 and DC–3 were designed and built using all-metal engineered design features first devised by Jack Northrop. It was Donald Douglas himself, who later said in praise, that every airplane built, "has a little Northrop in it." It may have been an understatement.

The new Northrop company quickly tooled up the production line to begin building the Northrop *Gamma*, the first plane rolling out in 1933. It, too, achieved fame almost immediately, becoming the first over-weather flying laboratory used to pioneer flying in the stratosphere. Equipped with newly developed blind flying instruments, the airplane was able to takeoff and fly in storms that in older days kept everyone on the ground. It foretold the days ahead when airlines could finally prepare flight schedules and actually keep them, regardless of the weather. The *Gamma* flew the coast-to-coast mail route in eleven and one-half hours, another record.

Commercial models of the Northrop *Gamma* were sold to TWA for carrying mail and cargo. Others were purchased by the Army Air Corps for use as transports. The *Gamma* was a favorite plane of famous pilots in the 1930s, much like the *Vega* in past years. Howard Hawks flew the *Gamma* over high passes in the South American Andes on his way to Chile from the United States in a well-publicized journey. Aboard as copilot with Hawks was Harvard graduate Gage Irving, newest member of the Northrop team. Lincoln Ellsworth flew the *Gamma* on his exploratory trips in Antarctica. Jacqueline Cochran broke several speed and endurance records in her own *Gamma*. The embattled Chinese, fighting invading Japanese in the late 1930s, bought fifty Northrop *Gammas* modified for use as attack bombers. During the early days of World War II, many of the Japanese fighter planes built in Japan exhibited an appearance that looked suspiciously like something borrowed from the older Northrop *Gammas*.

In 1935, the *Gamma* was modified to carry nine passengers and equipped with retractable landing gear. Called the Northrop *Delta*, it was the last of the prewar Northrop designed commercial airplanes. Shortly after its introduction in the market, the Civil Aeronautics Board ruled against the use of single engine transports in commercial passenger service. The Northrop company found itself again with one of the most efficient transport aircraft flying, but few customers.

Northrop had many ideas for new airplanes to replace the *Delta*. Like so many had before, Douglas discouraged him from spending any time working on his flying wing. Douglas felt that this would take him away from the more immediately profitable engineering projects the company was involved in. Potential new engineering work for the military was in the offing. As war clouds hovered over the horizon, military production increased, forcing the Northrop facility to move into the much larger, former Pickwick Motor Coach factory at Mines Field, later to become Los Angeles International Airport. Jack found himself in the same old box.

While at Douglas he designed a 300 miles per hour fighter intended for the U.S. Navy, and spent many hours developing a new dive bomber. This was the forerunner of the famous Douglas SBD *Dauntless*, which became the standard Navy carrier bomber during the first years of World War II, making history at the battle of Midway. He developed another pursuit plane, the Douglas 3–A and later designed the Douglas A–17 attack bomber, which was purchased in substantial numbers by the Army Air Corps.

With military work increasing at a rapid pace, it was decided to merge the Northrop subsidiary into the parent company and call it the El Segundo Division of Douglas Aircraft. As the majority stockholder, Douglas offered to purchase the stock held by Jack and Ken Jay. Jack decided to sell, in spite of a promising future as a shareholder in Douglas Aircraft and as Chief Engineer at the El Segundo Division. He left Douglas in 1938 without knowing what his next move would be. He had a pocketful of ideas for new airplanes and, for the first time, sufficient money from the sale of Douglas stock to do something about it on his own.

As far as Jack was concerned, the Northrop subsidiary of Douglas had been too successful for its own good. He felt that the change to a company that had become a primary producer of military planes no longer provided him with the opportunities he needed for his own satisfaction. His Douglas subsidiary had contracts with the U.S. Army and Navy, and the governments of China, Sweden, Argentina, Peru, The Netherlands, and Iraq. He was still not at ease with himself, did not consider himself fully successful. For a reason he could not understand, there was a continuing frustration in not being his own boss, in not being able to make the important decisions himself. No one seemed to appreciate his concept of flying wing aircraft. He was disappointed in not having the opportunity to proceed with flying wing designs, even while being credited with some of the most successful aircraft ever designed in the United States. He was a tireless upstream swimmer.

There was a very loyal cadre of professional associates, close friends who would follow Jack no matter what he decided to do next. It had been one of Jack's unusual traits as an engineer and a boss himself—he held strong feelings of loyalty towards those who were loyal and agreed with him, but he would often be annoyed by those who disagreed with him. Jack had a tendency to confuse an honest impersonal difference of opinion with disloyalty. Unlike a lawyer, he disliked argument. He never indulged in profanity or salacious stories, and was rather puritanical, commenting sadly on those who had told him a vulgar joke—especially if it was about flying wings.

Jack did not project a very magnetic personality, yet he inspired considerable loyalty. He was a deliberate kind of man, unemotional, one who never showed sudden anger. He was very reserved, calm even in the face of disaster and frustrating events. He had a stubborn, analytical, Norwegian mind, defending his ideas to the end, sometimes making very costly mistakes in the process.

He was definitely a "hands on" chief engineer. He headed the preliminary design team for every new aircraft. Before any project left his office, he would have made three-view layouts and decided on major dimensions and specifications. All his work was characterized by ingenuity and efficiency, never hesitating to suggest employment of new materials and processes to further his search for the most efficient and effective solutions. Surrounded as he always was by conservative engineers and accountants who thought themselves more practical, he felt that it was best to give free rein to innovative ideas. There were plenty of conservative thinkers ready to tell him why his ideas wouldn't work. Jack got along well with company test pilots who, while generally conservative and cautious, not ever taking chances, were always ready to fly something new.

Northrop was impatient with younger colleagues who tended to solve engineering problems the easy way instead of devising innovative solutions that might lead to a better, more efficient design. Jack's staff quickly learned that, while he encouraged a face-to-face discussion of difficult engineering problems, everyone soon understood they should not go to the boss with a problem unless they also were bringing along a possible solution. Jack never took credit for the work of these subordinates. He was quite the opposite, even to the extent of crediting the design patent for his flying wing in the name of the aerodynamic expert, W. R. Sears, who assured him of its practicality.

According to every past employee, Jack was a wonderful boss to work for, respecting every employee regardless of position, whether behind a drafting board or riveting gun. He insisted only that they be industrious and competent. When he wanted to meet with an employee the next day, his way of proposing the question was, "Do you plan to be in the plant tomorrow?" He worried about his employees' wives, children, their health—even their investments—and did so sincerely. Once when an engineer broke his arm cranking a rented concrete mixer at home over the weekend, associates heard Jack on Monday morning, saying, "Next time you need to mix cement for one of your projects, please let me send someone over to do it for you."

He was quiet, extremely modest, and very shy. He had enormous respect for generals, admirals, and people of authority—all those who had more education than he. Yet, he would have considered it presumptuous to attempt personal friendships with famous people. Clearly, he preferred the world of engineering, which he understood so well, to the world of people, politics, and management. Politically conservative, he was sometimes surrounded by younger colleagues full of liberal ideas and fervent disciples of the New Deal introduced by President Franklin Roosevelt. To them he presented an attitude that was tolerant and fatherly; he shook his head sadly over them.

Now that he had left Douglas, his past co-workers who could think of working with no one else but Jack Northrop, waited to learn what he might do next. They were waiting to follow wherever he went. Jack took his time. Being free of the responsibilities at Douglas and enjoying the financial independence achieved by selling his interest in the company meant, for the first time, he could carefully consider available opportunities. Unlike changes occurring in previous years, he could now afford to take his time deciding how to shape his future.

5

THE BEGINNING OF A BILLION DOLLAR CORPORATION

The word spread rapidly in the aviation fraternity that Jack Northrop had resigned as Chief Engineer of the El Segundo Division of Douglas. Eddie Bellande and Moye Stephens, Jack's old associates, called within a few days. They persuaded Jack to locate a qualified business executive with good connections in the investment banking field who would be interested in joining him in forming a new Northrop aircraft company. They assured Jack they would be at his door as soon as it opened. Jack agreed, with the understanding that stock in the new corporation would be widely held, so as to assure him greater independence at the drawing board and to give him an opportunity to build his flying wing.

Eddie Bellande, who had flown Jack's first flying wing prototype, approached La Motte Cohu, a director of TWA for whom Eddie worked. He suggested that Cohu and Northrop get together at an early date to discuss the idea of forming a new aircraft company. He would like to help. La Motte, whose brother, Wallace, was a partner in a Wall Street investment banking firm, had met Northrop a number of times. La Motte had been serving as president of Aviation Corporation, a holding company for aircraft industry securities. The corporation had been involved in a struggle for control by the auto maker, E. L. Cord, and La Motte had been forced to resign. He was looking for a new corporate connection.

La Motte was a different kind of man than Jack Northrop, with extensive experience in finance and administration. Since he looked up to anyone who was creative in a technical way, he was a longtime admirer of Jack for his special designing talent. La Motte was a director of TWA, which had flown many early Northrop aircraft. He had been introduced to Jack on the occasion of a Northrop *Gamma* delivery.

There was a marked difference, also, in the appearance and personalities of the two men. La Motte generally had a pipe in his mouth, exhibited the muscular build of a wrestler, laughed loudly, and appeared to be aggressive, often exaggerating stories about himself. Although the Cohu family were of French descent, and distantly related to the DuPonts of Delaware, La Motte rarely gave the impression of being a cultured gentleman. By contrast, Northrop never smoked or drank. He disliked cocktail parties and small talk. He was "straight laced," as some have said, and definitely not "one of the boys."

Jack Northrop traveled to New York at Eddie Bellande's urging. After talking with La Motte, Jack agreed to join in organizing a new aircraft company to be known as Northrop Aircraft Company. War had not yet broken out in Europe, and the conservative investors on Wall Street felt that the established aircraft manufacturers could produce all the airplanes the country would ever need. They reminded Jack and La Motte of Glenn L. Martin, Curtiss Wright, Grumman, Bell, Douglas, Consolidated, Lockheed, and Boeing. The idea of "going public" with the stock of a company that had no business on the books, no plant, and only a general manager and chief engineer as employees, made absolutely no sense to them. Jack and La Motte called on a number of Cohu's investment friends, but received little encouragement.

Discouraged, but still determined to find the necessary financial backing, La Motte returned to Los Angeles with Jack and contacted Eddie Bellande again. Eddie and Moye Stephens had been discussing the financing problems with several wealthy friends. They had concluded that they were in need of a good local investment banker to organize a syndicate in southern California to underwrite a public stock issue. This would preclude a few large private investors from insisting on retaining majority ownership and voting control over the new corporation. Jack had come to treasure his independence.

I had met Eddie Bellande earlier and frequently flew with him to Albuquerque, where my investment securities firm, Banks Huntley & Company of Los Angeles, maintained a branch office. Eddie mentioned Jack Northrop to me and asked if our firm would be interested in heading a stock underwriting group. As vice president and sales manager of Banks Huntley, I was immediately interested. I had previously heard about Northrop's plan to start a new company and thought the proposal had considerable merit.

I asked Eddie to bring Northrop and Cohu to our Los Angeles headquarters, and I would arrange a conference with Earl Huntley and his partners. It was August 1938 when we were introduced to Jack Northrop and La Motte Cohu in our Spring Street offices. Jack Northrop, led the way, talking enthusiastically about building airplanes. With an engaging smile, he said, "Aviation is a fun job. Every day you get up eager to see what can be done better, and at night I say to myself that I had not done my job well enough. Each day brings a new adventure." He was his own best salesman.

Banks Huntley & Company agreed to head an underwriting syndicate to sell the initial one and a half million dollars of stock and take the risk of the new venture. Jack insisted that a majority of the stock in his new company not be placed in the hands of a few large investors. He cherished his own dreams, and made it clear that his need to realize them had been his reason for leaving Lockheed, United Aircraft, and Douglas. He wanted to be free to design an entirely new airplane—a flying wing—and he felt that a larger number of shareholders with individually less money at risk would enable him to do it. He fully expected the new corporation to be profitable. He just wanted the flying wing to be one of those profitable airplanes.

With La Motte Cohu as the business head of the new firm, Banks Huntley was willing to proceed. La Motte and Northrop agreed to start work at modest salaries with the provision that they were to receive a special class of stock that would become valuable only after the company had proven its ability to make a good profit. Before the final commitment, I asked for permission to interview Donald Douglas and Robert Gross, the new head of Lockheed, in order to be able to insure my firm they would not put any obstacles in the path of Jack Northrop and his new venture.

The interview with Donald Douglas was very enlightening. I learned much about this outstanding aviation pioneer and was better able to appreciate his character and ambition. I learned also of Douglas' keen sense of humor. As we talked, the phone on his desk rang, and Douglas answered it, saying, "How are you Rube? It is nice of you to call." Douglas then put the receiver down on his desk and resumed the conversation with me. I could hear the caller carrying on an uninterrupted conversation unaware that Douglas was not listening at the other end of the line. Periodically, Douglas would pick up the phone and say, "Yes, Rube. That's fine Rube," and return the receiver carefully again to his desk while Rube continued his long monologue.

Finally, Douglas lifted the telephone, made a few brief remarks, and ended the call. After replacing the receiver on its hook, he turned to me with a smile and remarked, "Thanks for being here, Ted. As you may have guessed, that was Rube Fleet, president of Consolidated Aircraft in San Diego. He is always very long-winded, and without your presence he would have wasted my entire afternoon."

Donald Douglas assured me that there was plenty of business coming up for everyone in the aircraft industry. He considered Northrop to be a very talented engineer and he would put no obstacles in the way. He knew that Jack would lure away some valuable people from the El Segundo Division of Douglas. He would particularly miss Gage Irving, who might follow Jack if he was offered a key job. However, he now had someone to take Jack's place in engineering, and he was not afraid of competition. Douglas would put no unfair obstructions in the path of Northrop's future.

Robert Gross, a former banker, had come from the East in the early 1930s to take over an almost bankrupt Lockheed company. With newly received orders from the British for Hudson bombers and a popular commercial version, the Lockheed *Lodestar*, he had turned the company around. He told me of his friendship with La Motte Cohu in New York, and felt that he and Northrop would make an excellent team. Lockheed wished them well, and welcomed them as competitors.

With these assurances, Banks Huntley formed an underwriting group to sell 250,000 shares of Northrop Class A common stock to be offered to the public at $6.00 a share. Wallace Cohu's firm in New York City, O'Brian Mitchell Company in Buffalo and Lester Ryon's in Los Angeles were our partners. Key members of the Northrop management team were offered Class B shares as a bonus in exchange for accepting low starting salaries. The Class B stock contained the provision that it was of no value until the company earned its first million dollars. After this milestone, the Class B stock would be converted into Class A shares on a one-to-one basis.

Moye Stephens and Bellande cooperated with the underwriters by suggesting a number of prospective investors. Moye, who later joined the fledgling company, had flown Richard Haliburton around the world before the well-known author wrote his best seller, "The Flying Carpet." A former law student at Stanford University, Stephens learned to fly as a youth and chose to become an airline pilot rather than follow the family tradition in the courtroom.

Moye had a favorite story that he enjoyed telling, about the time when Haliburton and he arrived in New Guinea on their global trip in an open cockpit lightplane.

We had the plane equipped with floats so that we could fly into the interior and visit the primitive natives. We landed on a large river, and a tribe of pygmies were overcome with wonder when we descended from the sky. They thought that we were riding on the back of a huge bird, and when Dick and I climbed out, we were treated like gods.

That night, our pygmy hosts insisted that we sleep in a special straw hut, supported ten feet above the swampy ground on piling. Neither Dick or I could stand up in our hut, and as I prepared for bed my 190-pound body was too much for the fragile floor, and I broke through, landing with a splash in the swamp below.

After an uncomfortable night, we invited the pygmy chief to take a ride with us and, as we took off and circled their camp, I thought that our passenger would fall out of the open cockpit as he stood up and frantically waved at his cheering tribesmen below.

After landing and returning to the village, the chief was encircled by his faithful villagers, and he began to talk about his ten-minute flight. The talk continued for the next eight hours, long into the night, and the villagers sat in stony silence, fascinated by his account of the flight.

Moye said he wished that he could have understood what the chief was saying, as he apparently was relating what it was like to be flown to heaven.

Several months elapsed before the new Northrop company completed the necessary steps for incorporation and La Motte and Jack attracted an initial group of key employees to join them in starting the new firm. La Motte moved his family to California and bought a large home in Palos Verdes, in sight of cleared acreage ready for construction of the new plant in Hawthorne. The Northrop family continued to live in nearby Inglewood.

The chosen plant site was a 300 acre tract of vacant land east of

Prairie Avenue and south of 120th Street in the suburban town of Hawthorne. The plowed land, covered with weeds, had been used as a truck farm by Japanese farmers, and the majority ownership was held by a bank. Selling price was $3,000 per acre. After initially establishing the company headquarters in the Banks Huntley offices in downtown Los Angeles, temporary offices were rented in an old abandoned building in Hawthorne, a building nicknamed, "The Yellow Peril," on account of the closets being full of deadly Black Widow spiders.

In August, 1939, just two months before the European war began with Hitler's invasion of Poland, the underwriters, headed by Banks Huntley, made the initial stock offering. With war in the offing and an unpredictable economic future to consider, the securities market became unsettled. It proved difficult to sell the entire stock issue of 250,000 shares. After many months about 50,000 shares still remained owned by the underwriters.

At this point Jack Northrop came to the rescue of the underwriters. He recalled that Jackie Cochran, who had purchased and flown her first Northrop designed airplane and become famous as a woman air racer, had recently married Floyd Odlum, a well-known Wall Street financier and president of a large investment trust, the Atlas Corporation. Jack confided in me, saying, "I believe I can persuade Jackie to ask her husband to buy the balance of the Northrop Class A stock."

After a phone call from Northrop, Jackie Cochran agreed to speak to her husband. Wallace Cohu met with Floyd Odlum in New York and described to him the Northrop proposal. Atlas Corporation purchased the remaining 50,000 shares of stock, with the understanding that the underwriters would redistribute these shares after an over-the-counter market had been established for the new Northrop issue. In Jack's opinion, by this purchase, Floyd Odlum had made possible his new company. It was the beginning of a colorful and controversial relationship between the two men. In September of 1939, on the eve of Hitler's ruthless march into Poland, $1,500,000 was transferred to Northrop Aircraft Incorporated by Banks Huntley & Company, and ground was broken for the new manufacturing plant in Hawthorne. It was the beginning of the billion dollar Northrop company of today.

Moving in a minimum of furniture, Jack and La Motte began hiring key engineers to start work on the company's first project—the design and development of a true flying wing aircraft. First to be built would be an experimental prototype, designated the N–M1: Northrop mock-up number one.

One morning when surveyors arrived to begin laying out factory foundations in the Hawthorne field, workmen were surprised to find that overnight a fence had been constructed enclosing a narrow strip of land extending through the center of the property. After inquiry, it was learned that a paving contractor who owned the land directly south of the 300 acres purchased by the new Northrop company, had, a few days before, secretly acquired the narrow strip that bisected Northrop's plant site.

All work halted as negotiations proceeded with the interloping landowner. The fledgling Northrop company was informed they must buy an additional 100 acres owned by the contractor before continuing with construction. The price: $4,000 per acre, 33 percent higher than the $3,000 cost of the original 300 acres. In his desire to begin plant construction as soon as possible, Ray Madison, the company's new Secretary-Treasurer, had failed to make a title search. La Motte and Jack demanded his resignation, not realizing that Ray had actually done the company a great favor by forcing the purchase of an extra 100 acres. All of the land was very shortly put in use for expansion of Northrop's new manufacturing facility.

Ray's departure left three vacancies in the Northrop management team: a secretary, treasurer, and a vice president for sales. Eddie Bellande, who had initially been offered the sales position, turned the offer down when he learned the starting salary for the vice president of sales would be only $12,000 a year, much less than his salary as a senior pilot for TWA. Both Cohu and Northrop had agreed that the company should begin operations with low executive salaries, with a bonus for performance to be paid later in company stock. Their salary began at $15,000 a year, but their confidence in the success of the new company was so complete, they had little fear of not receiving substantial benefits when the stock bonus was eventually paid. Bellande was wary of this arrangement, and they could not convince him that his future bonus of 5,000 shares of Northrop stock would quickly make up the difference. He did agree to replace one of the Eastern bankers on the Northrop Board of Directors, serving until 1942.

At the time of incorporation in 1939, the board consisted of La Motte T. Cohu, Chairman and General Manager; John K. Northrop, President and Chief Engineer; James N. Wright, Vice President of Banks Huntley & Company, Los Angeles; B. P. Lester, President of Lester & Company, Los Angeles; Roland L. O'Brian, President of O'Brian Mitchell Company, Buffalo; and Henry Wallace Cohu, Cohu

Brothers, New York. Gage Irving, who had accepted the position of vice president and assistant general manager, with a $12,000 salary plus a similar bonus arrangement, was willing to leave Douglas and begin working at Northrop as soon as the plant was ready for production.

When Bellande's decision to continue flying with TWA was discussed in the next executive committee meeting, I offered to leave the higher paying position at my own firm, Banks Huntley, and join Northrop as corporate secretary, to later fill the sales position offered to Bellande. Jack Northrop was not convinced that I knew enough about airplanes to be able to sell them, and he was not sure I could adequately fill the job. All did agree that, if I demonstrated an aptitude selling airplanes to the government, I would be promoted to vice president for sales with membership on the board of directors.

This presented me with a major decision. I concluded that, with war breaking out in Europe it was indeed likely that the United States would sooner or later become involved. Perhaps now was the time for me to leave the investment securities business for a war-related job, even though it meant a temporary drop in my income. I could not deny that I, too, had fallen under the spell of Jack Northrop, and knew that I would surely enjoy the challenge of working with him, building the new company that I helped create into a major aircraft manufacturing corporation.

My decision proved to be a correct one. I accepted the position of corporate secretary in July of 1940, and three months later was promoted to vice president for sales. Within a year I replaced Jim Wright on the board of directors. I had found that selling airplanes during early World War II was an easy task.

The new company gradually began to take shape as more key employees were signed on. Claude Monson left Douglas to replace Ray Madison as Treasurer. Moye Stephens became secretary when I was named vice president and director. Stephens and Irving were also elected to the board, giving management five members on the board of nine.

We all knew that we must seek contracts for new airplanes that could be quickly designed and built, before anything as radical as the flying wing could be developed and sold. Our empty factory must be made to pay its own way as soon as possible. La Motte had been contacting the Norwegian government, following up connections his wife, Didi, a Norwegian native, had maintained. Officials in Oslo had

heard of Jack Northrop because of Bernt Balchen, the famous Norwegian airman who accomplished much of his Arctic explorations in
the Northrop *Gamma*.

La Motte decided to visit Norway to ascertain the interest in a
Northrop aircraft. Just as Cohu was ready to fly to New York, Hitler
began his march across Europe, and France and Great Britain declared war on Germany. La Motte decided to fly directly to Norway.
After departing London, his commercial airliner took a direct route to
Oslo, flying over the North Sea. The plane was intercepted by a
German fighter pilot, who, without warning, strafed the airliner with
machine gun fire. A fellow passenger, only two seats away from La
Motte, slumped over, mortally wounded by the burst of bullets that
easily pierced the unprotected skin of the airliner. Fortunately, the
plane was able to reach the Oslo airport and land safely. It was one of
the last commercial flights to Oslo, as this incident and others soon
resulted in the cancellation of all commercial flights to Norway.

La Motte returned to California from Norway carrying the young
Northrop company's first complete airplane contract, for twenty-four
N–3PB seaplanes. This was a rugged, fast aircraft, to be used as a
patrol bomber over the North Atlantic protecting vital sea lanes from
threatened submarine and aerial attack by Germany. Norway obviously needed the plane as soon as possible, and the plane had not yet
been designed, but to Jack Northrop this was no problem.

Jack quickly assembled an experienced engineering team, including Tom Quayle to head the project, and Fred Baum, who had worked
earlier on the design of multi-cellular stressed skin airplanes developed by Northrop. The airplane envisioned by Jack would be a
single engine, low-wing with NACA 2400 series airfoil, full cantilever
monoplane of aluminum alloy, semi-monocoque fuselage similar to his
Northrop *Gamma*, construction that had proven most efficient aerodynamically. Two pedestal mounted Edo floats allowed for water operations. The front cockpit was equipped with all necessary flight controls, engine controls, and flight instruments. The rear cockpit also
had basic flight controls and was designed for a gunner-observer in the
upper forward section and a gunner, radio operator-bombardier in the
lower rear section of the fuselage, where a small window was available
for lateral vision. The crowded quarters provided for a crew of three.
Over 300 design and production drawings were prepared.

Power for the N–3PB was the Wright Cyclone GR1820–G200
radial engine rated at 1,200 horsepower, giving the airplane a top

speed of 256 miles per hour at 17,000 feet, at the time the fastest military seaplane in the world. Actual flight performance exceeded Jack's design specifications.

The first Northrop N-3PB seaplane was designed, built, tested, and delivered in the record time of only eight months after signing the contract on March 12, 1940. The first plane completed was trucked to Lake Elsinore, southeast of Los Angeles, in December. Norwegian Air Force Commander Kristian Osthy was on hand to observe flight tests and accept the aircraft. Contract test pilot Vance Breeze made the first flight with Northrop test pilot Moye Stephens flying the remainder. By the end of March 1941, all twenty-four aircraft had been accepted by the Norwegian government, the fastest delivery on record and a remarkable achievement by the embryonic aircraft company.

German military forces were faster. Norway was invaded and occupied by German troops before the first plane could reach Oslo. A refugee government was established in the British Isles. The squadron of pilots who were to fly the 24 N-3PBs escaped from Norway and established a training base in Canada, where the fleet of Northrop patrol planes was finally delivered. The 330th squadron of the famous Royal Norwegian Naval Air Force, operated as a unit under the British RAF, based in Iceland. As originally planned by the Norwegian government, it was assigned to patrol duties in the busy sea lanes of the North Atlantic, where German submarines were raising havoc with Allied shipping. The first combat engagement involving a Northrop seaplane took place over Iceland on May 3, 1942. The aircraft accounted for itself in a very successful manner, driving off a German bomber and returned to base untouched. The Northrop aircraft established an enviable record in their operational missions of submarine patrol, convoy escort, photo-reconnaissance, and air-to-air combat. One patrol bomber assisted in the capture of a German submarine. Nine of the ten N-3PBs lost during the 1941–42 Iceland campaign were damaged beyond repair during water landings under severe arctic weather conditions. Not one N-3PB was lost to enemy fire in combat.

While tooling was underway for production of the first Northrop airplane, the only other evidence of activity in the new plant was the building of horizontal and vertical tail surfaces for Consolidated aircraft's PBY, a twin engine, long range flying boat being assembled in San Diego for the U.S. Navy, a contract that continued throughout the war. Major Rubin Fleet, Consolidated Aircraft Company's president, had moved his factory from Buffalo in New York to southern California. When he visited the new Northrop plant for the first time, he encountered La Motte Cohu enjoying his lunch hour practicing archery in the cleared area set aside for him in the largely vacant 122,000 square foot plant. Unaware of La Motte's considerable interest in sports, the receptionist ushered Fleet into the factory area without notice. Fleet confronted the Northrop chairman at a time when he was about ready to dispatch an arrow towards the distant target on the far wall.

"Is this all you're doing here at Northrop Aircraft?" Major Fleet shouted at La Motte. "I gave you some business to get you started, and when I come up to see how you're making out, I find you're playing Indian!" Major Fleet turned away without saying another word and left the building, ordering his chauffeur to drive him back to San Diego.

Word of the incident soon spread through the Northrop organization, everyone seeing the humor in the situation. La Motte enjoyed the incident immensely. "I know the old boy doesn't mean any harm. He's a bag of wind," La Motte later remarked. The receptionist was, from that time on, very careful about announcing his guests before escorting them into the archery section of the plant.

Even while the engineering staff were busy working long hours to expedite design of the Norwegian seaplane, they always took some time, with Jack's blessing, to continue preliminary work on the company-financed flying wing project. Unlike the 1929 model built with tail outriggers, Jack was now thinking of a true flying wing with no vertical fins or tail surface—his original concept. It would be a quantum step forward to demonstrate conclusively that an all-wing airplane with high lift and low drag would outperform any other aircraft flying. With the help of Dr. William Sears, Jack's friend, Dr. Von Karman conducted wind tunnel tests at Caltech, using a small scale model, more sophisticated tests than Jack had done earlier with a hand launched glider. His professional opinion was that the full-size flying wing would be easily controlled; it would be a practical aircraft.

The U.S. military were not very interested in Northrop's ideas for a flying wing. They considered it futuristic and commented privately that Northrop did not seem to understand their priorities. With war now raging in Europe, the brass in Washington wanted immediate production of conventional aircraft that would quickly build up their forces. There was little interest in entering into longterm development contracts for a new, and admittedly perhaps superior aircraft, no matter how persuasive Northrop's arguments. Nor did investment representatives on the board of the embryonic airplane company want to divert adequate engineering staff or capital to pursue such an expensive and long-range project. Without government financing, the company was unable to perform much serious work on a major flying wing program.

The U.S. Navy Bureau of Aeronautics decided to ask the new Northrop company to bid against the Douglas El Segundo Division for quantity production of 200 SBD-3 carrier-based dive bombers, the same airplane that had been designed when Jack served as Chief Engineer for the El Segundo Division. Many of the engineers and production employees who had worked on the plane at Douglas were now working for Northrop. It appeared to be a good idea for the Navy to consider Northrop for a second source. It would be a sure way to get the Navy's cost down by encouraging competition. In 1940, any of the southern California aircraft companies would be pleased to be awarded a contract for 200 airplanes that had already been designed and proven. Northrop badly needed a large production contract in order to produce additional revenue if there were to be any opportunity at all for Jack to work seriously on his flying wing and other new and better airplanes.

La Motte and I flew to Washington and submitted the company's SBD-3 bid to the Bureau of Aeronautics. Cohu returned home after introducing me to Captain Dick Richardson, officer in charge of navy procurement. Richardson asked me to supply him with a list of all Northrop employees who had previously worked on the SBD-3 at Douglas. The list included over 80 percent of Northrop's current employees, confirming Douglas' observation that many of his employees would move over to Hawthorne to work for Northrop.

I soon learned that Northrop would be the winning bidder, but was personally skeptical that Northrop could build 200 of the SBD-3 aircraft for the low $10,000,000 bid price. Even though Jack had been the chief designer of the SBD-3, the company was new and had no prior large scale production experience. With only $1,500,000 equity capital, most of which had already been invested in the new plant, a mistake in the bid of only 15 percent would send the company close to bankruptcy. My previous financial experience made me feel that our engineers may have been anxious to cut the price in order to get the business away from their former employer. Their desire to help Northrop beat Douglas might result in a serious financial loss if we were awarded the contract.

Admiral Towers, Chief of the Bureau of Aeronautics, told me to return to California and inform Jack Northrop that his company was the low bidder on the SBD–3, and the Navy was very pleased to have a second source for the plane. He advised me that Northrop should get to work planning for production immediately. A written contract and other paperwork would follow. News of the award was met with much jubilation at the Hawthorne plant. Northrop was personally very pleased at having won a contract in competition with Douglas and the many former Douglas employees in the new plant were quite elated.

The celebration was not to last long. Within a few days Jack received a call from Admiral Towers, requesting him to fly to Washington, where Jack was told that an obstacle had suddenly appeared, and the Navy must change its plans for the production of SBD–3s at Northrop. Donald Douglas, despite his earlier assertions welcoming competition from Northrop, was very upset when he learned that Northrop stripped his El Segundo plant by hiring most of the personnel, and then went on to actually secure the contract to manufacture a Douglas airplane. Douglas personally flew to Washington and raised hell with the Navy.

Jack and I returned to Washington and were told by Admiral Towers that, contrary to the previously announced arrangement, Douglas would be the prime contractor on the SBD–3. Douglas, acting under instructions from the Navy, would subcontract a major portion of the production work to Northrop.

Jack Northrop was outraged. As he sat silently listening to the change in plans, his anger mounted, and he informed Admiral Towers in very direct language unusual for Northrop, "You have gone back on your word. You told us to start working on the SBD–3 because we are the low bidder. We have already announced the award to our employees." He was adamant in his anger, saying, "I refuse to be a subcontractor to Douglas. If you go back on a promise to me, I will see to it that our company never does business with the Navy again."

He left the room without any opportunity for compromise, and returned to California. It was obvious that Admiral Towers was embarrassed, but it was also clear he had definitely decided to retain Douglas as the prime contractor, and was not about to change his mind again. Donald Douglas, over the years, had apparently been able to acquire considerable political clout among military decision makers. The small Northrop company had now met head on with the biggest in its very first armageddon. The admiral did feel he was amply fair in providing a large subcontract for Northrop in its stead.

I was quite concerned over the turn of events. After all, the Navy was a potential major customer for the future. I looked upon the incident from a more practical point of view, feeling that the revised contractual arrangement providing for Northrop to become a sub-contractor for Douglas would have been a break for Northrop, and eliminate the tremendous financial risk involved in producing the aircraft for a lower price than Douglas had bid. I kept these thoughts to myself, knowing that Jack was quite strong-willed, had meant what he said, and would never agree to the Navy's revised proposal calling for Northrop to be subordinate to Douglas. It was clear why Northrop needed a strong financial executive at the helm to prevent Jack from underbidding and refusing to compromise.

I stayed in the East to follow up on a sales lead given to me on my previous trip to Washington. An old friend, Dr. Albert Lombard, was working for the recently established War Production Board, and of-fered to introduce me to the British Purchasing Commission. The British were desperately looking for another manufacturer who could build the Vultee *Vengeance* dive bomber for them, under license from Vultee. Dick Millar, Vultee president, had recently called La Motte to inquire if Northrop would be able to build this new aircraft for delivery to the British at an early date. La Motte told me to go after the business.

The Vultee Nashville plant, where the *Vengeance* dive bomber was to be built, was working at its capacity. The Battle of Britain, then underway in the skies over London, was resulting in huge losses from German bombers and the frightening buzz bombs. The RAF badly needed more airplanes than Vultee was able to produce. Millar had offered a production license to Northrop, which provided for turning over the engineering and production drawings for use in building the dive bomber at Hawthorne. It was a great opportunity to fill the new plant with profitable work.

Vultee had received a contract for $17,000,000 to build 200 air-planes, planes about the same size and weight as the SBD–3. North-rop had just bid $10,000,000 for the same number of airplanes, belated evidence that the Northrop SBD–3 bid had been entirely too low. After contacting the British purchasers, I was sure that the contract to build the 200 Vultee bombers would indeed provide a real opportunity to put the new company on its feet financially. La Motte and Gage Irving agreed. Although Jack was still upset over the loss of the navy contract, he did accept the decision of the majority and cooperated throughout. Jack did not think much of the *Vengeance* design and made it clearly understood that he would have preferred to design and build an airplane of his own design, which he claimed would have been a better aircraft. But, as usual, no one wanted to wait for a better aircraft. Aircraft were needed immediately.

I had been able to negotiate a very favorable contract, with valuable assistance from Vultee, which provided for a 50 percent down payment, with the balance to be paid as the airplanes were delivered, ready to fly, on the ramp at Hawthorne. Chairman Cohu met me at the airport when I arrived home—with a signed British contract and a check in my briefcase for $8,500,000.

Cohu behaved like a delighted boy with a new toy when he was shown the sizable certified check. He was soon taking full credit for the accomplishment, ignoring the important role played by Dick Millar of Vultee. It was typical of La Motte, and a trait that was generally understood by those working with him. The important point was that, at last, the company had adequate working capital. Perhaps Jack could even work a little on his flying wing.

Northrop soon forgot his anger over the SBD contract, and did admit that his company should be grateful to their competitor, Dick Millar, an ex-investment banker who had previously known and admired Jack when they served together on the Douglas board of directors. The *Vengeance* contract with the British proved to be the major turning point for the new Northrop aircraft company.

Despite differences in their backgrounds, Jack and La Motte exhibited a great deal of respect for each other. Cohu delegated the engineering and technical side of the business to Northrop. Jack, in turn, was always ready to delegate financial and administrative matters to Cohu. On personnel matters they were in complete accord, making the Northrop company an excellent place to work.

1940 was the most significant year in Northrop aircraft history. The first 122,000-square-foot plant was ready for production in March when the N–3PB patrol bomber contract with Norway was signed; work was begun on the first subcontract with Consolidated for tails on their PBY flying boats; the N–1M flying wing prototype was begun with company funding; the Navy awarded Northrop the first gas-turboprop engine development contract, a forerunner of the jet engine; and profitable plant production was assured with the 200 aircraft order from the British for *Vengeance* dive bombers.

The year finally came to a close with another major achievement. The first contract was signed with the U.S. Army Air Corps for the P–61 night fighter, the Black Widow, a completely new aircraft, designed and developed by Northrop. It was to play a significant role in bringing an end to the war in the Pacific. The contract for two P–61 prototype airplanes was signed in December 1940, followed by contracts for over 700 of the successful night fighters in the following year. The Black Widow was the first airplane to be equipped with its own airborne radar guidance system. The ability of the P–61 to kill in the dark of night was a deadly surprise to the enemy. Jack Northrop's own company, and finally, his own aircraft design, were indeed unqualified successes. To be sure, visions of a flying wing were now within sight.

6

THE VENGEANCE, BLACK WIDOWS, AND THE WAR

With a healthy backlog of work assured, Jack Northrop delegated the responsibilities for manufacturing and general administration to Gage Irving and La Motte Cohu, and was able to concentrate on engineering and development of new aircraft for new customers.

Jack Northrop had many friends at Wright Field, where the responsibility for military aircraft procurement had been placed. Jack was the last person to claim he was a good salesman, but officers at Wright always wanted to talk with him personally, even though the sales department, and their representative, Tom Quayle, resident in Dayton, maintained daily contacts.

As a result, Jack Northrop was asked to submit a proposal to the Air Corps to design an entirely new, large fighter-interceptor, to be known as a night fighter, capable of shooting down enemy planes at night. Secret projects at the radiation laboratory of MIT had made practicable a new distant image generator called radar. Installed in an aircraft, the radar would be able to see the image of enemy planes at night or during periods of poor visibility, and shoot them down. The equipment's description and ability to see what could not be seen by the pilot, sounded like something lifted from the Buck Rogers futuristic comic strip. It would be Northrop's challenge to provide an aerial platform for the night-seeing radar.

A secret proposal from Northrop resulted in the award of a 1,000 plane contract to design, test, and produce the P–61 night fighter. Northrop engineers who had joined the company when their only office was in the abandoned Hawthorne hotel, suggested the name for the plane when they remembered seeing, and being uncomfortable with, the numerous black widow spiders in the closets adjacent to their working area. The name Black Widow proved most appropriate for such a deadly aircraft.

The large, twin-engine night fighter was painted a dull black, and was the first airplane designed for use of radar, providing night vision for the crew. The P–61 possessed a deadly sting from rapid-fire 50 caliber machine guns mounted in a gun turret and a 20mm cannon in the nose. Carrying a crew of three—pilot, gunner, and navigator—all riding one behind the other in a compact fuselage placed in the center of the wing and suspended from twin booms supporting the tail surfaces, the plane looked not unlike an enlarged version of the Lockheed P–38.

The Black Widow was considered by many to be Northrop's most important contribution to the war effort. The planes were delivered in quantity in time to play a decisive role in the war against Japan. Soldiers returning from duty on islands in the South Pacific reported that, after the Black Widows arrived, they were able to sleep for the first time without fear of a night air raid by the Japanese.

Before Black Widow airplanes started coming off the Northrop assembly line, I was kept busy going after new production work, spending considerable time in Washington, D.C., until Northrop established an office there in 1942. On one of my Washington trips I learned the Air Corps was planning a large contract for the Boeing B–17 bomber. When I learned that Philip Johnson, the president of Boeing, occupied the adjacent room in the Carlton Hotel where I was staying, I called him for an appointment and was invited to his room for a visit.

Johnson inquired about Jack Northrop, whose reputation always preceded him among a legion of admirers. Phil Johnson had resigned from Boeing and gone to Canada to organize Canadian Pacific Airlines, at the same time Jack Northrop left United Aircraft following the breakup of the large monopoly. He had returned to Boeing before the United States declared war on Japan, and was made president.

A major advantage of being part of a relatively small prewar aviation industry was that most of the principal executives knew each other on a first name basis. When war came, everyone cooperated with former competitors like members of a large family. The "family" included many of the prewar, Army and Navy career officers. This proved to be quite advantageous to the United States for, by cutting the usual government red tape, the production of warplanes could quickly be increased as demand dictated. High excess profit taxes took away incentives to overcharge. Most aircraft companies were taxed at the highest rate of 90 percent, and as a result retained only a modest profit while the war lasted. For corporate executives to informally meet in their hotel rooms to confer about new business, like Boeing's Johnson and myself, only made easier the cost-effective arrangements necessary to increase aircraft production and expedite contract letting.

After briefly discussing Northrop's idle plant capacity with me, Johnson called Seattle and talked with Clelland Gracey, head of Boeing's outside manufacturing department. He advised him to seriously consider the possibility of Northrop joining their B–17 bomber production team.

"Clelland," he began, "I would much prefer to do business with a fellow airplane company than to be told by the Air Corps that we must find our suppliers among the auto companies in Detroit. Northrop will know our problems." He continued, "The boys in the auto industry think they are the only ones who know mass production, but their methods of freezing designs do not work in building airplanes that must be continuously modified without slowing down production."

Phil Johnson turned to me and said, "Call your plant right away and get a good manufacturing engineer to meet you in Seattle. Go to see Gracey and pick out the parts you think you can build cheaply and quickly, and give us a firm bid. I have been told here in Washington that we have one of the two standard long-range bombers which the Air Corps will be buying in large numbers for the first time. The other one is Consolidated's B–24."

Dick Nolan, an experienced production man from the original Northrop team, met me in Seattle within the week. We picked out engine nacelles and cowling as being the most logical subassembly for us to produce in large quantities. They could be made in the Northrop Hawthorne plant without interfering with Northrop's own products. The informal Washington call on President Phil Johnson of Boeing had taken less than an hour of our time. During the subsequent short visit to Seattle the foundation was laid for work at Northrop that continued throughout the war. Later, the same B–17 parts were supplied to both Lockheed and Douglas, who had been given large production orders for complete Boeing B–17s. The incident was an excellent example of competitive companies cooperating in wartime, devising the best way to get the job done at the least cost to the American war effort.

Before the war ended in 1945, the manufacture of B–17 engine nacelles and cowling had run into the thousands. While the repetitive nature of the work caused prices to be continually reduced, profits from the Boeing subcontracts exceeded profits from the 1,000 P–61 Black Widow night fighters. A consequence of far greater long range importance to Northrop was the beginning of a profitable and mutually satisfactory relationship with Boeing that began in 1941 and still continues.

Shortly after the bombing of Pearl Harbor on December 7, 1941, an incident occurred at Wright Field in Dayton that caused much unnecessary delay in the production of the *Vengeance*. A junior officer at Dayton wired the Northrop plant to stop all production for the British, as Wright Field intended to take over all plant capacity for the U.S. Army Air Corps. This officer had taken it upon himself to interpret literally a telegram received from Washington, instructing the Air Corps to convert all plant capacity to the United States Government. The Washington wire did not say how this was going to be done, or where the contract money for the conversion was to come from. It obviously had been sent in a moment of war hysteria by an uninformed bureaucrat.

At the time of receiving the telegram, the principal production in the Northrop plant was the British *Vengeance* airplane. The Black Widow was still on the drawing boards, the N–3PB seaplane order from Norway neared completion, and, except for the N–1M flying wing demonstration flight model, the only other work was on parts for the B–17 and the Navy's PBY flying boats. It was hardly good news for Northrop, still struggling with growing pains. Realizing that it all was probably a serious mistake, I immediately flew to Dayton to straighten out the problem. Upon arrival, I learned that all aircraft companies with any British orders had received the same telegram, and production for our ally had come to an abrupt halt across the country. It took three weeks to get the mistaken Air Corps order rescinded. Valuable time and money had been lost. Gage Irving remarked, "If the Japs had dropped a bomb on Wright Field instead of Pearl Harbor, it would have done no harm. No bomb could have ever penetrated all the U.S. government red tape!"

On another occasion I decided to stay in Washington and assist our company treasurer in arranging for an additional advance payment from the British to cover the heavy expenses Northrop was incurring on the *Vengeance* dive bomber production contract. The original $8.5 million down payment had been exhausted, and our own working capital was insufficient to carry us until airplanes were delivered and paid for.

La Motte Cohu had taught me a valuable lesson. "If you need something important, always insist on seeing the man at the top. Don't allow yourself to be turned over to his subordinates." Accordingly, I called at the British embassy and asked to see the Ambassador, Lord Halifax. The receptionist asked why so important an official should be concerned with my problem. I replied by telling her that if the British wanted to receive *Vengeance* dive bombers from the Northrop company he had better find time to see me. Very soon a staff assistant ushered me into Lord Halifax's office, and a tall, gracious Englishman with a withered right arm, greeted me cordially and listened to my story attentively. He quickly understood, and explained that President Roosevelt had frozen all funds that the British had transferred to this country to pay for airplanes. The U.S. government wanted to be sure there would be enough money available to cover their large commitments. The British would have to obtain permission from the President, or his financial people, before they could release any more funds to Northrop. I asked him, "How can this permission be arranged?" Halifax smiled, and said he would call Harry Hopkins, the President's top assistant, and asked him to meet with me.

I was soon on my way to Hopkins' office in the White House, and was pleased to learn he was expecting me. I was ushered promptly into his office where I was confronted by a thin man of medium height, who was obviously very tired, as he had just returned from Europe on a long flight. His clothes were wrinkled and his face the color of ashes.

He too, quickly saw Northrop's problem. Picking up the phone, he called Jessie Jones, then head of the Reconstruction Finance Corporation, and asked him to meet with, "Coleman of the Northrop Aircraft Company of California." Our conference didn't last ten minutes before I was on my way again, this time across town to the RFC office.

Here, I was again greeted by a staff assistant, who carefully explained that because Jessie Jones was so busy, I should tell him what I wished to say to his boss. He would then summarize the message and obtain the answer. I did so, and we then walked into the large office, where Jones, who had helped elect Franklin Roosevelt, and been rewarded by appointment to head this important government agency, rose from his chair, and unsmilingly approached us. The assistant said his bit, "This man is an officer of Northrop Aircraft, and he needs more money from the British to finish their contract for dive bombers. Will you give them permission to release another $2 million to Northrop?"

Jones hardly paused long enough to look at me. "Mr. Coleman, we at the RFC aren't about to pull the British out of the hole they have dug for themselves by over-commitment of funds they have brought here to pay American contractors. You will have to find some other way to solve your problem." Jessie Jones turned his back on us, and it was the signal to leave the room. I resolved at that moment never to vote for Franklin Roosevelt again.

In despair, I again called on Lord Halifax. He was disturbed to learn that the U.S. government would not permit him to release more funds to Northrop. "But I have thought of a solution to your problem," he said. "If you can arrange a bank loan to carry you over until the airplanes are delivered and we are permitted to pay for them, I will agree to advise your bank that the British Government will guarantee the loan. That should get you the needed money without going back to these self-important American officials." The next day I flew to New York. With the British guarantee in hand, I successfully arranged for a $2 million loan from the Chase National Bank. Production of the *Vengeance* never paused.

While the *Vengeance*, designed and tested by Vultee, did not meet Jack Northrop's standards, the aircraft did serve the British well at a time when they desperately needed air support for their ground forces. By 1944, 400 *Vengeance* dive bombers had been built and test flown from the mile-long runway at Hawthorne without a single serious accident. This spoke well for Moye Stephens, chief of production test flying, who was meticulous, careful, and thorough, traits that he instilled in all the test pilots working under him. To insure that factory production was properly completed, Moye insisted that a flight mechanic from the factory fly with the pilot on all delivery flights. One of Moye's favorite sayings reflected this cautious attitude, "I want to be known as one of the oldest, not one of the hottest test pilots, when I terminate my flying career."

On August 22, 1942, a telegram was received by Wallace Cohu in Northrop's newly opened Washington office:

On behalf of the Minister of Aircraft Production, England, I should be grateful if you would convey to all workers of your Corporation our appreciation and gratitude for the magnificent effort they have made in completing the Vengeance contract six weeks before due time. The standard they have set is an inspiration to us all.

C. R. Fairey, Director General
British Air Commission

A rapid buildup in the number of employees at Northrop occurred following the Japanese bombing of Pearl Harbor and declaration of war by the United States. Government funds suddenly became available in large amounts. Many new contracts were awarded to aircraft companies for expanding production and the development of new aircraft and equipment. Thousands of women applied for work in southern California aircraft and shipbuilding companies to fill vacancies on the production line as men enlisted or were drafted into the armed services. It was the first time that many of these women had held a regular job.

In the Hawthorne plant and a new leased facility on Olympic Boulevard in Los Angeles where aircraft subassemblies were fabricated, women soon made up over 50 percent of the work force. The phrase, "Rosie the Riveter," became a popular expression. Men found themselves in the minority for the first time.

Northrop set up a separate manufacturing plant in an old four-story mattress factory at the corner of Olympic and Alameda in south central Los Angeles, on the edge of minority neighborhoods, to hire needed workers never before employed on an aircraft production line—mostly black and chicano. Jack personally visited the operation, often with La Motte, asking questions of employees as he walked through the plant, expressing his pleasure with accomplishments of the new work force trained by Northrop personnel to fabricate complicated aircraft parts. Jack was always concerned that everyone would feel he was part of the total Northrop production process.

The downtown operation fabricated subassemblies for the main Hawthorne plant, making cowlings for the P–61 *Black Widow*, and B–17. At its peak the plant employed 1,600 workers in the four-story concrete building. All work stopped on the morning after VJ day, the end of the war in the Pacific. The plant closed virtually overnight and everyone was laid off. The end of the war was not a happy day for many of the workers in south central Los Angeles, although it was not long before the Northrop company would be employing people of every race and culture in the postwar aircraft industry.

In 1942, though, the public, spurred on by hysterical reports in newspapers and on the radio, was concerned that the Japanese might attack southern California and the many aircraft plants in the area. There were numerous false air raid alarms, and every city in the Los Angeles area had volunteer neighborhood air raid wardens.

The number of security guards at Northrop was doubled. A huge wire screen was suspended over the main buildings to camouflage manufacturing facilities. Air raid shelters, consisting of covered trenches, were dug nearby to protect workers forced to evacuate the plant if there actually was a bombing raid. Anti-aircraft guns, manned by the National Guard, were placed around the plant. It created an atmosphere of considerable excitement, with air raid drills providing a midday diversion as production lines temporarily halted, and men and women workers filed into dimly lighted shelters to wait for all-clear signals.

When a real air raid alarm sounded, anti-aircraft gunners, thinking they had spotted enemy planes overhead, opened fire. To their apparent disappointment, nothing was shot down. Rumors persisted that a Japanese submarine had surfaced offshore, and was firing at an oil tank farm near San Pedro, a rumor that perhaps triggered the false alarm. Next day the newspapers were full of stories recounting the incident, but nothing was ever confirmed. For several weeks afterwards, all completed airplanes able to fly off the Hawthorne runway were flown to Muroc Dry Lake, and not returned to the plant until the war-induced excitement had subsided.

The entire Douglas plant in Santa Monica was covered with camouflaged netting, painted to make the plant appear from the air as if it were the location of the airport runway. The runway itself was painted in abstract camouflage designs of dirty yellow, mauve greens, and brown to make it look like nothing more than a field of weeds. This trick presented a continuing problem to transient pilots intending to land at the nearby Santa Monica Airport. Several planes were waved off as they approached the camouflaged buildings for a landing.

Gasoline was soon rationed, and most employees joined car pools made up of fellow workers. A spirit of goodwill prevailed among employees, continuing until the end of the war. True patriotism was the norm. Reports of war casualties were arriving daily, anxiously followed by the many employees with family members fighting in the armed forces overseas.

Any class separation between production line workers and office executives did not exist at Northrop. Jack and all other company officials, from La Motte down, carried their own trays from the food line in the company cafeteria to their table. There was nothing like an executive dining room at Northrop. Management entered their own teams playing against plant workers in the company softball and bowling leagues. As a result of excellent employee-management relations, with accompanying fringe benefits and wages often superior to competitors, as well as the considerable employee loyalty enjoyed by Jack himself, all attempts by labor union organizers to unionize the plant were unsuccessful. Wages and hours were frozen by government regulation, and employees of Northrop had no doubt of their fair treatment by Northrop management. It was always easy to meet with the boss, who listened carefully to complaints and suggestions from employees.

Baseball was one of La Motte Cohu's favorite sports. He found that one of the new plant security guards was John Miljis, a well-known, former professional baseball pitcher with the New York Giants, for whom he had pitched in the World Series. La Motte encouraged John to contact other professional baseball friends not yet in the service, offering them jobs at Northrop where they could help the war effort. Soon, the newly organized Northrop recreation club boasted the best team in California and won first place in the National Industrial League games played in Wichita, Kansas. There were so many top-flight players turning out for the team that no one could possibly make the Northrop team without big league professional baseball experience.

When Jack Northrop was told that recently hired security guards were taking a great amount of time away from work for baseball practice, he pointed out to La Motte that he should remember their primary business was manufacturing airplanes, and that government auditors would soon discover what was happening. The overemphasis on baseball was scaled back, much to the disappointment of the many enthusiastic company fans, and the guards, who in many cases had been chosen for their baseball playing ability.

Management found that, by working ten hours a day for five days a week, the employees produced better quality airplanes, than when working an eight-hour day for six days a week. This arrangement provided for two full days off each weekend. Only two ten-hour shifts were worked in a twenty-four hour day, giving maintenance crews four hours a day to clean up while the plant was empty.

Men and women from all walks of life applied for positions made available by employees leaving for overseas. Maurice McLaughlin, a former world champion tennis player, worked at Northrop. The brother of movie star Fredric March was employed as an accountant. All the girls in the front office would stop work and stare as the well-known movie star passed by on occasional visits to Hawthorne to chat with his brother.

Louis B. Mayer, head of the MGM movie studio, often arranged gatherings with his many stars to attract crowds at rallies selling war bonds. Movie and radio personalities visited the plant for noontime war bond shows, including Edgar Bergen and Charlie, Constance Bennett, Gary Cooper, Kay Francis, Hoagy Carmichael, Mickey Rooney, Esther Williams, Walter Pidgeon, and Loretta Young. Employees always came out to see them, returning home after work to tell their children about meeting the celebrities. Members of management were their most willing hosts for lunch in the Northrop cafeteria.

On one occasion Jack Northrop, always concerned about the welfare of his employees, was taken in by an enthusiastic salesman of vitamin pills, which had recently become popular. A local company had introduced an item called Stuart's Formula, a pill claimed to increase a person's energy. Jack listened and was convinced by the salesman that, if the vitamins were taken twice every day by all 6,000 factory employees during coffee breaks, their productivity would substantially increase. He was sure that employees would only take the pills if they were supplied by the company. Deciding it was a good idea, he authorized the purchase of sufficient vitamin pills to supply 6,000 employees for a month, his engineering mind forgetting to calculate the cost. When treasurer Claude Momsen received an invoice for the pills, he was shocked to find it came to $20,000 a month. A hurried conference convinced Jack he had made a mistake, and the pill order was cancelled.

Jack Northrop was naive in other ways as well, and was easily impressed by anyone who could intelligently discuss a subject in which he was interested. On one occasion before we entered the war, when Jack had accompanied me to Washington, we were invited to have lunch with a man introduced to us as a scientist from Switzerland. He wished to discuss the subject of boundary layer control as it applied to airplane wings, especially flying wings. Jack was flattered and impressed with his knowledge of aerodynamics. As we sat talking at our table in the hotel dining room near the lobby, our host from Switzerland was frequently interrupted. I noticed that he would go to the registration desk and each time meet a different attractive woman. These women apparently were being assigned rooms in the hotel. Before Jack and I departed, our host invited us to attend a party that he was giving in the hotel that evening. Jack, who generally avoided social events, was about to accept the invitation when he saw me shaking my head behind the man's back. Jack declined the invitation.

After we left the hotel, I expressed my suspicion that there may have been something going on behind our backs that Jack would find very uncomfortable, that our Swiss host was probably arranging a wild party for us. Jack was shocked by my candid comments, but agreed that we had been wise to decline the invitation. Upon arriving back home, Jack received a memorandum from the security office naming our Swiss host in Washington, and advising against making any contacts with him or discussing any subjects that might affect our national security. The FBI had discovered that he was evidently a German spy posing as a Swiss civilian engineer. The spy had been entertaining numerous government officials in Washington, and the FBI was advising government contractors to avoid him.

A U.S. Senate war investigating committee visited Los Angeles shortly after food rationing went into effect, conducting an investigation of those war plants operating company cafeterias to determine where they obtained food supplies. There had been complaints that some plants were receiving preferential treatment. La Motte asked George Gore, Northrop's legal counsel, to look into the matter and appear before the committee when public hearings were called. George duly made his usual detailed investigation. At the hearing, when he was asked where Northrop's cafeteria chefs buy their meat, he candidly replied, "We buy it on the black market."

Next morning all the newspapers carried a front page story featuring headlines saying, "Northrop buying meat on the black market." George was a relatively new member of the Northrop management, and upon arriving at work, cautiously entered La Motte's office to inquire, "Boss, am I fired?" La Motte laughed, telling George he had done absolutely the right thing. The investigating committee staff had already called to congratulate George for being honest. They had been given the information they needed to make vital changes in the government's rationing system.

*   *   *

A newly hired industrial engineer, concerned about production goals, decided that a recently developed uncomfortable toilet seat would add to productivity when installed in company toilets by discouraging lingering in the rest rooms. Without conferring with management, he authorized the purchase of several of these outlandish gadgets, installing one in La Motte's private toilet adjacent to his office. An executive committee meeting was in progress when Cohu excused himself to visit his restroom. Without warning, a loud roar issued from behind the door when he sat down, "Who installed this goddamned seat? I'll fire the SOB!" yelled La Motte. The next day all the toilets throughout the plant had their original seats reinstalled. By this time La Motte had cooled down and the engineer stayed on the job, but was told to be very careful about what he would do the next time he took it upon himself to improve plant efficiency.

La Motte was always informal in his relations with employees, a habit that caused the company serious trouble with one of the New York bankers participating in a major line of bank credit badly needed by the company. In addition to his habit of perfecting archery skills during the noon hour, La Motte found a skilled wrestler working in the plant on one of his visits to the plant machine shop, who offered to show him some new wrestling holds. In his younger days, Cohu had been a member of the Princeton University wrestling team, and was still powerfully built and very strong.

The mechanic was invited into La Motte's private office during the noon hour, where they would try new holds on each other, often resulting in one or the other being thrown to the floor. It soon became common knowledge that the big boss was enjoying his weekly workout with his wrestling friend whenever a loud thump was heard while passing his office door. A visiting vice president of the Bankers Trust Company of New York, one of the most prestigious banks in the country, was on one occasion ushered into his office just as the tough looking mechanic had succeeded in throwing the Northrop chairman of the board to the floor. The mechanic was sitting astraddle La Motte, pinning his shoulders to the rug. Making a hasty retreat, the banker backed out of the room, and ran down the hall calling loudly for a security guard to free the chairman from the clutches of a violent intruder. He was appalled when told of La Motte's unusual method of staying in good physical condition. Jack received a call from the banker, questioning him as to Cohu's qualifications to run the company as its chief executive officer in time of war.

*   *   *

Large numbers of North American manufactured AT–6 advanced trainers were being assembled in Canada and flown to southern California to prepare them for shipment overseas. When the nearby North American plant in Inglewood became overloaded with work, the Air Corps asked us to submit a bid for crating the trainers at Northrop for ocean shipment. A reasonable fixed price bid was submitted, but after several weeks passed without a reply, the shipping personnel were reassigned to other duties.

A few days later, a frantic call came from the Hawthorne airport control tower adjacent to the plant, informing the front office of an unexpected landing of ten North American AT–6s to be prepared for shipping overseas. Before the Air Corps' procurement officer could be located by phone, several more North American airplanes landed on the Northrop field. The planes taxied around the ramp with the pilots looking for parking spaces and asking for instructions, meanwhile informing the tower that more aircraft were on the way. The plant supervisor nominally in charge had not been notified, as no contract had been negotiated. He was as confused as the ferry pilots, now arriving by the dozen, according to the distraught airport tower controllers.

A telephone call from the Air Corps procurement officer finally came through, informing me that Northrop's bid for the new crating and shipping job had been received. "Mr. Coleman," began the officer, "We have decided that your bid price is too high. We must get two other bids so as to abide by regulations."

I had a ready reply. "I just called to tell you that the price has gone up. If you can't meet our price, please arrange to have the fifty planes that have already arrived at our airport flown out at once." The young Air Corps lieutenant at the other end of the line was suitably startled. "Please don't tell my boss about this," he pleaded. "There has been a terrible mistake. I'll call you right back."

In five minutes the phone rang again. "We will pay your new price and have a contract in your hands for signature tomorrow," he informed me. It was the first and only time the Northrop company was able to name its own price in dealing with the government.

Five-year-old Jack Northrop, Lincoln, Nebraska, 1900. Courtesy of John Northrop Jr.

Loughead-designed and built twin-engine biplane model F.1.A. First plane with engineering by Jack Northrop, 1916.

Young Jack Northrop with the Loughead brothers and Tony Stadlman in Santa Barbara, 1916.

First completely Jack Northrop-designed aircraft, the Lockheed S–1 *Sportsplane*, 1918, Santa Barbara.

Northrop's first airplane, the Lockheed S–1 *Sportsplane*, in front of San Francisco city hall, 1919.

Douglas U.S. Army *Cloudsters* return to Santa Monica in 1924, after completing first around-the-world flight.

Jack Northrop, 1925.
Photo courtesy John Northrop Jr.

Northrop family, 1928. From left: John Jr., Inez, Jack, Ynez. Photo courtesy John Northrop Jr.

The famous Lockheed *Vega*, designed by Jack Northrop. First of modern Lockheed company airplanes, 1927.

Amelia Earhart and her personal Lockheed *Vega*.

Wiley Post and his Lockheed *Vega*, the *Winnie Mae*.

The Lockheed *Air Express*, designed by Northrop in 1928. Courtesy of Harvey Christian.

The first Northrop flying wing aircraft on its maiden flight. Built in 1929 at Northrop's Avion company. While not a true flying wing, it represented a monumental step on the way toward the huge Northrop flying wing YB–49 bomber.

Jack Northrop with test pilot Bellande in the first flying wing, 1929.

First all-metal
stressed-skin
monocoque fuselage
of Northrop-designed
Alpha, 1928.

Northrop *Gamma*, 1936. Developed for high altitude "over-the-weather" flying. Flown by Frank Hawks, famous long-distance record holder. The *Gamma* was used by the Lincoln-Ellsworth expedition to fly over the South Pole for the first time.

The first Northrop engineering department employees gather at the "Yellow Peril," the Hotel Hawthorne, 1939.

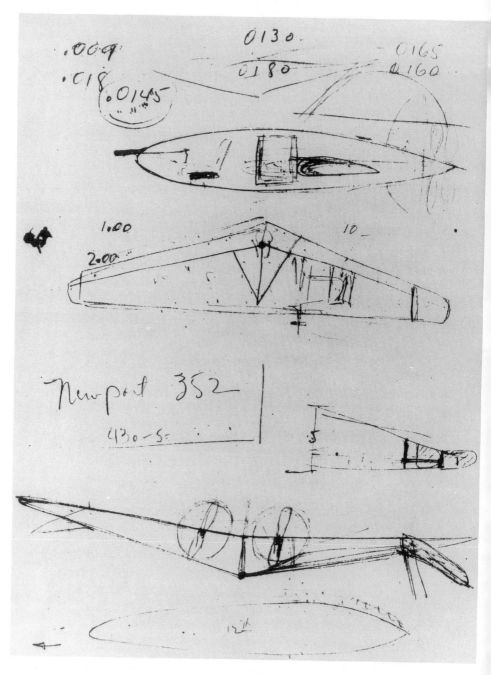

Original sketches by Jack Northrop of the first true flying wing, the N–1M, 1939.

First Board of Directors of Northrop Aircraft Inc., 1940. From left: James N. Wright, H. W. Cohu, Ted Coleman, Bert Lester, Rolland O'Brian, La Motte Cohu, (Jack Northrop not pictured).

Northrop Aircraft Inc.'s first Plant 1, at Prairie and Northrop Avenues, Hawthorne, 1940. Still part of today's large complex of Northrop buildings.

Gage H. Irving,
Vice President for Production
and Assistant General Manager,
1939–1948.

Northrop N–1M, final weight and balance check in the factory, 1940.

Northrop's first true flying wing aircraft, the N–1M, 1940.

Test pilot Moye Stephens ready for the first flight of the flying wing prototype N–1M in the Mojave Desert, 1941.

Thomas H. Quayle, one of the original Northrop engineers. Later served as both Washington and Dayton office manager, and manager of Turbodyne Corp.

Key men on flying wing program, William R. Sears, Walt Cerney, and Jack Northrop, 1942.

Ted Coleman on trail ride
with Conquistadores del Cielo.
Vice President-Sales
and Director, 1940–1946.

Jack Northrop (left) and James McKinley, Director of Northrop Aeronautical Institute, 1942.

General William Knudsen, head of War Production Board, and General "Hap" Arnold, Chief of Army Air Corps, visit Northrop in 1941.

Jack Northrop (right) and test pilot John Myers in the prototype flying wing N–9M, late 1941. Courtesy of John Myers.

Theodore Von Karman, consultant to Northrop, 1940–1944; Chief scientific advisor to U.S. Army Air Corps, 1944–1946; Chief scientist to UNESCO, 1947–1949. Photo courtesy of the Archives, California Institute of Technology.

7

THE SCIENTIST AND THE GENIUS

Jack Northrop entered into a consulting arrangement with the world's leading authority on aerodynamics, Dr. Theodore Von Karman. Von Karman left Aachen University in Germany and became director of the Daniel Guggenheim School of Aeronautics at the California Institute of Technology, popularly known as Caltech.

Von Karman had been a pupil of Dr. Prandtl, an early leader in the application of scientific reasoning to the problems of flight. At the time Von Karman left Germany, he held the Chair of Aeronautics at Aachen University. He had decided to take a leave of absence from Aachen and take a trip around the world, when the offer from Dr. Robert Millikan at Caltech came. As a prominent Jewish professor, Von Karman knew he would undoubtedly be persecuted as soon as Hitler came to power. He wanted to get his widowed mother and unmarried sister out of the country. The professor was single, and his family shared a home in Pasadena.

When the Nazi leadership began to rebuild the German war machine in the early 1930s (in violation of the Versailles peace treaty), Hitler personally addressed a letter to Von Karman urging him to return to Germany. He offered Von Karman a sizable salary increase and all expenses paid if he would return. Hitler urgently needed scientists like the talented Von Karman if Germany were to create a first-rate Luftwaffe and insure German domination of the air. Dr. Von Karman told Carlos Wood, a Caltech graduate student at the time, of the attractive offer, telling him how he answered the letter. "I went to the best portrait photographer in Pasadena, and had him make some profile pictures of my head, which emphasized my flying jib nose. I wrote across the lower part of the picture, 'To Adolph Hitler, best regards, from Theodore Von Karman.' I sent the picture to Hitler, and a couple of months later I read in the German newspapers that the Chair of Aeronautics at Aachen had been filled by someone else."

Von Karman's father had been a prominent Hungarian, who for many years headed the education system for the Austro-Hungarian government. His mother, with an advanced degree in philology, was reputed to be fluent in twenty-six languages and able to make herself understood in forty dialects. The sister, Pepa, also possessed a Ph.D., and liked to remind her brother that she had received a higher rating in her oral college examination than he.

Von Karman did much of his theoretical work in an office at home. It was a large room with a desk before a window overlooking the garden. In the middle of the room was a large brass pot at least thirty inches in diameter. He was a habitual cigar smoker, and, when finished with a cigar, he would throw it over his shoulder toward the huge ash tray. The cigar was supposed to hit the center. Sometimes it did.

Although Jack was credited with considerable aerodynamic knowledge, and was generally the first to try new ideas, he realized that his technical education was limited, and he admired the intellectual ability of recognized scientists. Jack strongly believed that Dr. Von Karman belonged at the very top of this select group. He felt fortunate to be able to work with him and gain from his knowledge. Von Karman in turn, was intrigued with Northrop's flying wing concept. He agreed with enthusiasm to spend two days a week with Northrop at Hawthorne, as a consultant on the flying wing and the new gas turbine airplane engine that a Northrop development engineer, Vladimer Pavlecka, had proposed to Jack.

The doctor possessed a large amount of practical, as well as theoretical knowledge, and had the courage to make difficult decisions. Caltech students and faculty admired him greatly. He was responsible for the establishment of the Jet Propulsion Laboratory in the Arroyo Seco in Pasadena. Here, in 1936, early rocket motors were fired experimentally by students working under his direction. Among this group were several budding scientists who became well known in the aeronautical field. These included Carlos Wood, later to become chief engineer for Sikorsky; Frank Malina, Apollo Smith, John Parsons, William Bollay; and Edward Forman, who organized the Aerojet

Corporation under Von Karman's leadership. There was Gerry Vultee and Richard Palmer, designer of the Howard Hughes airplane that set many early records; Eugene Root, who later became chief engineer for Lockheed's guided missile division in northern California; Arthur Raymond, who became chief engineer of Douglas; and R. C. Rockefeller, hired by Floyd Odlum as his consultant at Convair. Many of these scientists became instructors at Caltech during Von Karman's tenure.

Typical of many foreigners who had not grown up with the automobile, Von Karman was a poor driver and did not like to drive. He gladly accepted an invitation to commute to Hawthorne in the car pool with me, a fellow Pasadena resident and Caltech alumnus. Two other Northrop employees and I met together at alternate homes, taking turns driving the twenty miles between Pasadena and Hawthorne. We saved rationed gas and it was the beginning of a friendship enjoyed for many years.

Dr. Von Karman frequently stayed up late at night and was not an early riser. After several occasions when I arrived at his Pasadena home to pick him up for the ride to work, only to find him still eating breakfast, the regular members of the car pool decided that a revised arrangement must be made to avoid being continually late for work. As long as we were doing him a favor by driving to Hawthorne through heavy Los Angeles downtown traffic, it would not be unreasonable to ask the good doctor to first drive himself to the car pool driver's home, meeting there promptly for a 7:30 A.M. departure. Von Karman readily agreed with the new plan and promised not to hold us up.

The first morning that we inaugurated the new arrangement, he failed to show. Just as we were pulling out of my driveway to again pick him up at his house (Jack would have never forgiven us if we had failed to show up at the plant with his scientist), the sound of a distant auto horn could be heard. As we waited, the sound grew louder and louder as the horn continued to blow. A car soon appeared, racing up the street toward us. As Von Karman passed, with his horn still blowing, we waved frantically to attract his attention. Pulling his car to a sudden stop, several feet away from the curb, he hurriedly ran back to my waiting car and profusely apologized for being late. "I had forgotten where you live on this street," he said, "and I knew that my horn would attract your attention and you would come out to stop me."

He enjoyed smoking his ever-present morning cigar as he sat in the front seat of my car during the morning commute, frequently forgetting to use the car's ash tray directly in front of him. His coat and vest were generally covered with a light brushing of gray cigar ash when he arrived at Hawthorne, ready to meet with Jack.

Even after many years in California, the doctor spoke English with a very strong Hungarian accent. It required a good deal of exposure to his conversation before what he was saying was clearly understood. However, it was soon apparent to any listener that he possessed a great deal of wisdom, not only in the field of science, but about life in general. He was friendly with hundreds of students throughout the world who wrote to him regularly and looked up to him.

One of these students was Dr. William Sears, who joined Jack at Hawthorne as Northrop's chief of aerodynamics, where he made invaluable contributions to the success of Northrop during the war years. His work at Northrop was Sears' first and only job in the aviation industry, for he left California later on to head Cornell University's reknowned aeronautical research laboratory. Sears and Von Karman were perhaps the most important persons working at Northrop. It was these two scientists who confirmed Jack's long-held belief in the practicality of flying wing aircraft, and helped him design a flying wing that would fly.

Jack patented his flying wing on November 20, 1940. His patent drawings were published a year later in the November 18, 1941 issue of the international aeronautical publication, *Interavia*, receiving considerable attention in Germany. The Nazi government was sufficiently influenced to provide additional funds to support the German Horten brothers' imaginative flying wing aircraft. Beginning as a glider (before Germany was allowed by the Versailles treaty to build powered aircraft), the Horten plane had been under development for many years.

The idea of flying wing aircraft was not originally conceived by Jack Northrop. It was Northrop, however, who persevered against all odds and developed the concept into a practical, efficient aircraft. Perhaps the first true flying wing, shaped like an elliptical Zanonia seed, was designed and flown by a Czechoslovakian designer, Igo Etrich, in 1909. Etrich decided his plane would fly better with a tail like a bird and abandoned the pure concept. Almost all of the many so-called flying wing aircraft designed in Europe in prewar years were not true flying wings. Most had vertical fins and horizontal stabilizers, either mounted on flimsy tail booms, like Northrop's first experimental model, or at the tips of extremely swept-back wings. The only exceptions were the British 1910 Dunne D.6 monoplane with downward sweeping wing tips (resembling the bat-like appearance of Northrop's early flying wing designs), and famed English professor G.T.R. Hill's, Westland-Hill *Pterodactyl* Mk.IA of 1928, which incorporated pivoted wing tips serving as both ailerons and elevators. In 1910 Hugo Junkers of Germany patented an all-wing airplane, but the design was crude and the craft never built. Several true flying wings were developed as gliders prior to World War II in Germany, where Horten designs were commonly flown in competitive aviation events. Many were powered with small horsepower pusher engines like ultralight aircraft flying today.

Development of imaginative flying wing designs by the Hortens continued in Germany with enthusiastic help from the German Air Force. The U.S. military's interest in advanced aircraft development languished because of their desire to simply increase the numbers of aircraft available in the shortest time. The German military, with Marshall Herman Goering in charge, was alert to any new development that might be a breakthrough in making it possible for Germany to control the skies over Europe. Financial assistance by the German government resulted in the world's first turbojet-powered flying wing, the Horten HoIXV2, flown in January 1945. In the same year Alexander Lippisch at Messerschmitt designed the Me 163, the first operational flying wing fighter.

In 1943 Lippisch had become director of the German Aeronautical Research Institute in Vienna where he began research in supersonic aircraft, culminating in the design of the experimental P13 ramjet interceptor. A full-size glider prototype was unfinished when the war ended. When Von Karman was briefed by Lippisch in Paris about his flying wing designs, delayed American interest was revived. At Von Karman's urging, construction of the DM–1 glider was completed. The DM–1 was shipped to the United States where wind tunnel tests were performed.

Still on the drawing board when Hitler's Germany surrendered in 1945, was project P12, an experimental ramjet fighter bearing a remarkable resemblance to Lockheed's 1987 ATF Stealth fighter. During the war years Lippisch and his associates had spent fulltime developing flying wing concepts into actual full size flying machines for the Luftwaffe. Northrop was forced to confine his flying wing work to small prototype flying models since Washington was still not quite sure that a flying wing would fly. It was not until the frightening possibility of Germany winning the war became evident that Jack's proposal for an efficient, long-range flying wing bomber, capable of flying from the continental USA to Europe and return, suddenly opened the eyes of Washington military strategists to what advanced aircraft could offer in an intercontinental conflict.

Von Karman and Sears had available to them the extensive aeronautical library at Caltech, containing all of the technical data and information from foreign literature and NACA reports. Working with Walter Cerny, Northrop's assistant chief of design, they conducted extensive wind tunnel tests, utilizing a wide variety of models to test various configurations of flying wings. The result reflected very closely Jack Northrop's early sketches of a highly efficient aircraft with engines buried in the wings and various flaps, high-lift devices, and airfoil lift spoilers along the entire trailing edge of the wing.

In an article published in the March 29, 1930 issue of Aviation Magazine, under the title, "The All-Wing Type Airplane," Jack anticipated the aircraft his company would eventually build. He wrote,

> It has been apparent for several years to the designer of aircraft that some radical changes in the general arrangement will be necessary if any large increase in the overall efficiency of the average airplane is to be accomplished . . . The flying wing in various forms has been a well recognized dream of designers since man began to fly, but it has been pictured in prohibitively costly and mammoth sizes. However, certain comparatively recent developments have made many of its advantages immediately applicable to planes of moderate size.

The original Northrop N–1M flying wing prototype was a totally company-financed and company-sponsored project. Actual engineering design for the plane was assigned by Jack to the small group of engineers who had worked with him at Douglas and followed him over to Hawthorne to work with the new Northrop company. It was the first actual aircraft design work begun by the new company, before they received any outside contracts, while plant and production space was still under construction. The first N–1M was built as a "flying mock-up" with wood structure that could be easily modified and changed after it had been flown, its flight characteristics studied, and the data evaluated. As soon as the design was completed, many of the same design engineers were assigned to supervise construction of the little plane they called the "Jeep," after the small military vehicle of the same name. The N–1M was the first aircraft to be built in the new plant. Its existence was kept secret but after it was flown several times by company test pilot Moye Stephens, word got around the southern California aircraft industry that Jack had indeed done something revolutionary. It was not until a year later that Army Air Corps General "Hap" Arnold called Northrop, asking about the new plane, saying he wanted to see it fly.

It was Irv Ashkenas, assistant to Bill Sears, Jack's Chief Aerodynamicist, who did much to make the flying wing successful. Ashkenas, working closely with Jack, did most of the innovative work devising entirely new controls for the later flying wings. The little N–1M had used conventional wire cables and pulleys to connect various control surfaces with the pilot's stick and rudder pedals. After the second N–9M, the planes were flown with the first fully powered hydraulic control system installed on any aircraft. This system gave pilots the feel of aerodynamic forces on control surfaces—sort of a synthetic "seat of the pants" system later to be incorporated in every large aircraft. The new system also assisted the pilot in overcoming excessive forces imposed when the flying wing went into a dive. These forces thrust the stick violently back into the pilot's lap, an unnerving and unexpected characteristic of all flying wings.

With a government contract for building small prototype airplanes finally in hand and theoretical work behind them, Northrop engineers were ready to build as many flying models as necessary, preparatory to development of the full-size flying wing, actually one-third aerodynamically scale models of the future flying wing bomber. The government continued to place such a high priority on immediate projects needed for the war effort that little time could be spared on new designs. The Air Corps placed greater emphasis on building more fighters than development of long-range bombers. Britain was still there, Germany hadn't won, and the English isles remained as principal bases for Strategic Air Command. With their very successful Boeing B–17 *Flying Fortress* and Consolidated B–24 *Liberator* the SAC was doing an excellent job bombing Germany. A newer long-range bomber, no matter how efficient, was no longer urgently needed, especially with the newer B–29 *Super Fortress* going into production.

Northrop would not allow work on his flying wing to stop altogether. He was aware that Consolidated Vultee placed great faith on the development of their giant B–36 as a conventional replacement for the B–29 in the postwar era. As Consolidated Vultee proceeded with preliminary design work for their B–36, Northrop, at times working in secret, keeping his efforts unknown even from the Air Corps, proceeded with preliminary engineering work on a full-size flying wing bomber.

The Northrop aircraft company later submitted to the Army Air Corps a proposal for two flying wing bombers, designated XB–35, to be developed and flown under a cost-plus-fixed-fee contract. The Army at the time used the letter "X" to designate experimental, the letter "B" for bomber, "P" for pursuit, and later, for the same type of plane, "F" for fighter. There were usually two experimental aircraft of one model built. In the case of the flying wing, which the procurement people evidently felt was a little too ingenious to even make two of, Northrop received a contract for only one aircraft. This occurred in December 1941, shortly after the bombing of Pearl Harbor. A few months later the second XB–35 was added to the contract, after the generals returned from the Mojave desert test hop with proof that the flying wing "really does fly!" A year later, after many hours of flying the flying wing N–1M produced considerable actual flight data and the company received a third contract for thirteen additional YB–35s, the "Y" designation indicating they were to be assigned for service flight testing. The usual procedure of the Air Corps was to drop the "Y" after service tests were completed, quantity production was underway, and the plane became operational. It would not be until a much later date that the bomber designation was changed to YB–49, after jet engines were installed in place of the original air-cooled piston engines. A single flying wing was designated YRB–49, for photo reconnaissance, the last of the line of flying wings to be built.

The competition between Northrop and Consolidated Vultee was now real. In the same month Northrop was awarded their first contract, Consolidated Vultee received an order for 2 XB–36 bombers. The next year Consolidated Vultee also received a contract for thirteen YB–36s. A future production order for 100 Northrop B–35s was given to Glenn L. Martin to manufacture, but the order was cancelled before the war ended. Consolidated Vultee received an order for 100 B–36s but did not begin producing any until 3 years later.

After having been dissuaded by all his previous employers from doing any design work on a flying wing, it was a happy day at the

Northrop plant when the Air Corps mailed in a contract for the first flying wing bomber. As if to underline their sudden acceptance of the flying wing idea, the Air Corps indicated to Jack and several of his key engineers, that it would probably be worthwhile to begin thinking of fighter applications of the flying wing concept. Northrop was encouraged to stretch the state-of-the-art as only he could, and some far-fetched projects resulted. He designed and built several special purpose pursuit aircraft and interceptors that were in essence, tailless, and incorporated features of a flying wing. For this purpose, the government issued a number of research and development contracts to cover the cost of experimental projects involving theoretical work by Von Karman and the special services of a number of highly skilled test pilots able to fly some of the most incredible aircraft ever sketched on a drawing board.

These strange aircraft included: the first American rocket-propelled airplane, using an engine designed by Von Karman, the MX–334 *Rocket Wing;* the MX–543 *Buzz Bomb;* the MX–544 *Jet Bomb;* the XP–79B *Flying Ram* intended to ram enemy aircraft in flight, the aircraft that killed Northrop test pilot Harry Crosby; and the stubby, beer bottle shaped XP–56 *Silver Bullet* pursuit plane. The war was over before any of these secret airplanes were perfected to the point of being placed in quantity production, much less flying successfully, but all provided an exciting, if sometimes tragic, experience for the test pilots who elected to fly the aircraft.

In some of these strange machines, the pilot was required to lie prone in the narrow cockpit compartment. The slender thickness of the wing did not allow him to sit in an upright position. Also, it was believed the prone position would enable the pilot to withstand maneuvers producing up to 14Gs without blacking out. The rocket propelled *Flying Ram* was designed with wing leading edges of stainless steel, so the pilot would be able to simply dive on an aircraft, fly through the tail or wings, ram the enemy airplane and destroy it without guns or gunsights. The *Silver Bullet* was a tailless pursuit plane constructed entirely of welded magnesium plate, driven by contra-rotating pusher propellers powered by a huge Pratt & Whitney double-row radial engine buried in the fuselage behind the pilot. Exhaust ports ended a few inches from the propellers, causing a loud, sharp roar whenever the aircraft engine was warmed up on the Hawthorne airfield. Complaining phone calls from nearby residents were frequent. They always knew when the "Bottle" was about to fly.

There was so much activity in the Sears research section that, on occasion, some of the engineers would get careless about locking up confidential and secret report data when leaving for home. The rules were clear that all such documents were to be kept under lock and key, to be secure from prying eyes. Late one evening when Jack was looking around the engineering department, he noticed some confidential material lying around. He collected all the classified papers and locked them in his office, not telling anyone what he had done. When the items were missed, there were some worried engineers. He let them worry for a week before informing them of his evening stroll. It was not a joke to Jack Northrop—it was a way to enforce security, and further evidence of Jack's unusual way of handling employee relations.

The combination of Jack's imagination, scientist's calculations, and the test pilots' skills produced some amazing aircraft, all of them far ahead of their time. Doing all this work within a short time span, it was not unexpected by Northrop management to realize by late 1942 that the original dates promised for completion of engineering, testing, and delivery of two full scale experimental XB–35 flying wing bombers, and thirteen service model YB–35 bombers would not be met. Estimates had been given to the Air Corps before Northrop was committed to all-out production of the P–61 *Black Widow* night fighters. The entire manufacturing capacity of the plant was involved with the P–61s along with the last of the *Vengeance* dive bombers for the British, and the experimental aircraft. Shirting war requirements were demanding even more fighters, not bigger bombers. Jack would have to wait awhile longer for his own flying wing to fly.

Jack and the financial organizers of his company did not wait long for Northrop's first profit. By the end of their second year in business manufacturing the Vultee *Vengeance*, beginning work on the P–61 *Black Widow*, doing subcontracting work on assembling tails for Consolidated PBYs and Boeing B–17 cowlings, corporate accountants were able to report that Northrop had made its first million.

8

THE WORLD OF THE TEST PILOT

The opportunity for a test pilot to display his skill is always present. The financial awards are above average. And the test pilot's public image, appearing heroic to those who read of their exploits, can be very satisfying. While these rewards are attractive, the greater return is the simple satisfaction of getting the job done successfully and the confidence developed during emergencies. When their job is done well they will be saving the lives of those who will later fly the machines they have tested. All the successful test pilots I have known have one trait in common—they are self-confident fatalists.

During World War II and the immediate postwar years, Northrop's staff test pilots were a dedicated group of men with similar skills, but with marked differences in personalities. They ranged from the conservative Moye Stephens, their senior member, to colorful Harry Crosby, the former air racer.

Reporting to Moye Stephens, in the more conservative production test pilot category, were a pair of ex-airline pilots, Dick Rinaldi and L. S. "Slim" Perrett. Perrett was killed shortly after the war ended when an experimental fin tore loose from the tail structure of Northrop's quite conventional N–23 trimotor *Pioneer* transport. He stayed with the plane at low altitude, long enough to see his fellow crew members parachute to safety, too late to save himself after flying into the ground to avoid crashing into an oil refinery. Perrett's trio had flown hundreds of production military airplanes out of the short Hawthorne airport without serious accident.

Engineering test pilots who flew the more radical Northrop prototype aircraft were Harry Crosby, John Myers, Max Stanley, Alex

Papana, Max Constant, Charles Tucker, and Fred Bretcher. Of this group, who risked their lives on every first flight, there were two casualties, Harry Crosby and Max Constant. Max was killed when he crashed in one of Northrop's prototype flying wings, the N9–M. John Myers had a close call when he was involved in the crash of the XP–56 *Silver Bullet* tailless fighter, but fortunately he survived.

Northrop's *Silver Bullet* was the kind of aircraft that, at first glance, would quicken the pulse of any prototype test pilot even if it did look like trouble. In those days test pilots were not issued crash helmets. John Myers had played polo at Stanford University, a dangerous sport where protective head helmets were required, so he dusted off his old polo helmet and took it to Muroc. The ground crew riveted two small "Mercury" wings on the sides as a possible comment on what John later said was "my courage, competence, or sanity, or an expression of an affectionate realization that I had something in common with Buck Rogers." The first few test hops of the *Silver Bullet* were without incident although landing was always something of a problem.

The *Silver Bullet* behaved the way it looked—vicious. Stability was a major question and landing took more than usual skill. On landing after the sixth flight, the left tire disintegrated at very high speed during the roll-out, and the airplane—with no tail at the time—was totally uncontrollable. It immediately swapped ends, rolling backwards end over end, two-and-one-half times. Each rollover being actually a backward leap up into the air followed by a crash back down on the nose. On the second revolution, the pilot's seat came loose. Seat and pilot were projected together out through the plexiglas canopy. He landed hard on the pavement, his only protection being his polo helmet. The airplane followed on its back, smashing the pilot's cockpit. One of the Mercury wings broke off the helmet, and John suffered a broken back. John's foresight and his polo playing had saved his life.

John Myers did most of the engineering test work on the various miniature flying wings. After Constant was killed in the N–9M, John recommended that Max Stanley, whom he met while working at Lockheed, be hired to fill the shortage of capable test pilots. It must have been difficult for Myers to convince Max that there really wasn't much danger in test flying while he was lying in a hospital bed with a broken back. Max was not so sure, but they compromised. Max would do the P–61 production testing, but would not be required to ever fly a flying wing. Max was hired, and later changed his mind about the flying wings. He took the XB–35 flying wing bomber aloft on its first flight from Hawthorne, and eventually did almost all flight testing on the XB–35 and YB–49 flying wings.

Max Stanley first tested a new installation of wing flaps on the P–61 Black Widow, an experimental type to enable the airplane to slow down quickly in the event of the night fighter overshooting its target. Special flaps, called fighter brakes, were installed in the center of each wing. These flaps, when extended by the pilot, would immediately produce an excess of drag, slowing the plane.

A flight engineer and navigator accompanied Max on the flight. The engineer sat directly behind the pilot, and the navigator in the so-called "greenhouse" in the rear of the fuselage with no forward vision. The navigator depended on his instruments to determine the plane's position.

When Max pulled the control lever to extend the fighter brakes, a flap came out on one wing but not on the opposite wing. This suddenly threw the P–61 into an unusual attitude, pitched to one side. Max's first reaction was to reach for the hatch release lever above his head so he would be ready to bail out and parachute to safety. However, he quickly regained control of the airplane and decided not to jump.

The Black Widow was designed with an unusual configuration of twin booms extending back from the radial engines on each side, the booms supporting both horizontal and vertical tail surfaces, with the fuselage occupying the space between the booms. Crew members were concerned with the hazard of leaving the plane without hitting the tail surfaces in the rear. The engineer's position directly behind the pilot was considered to be particularly hazardous.

When the engineer saw Max Stanley reach for his escape hatch lever, he did not wait for instructions to bail out. He immediately released the hatch cover over his own seat, unfastened his seat belt, and was quickly ejected from his seat by the force of the rushing air around him. Out he sailed, clearing the gun turret and the tail before his parachute opened, floating him safely to the ground.

Max, realizing what had happened to the engineer, circled the engineer's landing place and returned to the Hawthorne airport for a safe landing. He quickly climbed out of the cockpit and rushed to the rear of the plane to find out if the navigator had also bailed out. He found the young navigator sitting in his seat, looking puzzled. "Mr. Stanley," he asked, as he opened his hatch. "Did we lose something back there?" "Yes, we did," replied Stanley. "We lost Hetzel, the engineer."

Hetzel was gathering up his parachute and grinning from ear to ear when he was picked up a few minutes later. It was his first parachute jump and he had proven that one could safely bail out of the gunner's seat in the P–61 Black Widow, a procedure that had not been listed on Max Stanley's test flight plan that morning.

Jack Northrop was the first passenger to fly in the Northrop prototype flying wing. He insisted on a ride in his engineering child, a plane that had been built without a second seat. Factory personnel found that by removing a second fuel tank installed behind the pilot, a passenger could sit on the floor, and that is what Jack did. Of course, he did not let the board of directors know of the flight, but John's friends on the flight line took a snapshot of a very pleased Jack Northrop with pilot John Myers in the N–9M to prove it.

On a subsequent day when the N–9M flying wing prototype was scheduled for testing, Bill Sears, Northrop's chief aerodynamicist, asked Myers if he could accompany him on a test flight. John agreed, as the small flying wing had proven to be quite controllable in several previous test hops and was now equipped with an observer's seat behind the pilot. John felt that the risk of carrying a passenger in the experimental airplane was no more than in any other airplane, considering the number of hours he had been flying the plane. Bill, as one of the key engineers responsible for the design, wanted to see for himself how the little plane behaved in flight.

They took off without incident from the Hawthorne airstrip, and after a half hour in the air John prepared to return for a landing at the airport. He pulled the lever to lower the retractable landing gear, but only one of the main wheels came out of the wing. The control tower saw what had happened and immediately radioed John of the malfunction. He circled the field thinking of how he could best bring the small airplane in for a safe landing on the remaining wheels. He also didn't want to bend the propellers, or otherwise damage the only plane of its kind. Word of the trouble spread rapidly through the plant. Soon hundreds of employees were standing on the ramp to watch John and Bill touch down with only the nose wheel and one of the two main wheels lowered for landing.

There was no way John could correct the problem while still in the air. He determined that the best of two difficult alternatives was to attempt a landing with what he had, the two wheels that were down, rather than risk a belly landing by retracting the wheels into the wing and sliding across the runway on nothing but the wing. By this time,

Jack Northrop had joined the observers looking on. He held his breath as they approached the field with his chief aerodynamicist riding as a passenger.

To bring the propellers to a stop immediately before touchdown required that two levers controlling the propeller brakes, located on the front instrument panel, be pulled at the proper time. "These were too far forward for Bill to reach from the rear seat, so I asked Bill to take off his tie and I took off my belt, tied one end of each to a propeller brake lever and gave Bill the other ends. I told him when to pull, and to pull hard," John explained.

It was then Myers' turn to demonstrate his skill and cool nerves as he brought the little flying wing down to the runway. Everyone stared in disbelief as he balanced the airplane on only two wheels, gliding smoothly along the pavement. At the very end of the landing roll-out, when he had lost forward speed, Bill stopped the propellers and a wing tip dragged along the runway, with very little damage beyond some surface scraping. Bill remained composed throughout what could have been a disaster. The crowd of spectators let out a cheer as John and Bill crawled out without a scratch. Jack let it be known that henceforth only test pilots should test airplanes. John Myers was flying again the next day.

Jack was not in the habit of flying with test pilots except on rare occasions. He did accompany Myers again, on a flight to Fresno, California, where P–61 night fighter pilots were trained. Myers flew up to help give the military pilots more confidence in learning to fly the twin engine *Black Widow* like the fighter it was. The plane was capable of being maneuvered in much the same manner as smaller fighters. Its landing and takeoff characteristics were not much different—just a little faster on touchdown—even though the airplane had the weight and dimensions of a medium bomber.

Myers asked Northrop, on the way to Fresno, if Jack would like him to demonstrate some of the unusual flight characteristics of the plane he designed. Jack agreed, providing that John would maintain adequate altitude and give him a warning over the intercom as to what he should expect. John executed a slow roll, in which the pilot and passengers hang briefly by their seat belts in an upside down position. He then demonstrated a loop, when both were thrust into their seats from the high gravity forces imposed and the ground seems to revolve around the airplane.

Becoming more confident that his passenger was appreciating

this demonstration, Myers said he would like to execute a stall after shutting off one engine and pulling the nose up into a steep climbing turn. John explained in a reassuring voice, that, "In most airplanes of this weight this maneuver would be suicidal." Jack tightened his seat belt and bravely got ready for the ordeal. John cut one engine and feathered the propeller, at the same time pulling the nose up into a steep climbing turn. As he had intended, the airplane suddenly fell off sharply to one side and started to spin rapidly. John quickly recovered from the spin and returned to level flight in the direction of Fresno, grinning back at his boss who was sitting silently, very white in the face.

On the return flight from Fresno they decided to detour from the direct route and do some sightseeing over the snow-capped high Sierras. It was a beautiful day and, as they flew peacefully over the mountain peaks, Jack asked John, "Have you checked out the ceiling of the *Black Widow* while flying on only one engine?" John's reply was negative, and he asked Jack if he would give him permission to try it as they were then flying at an altitude of 20,000 feet. Jack gave his consent and, after shutting down an engine and feathering the prop, they proceeded to fly at above 18,000 feet for the entire remaining distance to Hawthorne.

Both of them were elated. When John Myers was criticized for experimenting while Jack Northrop was aboard, he brushed it off by reminding his critic that the highest peak in the area was only 14,000 feet high, and he already knew that the P–61 could fly higher than that on one engine. He also pointed out that he could have restarted the other engine in plenty of time to avoid trouble in case of an emergency.

After the P–61 *Black Widow* was placed on active duty in the war against Japan, John Myers was transferred to the sales department and sent to the Pacific war zone, where he demonstrated the new plane's capabilities, actually flying a number of combat missions. He became a good friend of another civilian pilot also flying in the war zone at the time, Charles Lindbergh, doing similar work for Pratt & Whitney, whose engine powered the Vought *Corsair* Marine Corps' fighter.

Dick Rinaldi, a Northrop test pilot who had been an airline pilot, had been associated with Moye Stephens before the Northrop company was formed in 1939. He was hired as a test pilot to try out the *Vengeance* and *Black Widow* airplanes as they came off the production lines. Since Dick was very short in stature the other pilots often referred to him as "the pilot with the greatest amount of blind flying time," because he had difficulty seeing over the edge of the cockpit. He had conservative political views, and disliked the liberal president, Franklin Roosevelt. One morning he came to work, announcing, "I'll have to get a new carpet for my living room today. Last night, as I listened to Roosevelt giving one of his weekly fireside chats, my radio began to drool all over my valuable carpet."

The test pilot's conversation was always light and easy, peppered with humor and a casual approach to the most frightening emergencies they encountered in flight. Death was never discussed. A test pilot was always winning, whatever the odds. Flying into difficulties was never a problem, only a momentary challenge to be solved. When the test pilots joined sales and engineering personnel at lunch time, as they often did, their experiences with aircraft could be quite demoralizing. It made all of us nervous when we flew on business trips, wondering what might go wrong with the airplane we were depending on to carry us safely to our destination. One received the impression from listening to test pilots that airplanes were far from being perfected. Even Jack Northrop appeared to be concerned about flying. In spite of his many years in aviation, Jack was never completely relaxed when he flew with even the best pilots. He never learned to fly himself.

As an officer of a major aircraft company there was sometimes implied criticism of the fact that I didn't know how to fly, but it wasn't necessary for me to fly the airplanes I sold, nor fight in them for that matter. When the company installed a Link Trainer to provide a facility for Northrop company pilots to practice blind flying by instruments, I decided to practice some flying on my own in the Link. I found that I was soon quite capable of flying by instruments while sitting firmly on the ground. When John Myers learned I had been practicing, he asked me to join him in the cockpit on our next trip and sit in the copilot's seat.

After takeoff and climbing to cruising altitude, he suggested I take the controls. He instructed me to follow the route by watching the needle on our radio compass, which was tuned into the San Francisco radio beacon. When he confirmed for himself that I could hold the airplane in a straight and level flight toward our destination, he left the cockpit and took a seat in the rear cabin of the transport we were flying. Northrop's public relations director, Dale Armstrong, was the only other passenger. He was sound asleep and didn't notice that John had joined him in the cabin. John also fell asleep.

All went well until I flew directly into a cloud, as I continued straight ahead on a direct course to our destination, watching the needle, concentrating on the instruments in front of me. Suddenly, rain started pouring down on the plane. The noise woke up Dale with a start. Seeing John asleep beside him, he let out a scream, "My God, John. Have you lost your senses? Ted doesn't know how to fly. He will kill us."

Johnny sat up from his sleep and laughed, but quickly came forward and took over the controls. He turned the plane out of the rain cloud and proceeded to lecture me on how to avoid blind flying unless absolutely necessary. I never did learn how to fly in the sky.

Northrop test pilots were also required to be checked out in the altitude simulator at Wright-Patterson Air Base in Dayton, before they were permitted to fly at extremely high altitudes in military airplanes. In the 1940s, before airplanes were pressurized, any altitude over 30,000 feet was considered high.

Harry Crosby had gone to Dayton to be tested in the simulator, because he had been selected to fly the P–61 Black Widow at 45,000 feet, or higher if it would go, to determine its true ceiling. Since I was also in Dayton on company business, we had dinner together one evening after his testing in the simulator. "I just set a new altitude record today, in that contraption they put me into at Wright Field," was Harry's casual comment. "What happened, Harry?" I inquired.

They put me in the pressure chamber with three young pilots and closed the door. The altimeter began to climb, and soon we were at 30,000 feet. I felt comfortable in my oxygen mask, but one of the younger men began to hold his belly, and complained of cramps. The decreased atmospheric pressure in the chamber made his stomach feel like it would burst. He was full of gas. We nodded to the operator outside our window, and he decreased the pressure in the chamber to sea level, and opened the door for the young pilot to get out.

Up we went again, and when the altimeter showed 40,000 feet the other two pilots began to groan and hold their bellies, so we came down again and let them out. The operating technician asked me how I felt, and I said fine, so up we went again until I reached 50,000 feet. I signaled the operator that I had enough, and when he opened the door, I asked him, "How high does this damned thing go?" And he said that it went to 55,000 feet, and I had just set a new altitude record."

*   *   *

It was the typically matter-of-fact attitude of a test pilot describing his amazing exploits.

Harry Crosby had been an air racer, had built and flown his own planes, and was extremely confident of his flying ability. He was well paid, like all the test pilots, and was saving his money for the future, planning to buy a ranch on the desert near Muroc for his retirement, before anything unfortunate could happen.

Crosby flew all the radical new airplanes being tested at Muroc Dry Lake, including the MX–334 *Rocket Wing* experimental plane, destined to become a rocket propelled buzz bomb. After being towed aloft and then released to glide back to the desert runway, the plane flipped over on its back. Harry miraculously escaped by climbing upon the center section and sliding off the wing, successfully opening his parachute for a different kind of ride back to Muroc. Harry later made the first flight in the Northrop XP–79B *Flying Ram*, in which the pilot rode in a prone position in the flying wing.

Harry was the first and only pilot to fly the Northrop XP–79B *Flying Ram*, the experimental flying wing built to dive on enemy bombers and destroy them by slicing off their tail assemblies without inflicting any damage to itself. With Harry at the controls, the plane took off routinely from the Muroc Dry Lake runway for a test flight, rapidly climbing to 8,000 feet. Here he made a climbing turn that soon became a roll, causing the flying wing to stall. The XP–79 fell off into a spin from which it never recovered. Observers on the ground saw Harry free himself from the small cockpit and jump, just as the spinning plane struck him with the rotating, slashing wing. His parachute never opened.

9

THE XB–35 STAYS MAINLY ON THE DRAWING BOARD

While Jack's imagination went wild on smaller tailless projects, he did keep an able staff of engineers busy on detail design work for his preferred project, the XB–35 flying wing. A new and separate engineering and manufacturing facility, Plant 3, was constructed at the corner of Crenshaw Boulevard and Broadway, financed by the government's wartime Reconstruction Finance Corporation. The entire engineering department moved to the new location. It was originally planned to build the big bombers in the new Plant 3, as well. In a very short time the new building was seen to be obviously inadequate for large-scale production of the flying wing bomber. It was filled with all sorts of other experimental projects long before engineering on the XB–35 was finished. Jack had an unending quantity of new ideas coming off his drawing board and during the war the Air Corps was always interested in financing a flying version, no matter how radical the design appeared to be.

Employees understood why the flying wing project must remain a secret, but a frequently heard complaint from both employees and shareholders during the early war years was why Northrop didn't receive more publicity. Newspapers, magazines, and the radio were full of stories about Lockheed P–38s, North American P–51s, Boeing B–17s, and just about every other aircraft manufacturer, but Northrop was never mentioned. The pleas were insistent to do something to get recognition.

The lack of press coverage was particularly annoying to La Motte, who was anxious to have Northrop become well known. It would also make it easier for me to sell airplanes. Jack, as it turned out, was often disturbed by too much publicity, generally turning inquiries by reporters and outside shareholders over to La Motte. There were some writers who thought that Jack was still the chief engineer for Douglas.

The company name was frequently confused with the older North American Aviation Company, whose famous fighter plane, the P–51 *Mustang*, stole most of the headlines. Their advanced trainer, the AT–6, was flown by all new Air Corps and Navy pilots.

La Motte had at one time persuaded the directors to appropriate more money for advertising. Air Corps' auditors disallowed the expenditure as unnecessary, and the funds were soon cut back. Northrop directors remained convinced of the desirability of good publicity, if only to get their name spelled right. Eventually they hired one of the best public relations men in the country, Steve Hannigan of New York. Hannigan agreed to become a Northrop consultant for a fee that was a fraction of what had been paid for the previous national advertising.

One of Hannigan's top associates was assigned to the Northrop account. He advised La Motte to hire Dale Armstrong, a Hollywood film publicist, as a full time public relations director and to assign the less experienced advertising director then on the payroll as his assistant. This move also gave the former advertising director time to serve as editor of the employee newspaper, *The Northrop News*.

Before long the company name began to appear in print, properly spelled; Northrop, not Northrup. Numerous articles were seen in national magazines, the first stories describing the exploits of Northrop's patrol bomber being flown by Norwegian pilots on dangerous North Atlantic patrols. Later in the war there were stories of the deadly Northrop P–61 *Black Widow* fighter keeping night skies in the Pacific free of Japanese bombers. The stories appeared in newspapers throughout the country, along with magazine features complete with dramatic photographs of the aircraft. A nationally known cartoonist, Leslie Turner, began to feature the Black Widow in his syndicated comic strip. The exploits of "Captain Easy" flying his faithful P–61 were followed by newspaper readers on a daily basis.

While the Northrop name is well known today, and its reputation considerably enhanced, misspelling of the company name persists, an "o" commonly replacing a "u," a frequent phonetic mistake. It all began when the U.S. patent office spelled Northrop's name "Northrup," on the patent Jack took out for his first all-wing airplane. It has occurred many times since on official records and publications. Ira Chart, Northrop historian, says, "I think the reason is people tend to say "North-rup," so they spell it the same way."

At the White Sands Missile Range in New Mexico, where Northrop and the Air Force tested missiles, there are two seven-mile long runways that were originally graded by Northrop. These were named Northrop Landing Strip in the late 1940s. Through clerical error all charts and official records have over the years been changed to North-*rup* Strip. The New Mexico strip would be an alternative landing place if an aborted Space Shuttle flight required an emergency landing site, or if too much rain at Edwards Air Force Base flooded the California landing area. The old airstrips would then become the next choice and the Northrup Strip would suddenly become the center of national attention—spelled wrong.

Henry J. Kaiser, the celebrated industrialist, dropped by the plant in late 1942 and suggested a much larger flying wing aircraft than even Jack had imagined. Shipping losses to enemy submarines were particularly heavy in the Pacific after war was declared with Japan. Merchant cargo ships were the most vulnerable. Kaiser was building and launching Liberty Ships at the rate of one every four days from his shipbuilding yards in San Francisco Bay to replace ships lost to enemy torpedoes. He perceived what he thought was a brilliant idea for solving the problem: fly troops and supplies over the ocean in huge airplanes, thus avoiding the dangerous ocean entirely.

He made a special trip to southern California to promote his idea with Douglas and Lockheed, but was not successful with these old-line companies. Kaiser called Northrop for an appointment, and Jack invited La Motte, Gage Irving, and myself to join them for a conference.

All were assembled in the board room and introduced to Henry Kaiser and his staff. Kaiser, who was noted as being a very successful entrepreneur and an excellent salesmen, dominated the meeting. He began with an outline of the considerable problems our country faced in the war and the absolute necessity for the United States to supply ever-increasing tonnage and manpower to overseas allies, as well as to the country's own front line war zones in the vast Pacific. Kaiser impressed on us that he had talked privately with Vance Breeze, the test pilot who had flown the first prototype flying wing. Breeze had told him about the promising future of Northrop's radical design and the plane's potential ability to carry huge loads of cargo over great distances. Kaiser proposed that a new company to be called Kaiser-Northrop be formed, with Northrop supplying the engineers and Kaiser supplying manufacturing facilities. He offered Northrop 50 percent interest in the new subsidiary. His close friendship with President Roosevelt would assure that the new company would obtain contracts for the aircraft and working capital, even if the military services were not enthusiastic about the idea of building huge new flying wing cargo planes.

Jack reminded Kaiser that the flying wing project, and the development of a long-range bomber of Northrop's design, was classified secret by the Army Air Corps. Kaiser, in his typical way of always doing what had to be done immediately, asked to use the telephone. In the presence of the Northrop executives, he called Assistant Secretary of War Lovett in Washington and explained his need to discuss the secret flying wing with Northrop. Jack was called to the phone and told by Lovett that it would be all right to proceed with the discussion.

Gage Irving then pointed out that aviation fuel would need to be transported by ship to many distant parts of the world to enable cargo planes to make the return trip home, as no fuel supplies would be available at many of the proposed distant landing sites. These fuel tankers would offer enemy submarines with more new targets. Kaiser persisted with his plan, paying little attention to Gage's reasoning. The meeting was adjourned without any conclusion being reached. Kaiser and his staff departed, promising to return after Northrop had more time to check the idea with the Air Corps.

Next day the Northrop management, after talking again with Lovett in Washington, decided to turn down Kaiser's offer. Entering into the joint venture would in all probability delay the existing flying wing program for the Air Corps, and that would not be permissible. None of those present at the conference with Kaiser in 1943 ever thought of the possibility that the flying wing program would ever be cancelled or that Northrop was giving up the chance to develop a large flying wing cargo plane with Kaiser's sponsorship and the opportunity to keep the project alive in postwar years. The cargo airplane would have been an ideal application for the flying wing design, a far more practical and useful airplane for peacetime use than a long-range bomber. Jack called Kaiser a few days later, advising him that the government had discouraged him from entering into a contract for the Northrop-Kaiser flying wing cargo plane, and that he must turn down the proposal.

A short time later Kaiser called back to tell Jack that he had entered into an agreement with Howard Hughes to build a huge flying boat of conventional design. He thanked Northrop officials for their gracious attention to his proposal. Jack was relieved, and wished him well in his joint venture with Hughes, not realizing that slipping from his grasp was his only opportunity to build a flying wing cargo and passenger transport, an aborted dream subsequently killed by the Air Corps.

Howard Hughes' Spruce Goose, as the plane was popularly called (a name that Hughes disliked) was constructed of wood. The military, who were not supportive of Kaiser's idea, refused to allocate scarce aluminum for the project. Kaiser was also denied a contract that would have provided military contract monies; the plane was built using Defense Plant Corporation funds. Henry Kaiser terminated his relationship with Hughes after the war ended, and the $18 million contract was changed to pay for only one of the three flying boats originally called for. Hughes was forced to pay out an additional $8 million of his own money to collect the balance due him from the government. The Spruce Goose flew only once; it is now a popular tourist attraction at Long Beach. One can speculate what the outcome would have been if a large Northrop–Kaiser flying wing cargo plane had been designed and built in the 1940s instead of the ill-fated Spruce Goose. Decisions of this kind were hard ones to make in the demanding times of war.

Northrop production lines were chronically short of essential aluminum. During the early years before the United States entered the war, production of the *Vengeance* dive bomber was occasionally slowed because of lack of needed metal. No effective priority system for scarce materials had been worked out by the government. The nation's only supplier of aluminum 24ST for aircraft construction, Aluminum Corporation of America (Alcoa) had adopted a policy of favoring manufacturers who were building airplanes for the U.S. government, and who had been Alcoa customers in the past. Northrop's only major airplane contracts in 1940 were with the Norwegians and British.

Alcoa, controlled by the powerful eastern industrialist, Andrew Mellon, had a virtual monopoly on aluminum. The Reynolds Metals Company had not become a major supplier and Kaiser Aluminum was not yet organized. Northrop's continued plea for additional allotments of aluminum fell on deaf ears at Alcoa, and shortages at the Hawthorne plant became common. One morning, La Motte read a story in the *Los Angeles Times*, "War Production Board Director Edward Stettinius assured that there is an adequate supply of aluminum for the war effort." The article went on to quote Stettinius, "I have been assured by Alcoa that they can supply the aircraft industry with all the aluminum they need."

La Motte was very upset at what appeared to him to be an attempt by Alcoa to prevent its competition from building new production facilities. He called me into his office and directed me to call all the wire services and local papers with a story about Northrop, and to quote him, "Due to a shortage of aluminum, Northrop Aircraft is shutting down its production line of dive bombers for the British next week. This order from the general manager will necessitate the cutting of hours in the factory at Hawthorne from 10 to 8 hours a day and the laying off of our night shift. In addition, several hundred workers must be laid off, and all remaining employees will be assigned to other projects."

The following day newspapers across the country carried front page stories with supporting headlines about Northrop's defiance of Alcoa. An article appeared in *Time* under the heading, "Tiny Northrop Takes on the Aluminum Trust." WPB Director Stettinius was on the long distance phone as soon as the headlines appeared in the *Washington Post*, demanding that La Motte retract what he claimed was a misleading story. "Mr. Stettinius, the story is true, and only when we receive sufficient aluminum from Alcoa to enable us to resume full production will I make any further announcement," was La Motte's reply.

Within a few days, carloads of aluminum began to arrive at the plant in Hawthorne. It was not necessary to close down the production line. Within a few months Reynolds Metals expanded enough to give the industry a large second source of aluminum. The Alcoa monopoly had been broken.

Engineers wanted to utilize another metal in manufacturing, magnesium, which has many qualities ideally suited for aircraft structures that needed light weight with strength. However, magnesium was difficult to fabricate because of its tendency to burn and explode when exposed to the flame of a welding torch. No one had been able to weld magnesium parts together prior to Northrop's experimentation with various methods. A Northrop fabrication engineer, Tom Piper, discovered that magnesium could be welded if the flame was contained within a helium atmosphere. He developed a special torch connected with a helium source that fed the gas under pressure so that it surrounded the flame emitted by the welding tip. Heliarc welding was born.

Union Carbide negotiated a license to use the process and manufacture the necessary welding equipment. Heliarc welding of magnesium and other flammable metals became a common procedure used in a wide variety of applications. Northrop employed heliarc welding in building the first all-welded magnesium airplane, the tailless XP–56. Important key magnesium parts, such as landing gear struts, were fabricated for the flying wing XB–35 using the heliarc process.

Production at Northrop increased dramatically. New buildings were built to house the Northrop employee training school and a newly designed wind tunnel facility for aerodynamic testing. The original Northrop plant, now called Plant 1, and a facility across the street near Prairie Avenue called Plant 2, were busy doing machine work, subassemblies, final assembly of the *Vengeance* dive bomber, vertical rudders for Consolidated PBY flying boats, parts for Boeing B–17 bombers, and Northrop's own *Black Widows*. A large building on Olympic Boulevard near downtown Los Angeles was leased for manufacturing parts, including work for Boeing, Douglas, and Lockheed.

Northrop was plagued by a shortage of facilities and manpower, a problem affecting every aircraft manufacturer in the country, making immediate postwar adjustments difficult. When World War II ended in 1945, the company adopted a policy of owning all its plant facilities. Northrop purchased Plant 3 from the RFC, hoping to maintain its freedom of operation and ultimately remove itself completely from too much dependence on U.S. government business. This policy left the company short of space for expansion when the two XB–35s were ready to be built.

Secret experimental aircraft were built in Plant 3 where Jack could keep a close eye on them. A full scale wood mock-up was built of the XB–35 center section, impressing all who saw it with the unexpected roomy pilot's cockpit, with ample space on all sides in the huge flying wing for the navigator, engineer, and gunners. One impressive feature was the forward and downward vision enjoyed by the pilot and copilot. Both forward and rear gunners were also assured of clear visibility over wide arcs, ahead and to the rear, without any obstruction to interfere with their line of fire, as in conventional aircraft. A comfortable lounge and bedroom for the extra crew carried on long missions was located in the inner center section of the thick wing. As one observer noted, the inside of the flying wing was not unlike a small apartment, with all conveniences included.

Northrop was quite pleased after the Air Corps' "mock-up" board from Wright Field visited Plant 3, reporting to Jack their strong approval and unexpected surprise at the roomy interior—a six foot pilot could stand upright—very different from the stooping attitude necessary in every bomber then flying.

Jack was so enthusiastic over this spacious mock-up that he authorized the construction, at company expense, of a full-size mock-up of the flying wing designed as a civilian airliner, for use in a motion picture promotional film. It would have been an excellent time for Henry Kaiser to show up with his grandiose plans and money. The Northrop flying wing transport boasted a passenger cabin that fired the imagination of everyone who walked around inside. This was one of the more amazing features—being able to walk around. The airliner's seats were arranged as they might be in a small theater, with aisles and ample headroom. There was room to stand up and converse and to enjoy the view ahead through large greenhouse windows in the forward section of the wing. The civilian flying wing was an amazing glimpse of the tremendous possibilities inherent in the flying wing design. A commercial motion picture firm was hired to photograph the interior with models posing as passengers enjoying the view and cocktails. It was a photographic documentary of the future aboard a Northrop flying wing airliner. Unfortunately, this airliner was never to leave the drawing board.

When it came to building flying wing mock-ups and experimenting with new ideas, Jack could be somewhat extravagant. When it came to company expense accounts, it was a different matter. It had seldom seemed necessary to invite Air Corps' officers who came to the plant on Air Corps' business out to dinner with company executives at company expense. In any case, the practice was discouraged by government regulations.

After Jack had shown the Air Corps officers the XB–35 mock-up for the first time, and they had remarked so favorably on the project, Jack's enthusiasm got the better of him. He asked that I take the entire mock-up board, all fifteen of the officers, to Earl Carroll's restaurant for dinner. Jack said the company would reimburse me for the check. Jack was not much good at these affairs, and said he did not plan to be there. I was surprised that Jack would suggest a nightclub noted for its sparsely dressed chorus girls, and asked him if he had ever been to Earl Carroll's in Hollywood. "I have never been there," he replied, "but I have heard they have a good floor show and feel these men will appreciate it."

I took the fifteen officers to Earl Carroll's, reserving a table down in front near the stage. The food was good and the entertainment was obviously enjoyed. I paid the $525 check out of my own pocket. When no one at the plant offered to reimburse me, I took a duplicate of the bill to Jack, who almost fainted when he saw the amount. He reluctantly authorized its inclusion on the company expense account, signed it, and I was paid. Thereafter he did insist, however, that visitors pay for their own entertainment, to the relief of our Air Corps' auditors.

When design engineering was almost completed on the XB–35s, it became apparent that preparing production drawings for final assembly of the aircraft was beyond the capacity of Northrop's already thinly stretched engineering department. The Air Force, having cut back work at the Glenn L. Martin Company in Baltimore, directed Northrop to transfer all production engineering work to Martin. As an inducement, the Air Force gave Martin a contract to build 200 B–35 airplanes. These could be produced in a government owned plant in Omaha, already built for a cancelled Martin bomber contract. As the war ended before the first XB–35 had been flown, all the Martin contractual arrangements were cancelled, and the production engineering returned to Northrop.

It seemed to be a strange way to build airplanes. The various developments would have perhaps been of considerable discouragement to a less dedicated man than Northrop, but Jack was determined to prove that he had the world's best bomber and the finest airliner in the world. As soon as priority war production slowed and he was permitted to do so, he completed assembly of the first XB–35 flying wing bomber, using his own production engineering staff. The plane was ready to fly by 1946.

When Jack learned that Consolidated had been having similar problems completing work on its own rival long-range bomber, the conventional XB–36, Jack pushed his employees to complete early preparation of the XB–35 for flight, as he anxiously awaited the time when his bomber would finally be in the air. He was sure his flying wing design would easily prove its superiority over the rival aircraft.

10

THE FLYING WING TAKES TO THE AIR

Since the beginning of high-speed taxi tests two months ago, a small crowd had gathered outside the Northrop factory, observing with considerable curiosity the strange looking "bat bomber" parked on the Hawthorne airfield. They were waiting for the airplane to fly and activity on the ramp this morning gave every evidence it soon would. Newsreel, newspaper, photo press services, and *Life* magazine photographers clustered together on the gently sloping hill east of Crenshaw Avenue, as flight crews warmed up the aircraft engines in the early morning mist, their loud exhaust roar echoing back from nearby buildings. Traffic on Prairie Avenue was temporarily blocked and it was evident that the first flight of the secret flying wing would soon occur. World War II had ended almost a year earlier. It was June 1946.

Max Stanley, veteran Northrop test pilot and the most experienced pilot of flying wing aircraft, having flown the small-scale prototypes on numerous test flights, would take the huge XB–35 into the air for the first time, backed by copilot Fred Bretcher, a heavy aircraft pilot during the war. Orva Douglas, the very meticulous Northrop flight engineer seemed to have been warming up the engines for hours, enveloping the entire Northrop plant in exhaust fumes of oil and fuel mixed with the morning haze. As engine throttles were edged forward one engine at a time, for rpm and propeller checks, a swirling tornado from the prop wash battered at the barrier fence erected along the west runway threshold, diverting the artificial wind storm up and away from Prairie Avenue. Ordinarily, Stanley would be taking off into the prevailing wind, toward the west, but this morning the air was calm. In any case he thought it best not to risk taking off on the first flight over populated downtown Hawthorne.

Stanley was already settled in the enclosed cockpit, having made the difficult climb up through a hatch in the bottom of the wing into the crew seats that would only be comfortable enough for the short flight to Muroc. With the engines at full throttle, vibration was a problem, but Stanley was pleased with the overall low noise level in the cockpit area. He once again glanced over the array of flight instruments, checking to see if all the needles were in their normal indicating position for takeoff. It was not necessary to read every instrument, only to look for a needle out of line. He found none.

The pilot's seat was below a non-jettisonable Plexiglas bubble to the left of the center of the wing, with the copilot seated to his right at a lower level completely within the wing. Stanley spoke with his copilot and recalled his previous flights in the smaller flying wing prototypes, scale models that were not merely smaller sized, but also dynamically scaled, proportionally, to the full-size flying wing. He remembered that all the control and stability characteristics of the small models were slowed down by a factor of almost two in the big flying wing (1.732 as determined by the mathematicians). This meant that the annoying lateral directional oscillation, the yawing back and forth of the small plane, should be smoothed out into wonderfully stable flying in the big plane.

The remarkable flying wing was made of many new materials, placing the aircraft on the leading edge of almost all technologies of the day. It was the first use of 75ST specification aluminum, more critical to fabricate because of increased notch fatigue, but considerably stronger and lighter than the commonly used 24ST aluminum. There was the first use of Alclad control cables by Roebling, positioned within the long span wings to manage changes in cable length resulting from temperature ranges to be encountered at different altitudes. The flying wing was no doubt a state-of-the-art aircraft.

The eight counter-rotating propellers bit into the hazy air as the huge plane throbbed impatiently behind the wheel chocks, wanting to be released. Stanley's head could be easily seen beneath the Plexiglas bubble protruding above the wing surface. He remained alert to every sound penetrating the flight deck, ready to react instantly to any anomaly that might warn of an aircraft or engine malfunction.

Flight engineer Douglas, unable to see outside the aircraft from his position at a lower level behind the pilots, faced the complex array of jittering engine instruments. He had started the four 3,000 horsepower radial engines buried in the wings, one-by-one, as ground crew members stood by with fire extinguishers ready. The engines roared in response as the engineer slowly pushed individual throttles forward for a full power propeller feathering check, joining finally in a raucous exhaust from all four engines at full throttle, blowing hot oil and swirling clouds of bluish smoke into the air, as if in a grand celebration. The pilot relaxed, as only a skilled professional can do in an aircraft he has never flown before, looking forward to a successful first flight of Jack Northrop's lifelong dream. It would be his responsibility to help make the dream come true.

Northrop's first XB–35 flying wing bomber had been parked on the preflight preparation ramp at the Hawthorne plant for almost a year after being rolled out of the production hanger. In recent weeks it had become quite evident to employees that the huge craft was finally being prepared for its first flight. Reports circulated through the plant that the momentous event was imminent, and the employees grapevine communications system had been alerted that the first flight may soon occur. There was not a single employee who had not made plans to be standing alongside the runway to watch the takeoff as soon as the word came that the plane was ready to roll. This presented the company with a problem in crowd control possibly beyond the capability of plant security personnel to handle. The safety of all concerned as well as the aircraft's large size (it had a wing span extending beyond each side of the paved airport runway) had to be considered.

A memorandum was issued by the general manager, to "all personnel," stating, "On the occasion of the first flight, no one will be allowed in the vicinity of the flight line. All employees will remain at their work stations." To soften the disappointment resulting from this directive, the memo stated that, as soon as feasible, the flying wing would return to Hawthorne. At that time all personnel would be released to watch the flyby. When Jack Northrop read the memo, he felt, with his usual sense of obligation, that the order also applied to him although the first flight of the full-size flying wing was, in a very real sense, the culmination of a lifelong ambition. Jack did not step out to the flight line, a decision that says much about the character and sense of values of Jack Northrop. He stayed at work over his drawing board, perhaps sketching a new dream.

As far as the other employees were concerned, the memo was a request difficult to obey, and no one did. After all the work and personal involvement in the flying wing project they were going to watch their airplane fly, no matter what. The plant emptied quickly as the motor noise grew louder, everyone anticipating the takeoff. Soon the entire length of the Northrop runway, from Prairie Avenue to Crenshaw, was lined with hundreds of employees, waiting for their creation to fly. When a sustained engine roar signaled that the flying wing was about to roll, a cheer rose from the crowd, a cheer that even Jack must have heard back in his office, alone, undoubtedly wanting as much as anyone else to be outside on the ramp. The paved runway was only 150 feet wide. The span of the flying wing was 172 feet, half the length of a football field and overhanging the runway. The takeoff would be quite an exciting event. Max Stanley expected to use all the runway, from one block to the next.

Max had mentally rehearsed this first takeoff and flight many times, trying to anticipate possible problems that would arise and what his corrective response would be. He knew how the airplane would fly and had complete confidence in Northrop's engineering staff and the men and women responsible for building the first large size airplane of its kind. He had every reason to be assured all components would function properly, yet he was aware of the numerous engineering problems that had already delayed this flight for months. In an aircraft of this complexity, failure of a minor part could prove disastrous.

The flying wing originally had been designed in 1942 as a long-range bomber capable of flying nonstop from the United States to Europe and return. The government assumed at the time that England might be invaded and occupied. But Nazi Germany had now been defeated and a long-range bomber satisfying the original specifications was no longer a high priority. However, work continued on what the military considered to be an experimental aircraft. In the eyes of the inventor, Jack Northrop, there was still the possibility of a civilian postwar transport to consider. The tremendous potential of the flying wing on the Hawthorne ramp waiting to fly seemed enhanced by the sheer streamlined beauty of the aircraft. It was surely the proof of Jack Northrop's often expressed engineering philosophy, that if it was beautiful it had to be right. No one debated the plane's exciting beauty. Now it was Max Stanley's job to make it fly.

The XB–35 was the largest aircraft Max had ever flown, larger than any land aircraft anyone had flown at the time. It was the largest

American airplane ever built. He had piloted B–29 and B–24 bombers, but had not flown in the war. When war broke out in Europe he took a job flying Lockheed *Hudson* bombers to eastern Canada, where they were picked up by Royal Air Force pilots for delivery to England. He was loaned by Lockheed to Pan American Airlines, gaining more experience ferrying warplanes from Florida to North Africa. He had decided to apply for a commission in the Navy, but while waiting for it to come through, Northrop chief test pilot, John Myers, called to ask that he become a Northrop test pilot. He was selected for the first flight of the flying wing because of his skill, cool head, and good judgment.

The XB–35 was a much larger airplane in every dimension except length. There was no length. No ungainly fuselage and tail stuck out in the rear. The very simplicity of its appearance hid the yet unfulfilled ability within the sleek aluminum wing, where all four engines lay buried, as if they preferred not to display the tremendous power hidden deep inside. It was a secret airplane with character and a personality yet to be revealed.

While the 5,000 foot Hawthorne runway was adequate for a normal takeoff, there was no room for error—no room for loss of power. Max was apprehensive about the performance of the engine drive shaft, the counter-rotating gear box arrangement, and the controllable pitch propellers. These all important parts of the aircraft had not been designed by Northrop engineers. A major obstacle for the XB–35 had been the provision that the government would contract for and furnish engines, the power train, and propellers. Each of the four Pratt & *Whitney Wasp* Major engines were located in the wing almost thirty feet from the two sets of four-bladed counter-rotating propellers, power being transmitted to the propellers through long driveshafts and complex gear boxes. The unusual arrangement had presented entirely new design problems to the Hamilton Standard propeller company, which was doing the development work for the government in Hartford, Connecticut, across the continent from Northrop. The propeller governor and gearbox problems had never been adequately resolved, and they had been the single primary source of grief, beginning with late delivery. More hours were spent attempting to solve problems the new design presented by adapting standard off-the-shelf hardware to get the moving parts to move, than from Northrop's radical aircraft design itself.

The considerable distance between the two companies, both of them developing entirely new products to be combined into a new aircraft design in advance of the current state of the art, proved to be an almost unsurmountable problem. The East Coast-designed power transmission shafts, gear boxes, and adjustable pitch propellers never worked properly on the ground. It remained to be seen how they worked in the air. The military procurement procedure made Northrop dependent on an East Coast supplier with only a passing interest in the flying wing project, a supplier already overloaded with other work. Newly developed jet engines not requiring propellers or complicated power transfer systems would have eliminated these troublesome problems. The Air Corps, however, felt that low fuel consuming piston engines were necessary if the bomber was to fly the specified 10,000 miles nonstop.

The decision of the Air Corps to order Northrop to subcontract with the Glenn L. Martin Company in Baltimore to do production engineering work for the flying wing, presented even more of an obstacle to getting the XB–35 airplanes into the air. To carry out this decision, a letter of intent was given to Martin to build 200 B–35s in Omaha, Nebraska. As the war ended, Northrop's own plant was working at capacity converting wartime *Black Widow* P–61s to postwar reconnaissance RP–61s, stripping military surplus C–47 cargo airplanes to convert them into civilian DC–3s for airline use, as well as the design and production of the first cruise missile, the Northrop *Snark*. Northrop, as a consequence, was awarded contracts to build only fifteen of its own aircraft. It was responsible, as prime contractor, for Martin's engineering work on all the flying wing XB–35s. There were numerous frustrating delays on the production line. After the war's end the letter of intent to Martin was withdrawn, but production engineering snafus remained to plague Northrop.

Martin, like so many others, demonstrated little interest in Northrop's flying wing. Martin's failure seriously to accept the manufacturing responsibility involved in planning production engineering for Northrop's XB–35 may have resulted from Northrop having been selected to produce the new generation heavy bomber over Martin's own XB–33 *Super Marauder*. Troublesome management behavior, from the Air Corps point of view, was not unknown at Martin. Before long the Martin company had soured on the idea of building Northrop's aircraft, as requested by the Air Corps. They subcontracted a significant portion of the XB–35 production engineering work to the Otis Elevator Company, far away on the East Coast. The awkward arrangements presented Northrop with continuing communication problems, as California engineers attempted to coordinate fabrication of the most advanced aircraft of the day with a manufacturer of elevators. In an era before conference telephone calls and computers, it was to Northrop's considerable credit that the first XB–35 aircraft actually had been built by 1946, with the airplane now on the Hawthorne flight line, engines running, ready to fly.

Max Stanley waited patiently for his flight engineer, Orva Douglas, to advise him that all four engines were running properly. The transparent bubble and flight deck had been transformed into an aeronautical oven in the hot morning sun. Stanley's khaki shirt was dripping with sweat and exposed metal surfaces became too hot to touch. Stanley wrapped a rag around the control wheel to buffer the heat and allow a firmer grip. Engine and propeller noise, however, were minimal. In the flying wing, exhaust and propellers were far behind the crew, making the flight deck a relatively pleasant place to work.

Since there was no fuselage, the crew's flight stations were contained wholly within the thick flying wing. The seven foot head clearances were quite a luxury compared with crowded cockpits of conventional aircraft. Designed for long-range flying over many hours with fifteen men aboard—three complete crews—the flight deck could be described as a small apartment. There were bunks for sleeping, toilet facilities, even a kitchen. The flight engineer occupied space on a lower level ten feet behind the pilot, adjacent to the navigator's table. Of the crew, only the pilot's head could be seen in the above wing bubble; the copilot looked straight ahead through a greenhouse window in the wing's leading edge. The engineer faced the rear, unable to see outside. He watched only his engine performance instruments and fuel management gauges, duplicated for each of the four engines, a total of sixty-two instruments for him to monitor continually in flight.

Flight engineer Douglas passed his "OK for takeoff" to Stanley on the intercom as the cockpit check was completed with copilot Fred Bretcher. Engine run check had been completed at maximum takeoff rating. The ground crew stood by to remove wheel chocks. Brakes were set to hold the airplane in place until ready to roll at full throttle. There would be no taxiing anywhere. Northrop's airplane was waiting with its back to the street. No portion of the runway would be wasted moving away from the streetside fence. Stanley wanted all of the 5,000 feet of available runway. Straight ahead was where he was going, into the clear sky above. He called the Northrop control tower, "We are ready," he said. "Here we go."

Inboard fuel tanks were full; nose-up trim set at the prescribed three degrees; rudder trim in neutral; flap indicator "UP;" wing slot door switch "OPEN." Wheel chocks were pulled free. Stanley took over engine operation from the engineer, pushing the four individual throttles full forward in one continuous movement. Brakes were released and the plane surged forward as Max guided the flying wing along the painted runway centerline, putting forward pressure on the control column to keep the nose wheel tight on the pavement until flying airspeed was reached. Copilot Bretcher began calling out the airspeed as the flying wing rapidly accelerated down the Hawthorne runway to begin its first flight. Stanley kept his eyes on the rapidly diminishing runway, listening for his copilot to call out 75 miles per hour, the airspeed when the split-flap wing tip steering rudders became effective. Northrop's dream was on the way to reality.

"Suddenly," recalled Stanley, "a wild jackrabbit jumped out of the weeds alongside the paved runway. With great leaps the rabbit ran ahead of the plane as we increased speed. The leaping rabbit did nothing to mitigate my apprehension as I realized the plane was not gaining on the rabbit. Either he was a very fast rabbit or the flying wing was in serious trouble! As I thought of the possible consequences, the rabbit, just as quickly as he came, jumped clear of the plane, off the runway, and disappeared back in the weeds."

About half way down the runway, at 100 miles per hour, satisfied with the "feel" of the controls as the aircraft began "running light," Max Stanley slowly pulled back on the control yoke, raising the nose wheel. At 115 miles per hour he pulled the 200,000 pound XB–35 smoothly into the air in a cloud of swirling smoke and was flying, having used 3,000 feet of the runway, exactly as calculated. It was 10:30 A.M. No one had ever seen anything like this fly before. It was truly an emotional event. Everyone watching along the runway must have felt a shot of adrenalin—a clutch of the stomach. The common murmur was, "Oh, my God." Jack Northrop's office was on the plant's east side. A face momentarily appeared in his window, watching the flying wing climb toward the morning sun, a beautiful bird on its first flight.

Retraction of the landing gear required almost a full minute, during which time red fire warning lights flashed on due to the low air speed and high power settings as the XB–35 continued to climb. The wheels were completely within the wing at the planned 5,500 feet. The plane passed over downtown Los Angeles on a straight eastward heading, leveling out at 8,500 feet to turn inland toward Muroc over Cajon Pass. Enroute to Muroc the crew ran a dozen flight tests of various controls and handling characteristics before calling the Army control tower at Muroc. Forty-four minutes later, at 11:14 A.M., Stanley landed the flying wing at Muroc Dry Lake, the sprawling military base in the Mojave high desert inland from the southern California coastal range. "A simple, uneventful ferry flight," Stanley would later describe the pleasurable jaunt. "No bugs— no squawks." Jack Northrop learned by telephone that, on the morning of June 25 in the summer of 1946, his dream had come true.

In the following hours and weeks of flight testing over the Mojave Desert, the XB–35 quickly proved Northrop's flying wing to be superior to any other contemporary aircraft design. However, Northrop test pilot Stanley commented, "the flight test program was plagued with problems from the very beginning. Like controllable pitch propellers that would fail to govern themselves or would not feather, and, if they did feather, would not unfeather. The driveshaft would continue to develop unacceptable vibration. The gearbox would overheat." All of these malfunctions forced program delays.

Fortunately, none of the propeller or gear failures resulted in any loss of the airplane or crew. Both Stanley and military test flight crews always brought the flying wing back to base, sometimes on only one-and-a-half engines. But the plane returned to where East Coast factory engineering consultants waited to correct the problem.

The recurring inflight failures, while not serious in terms of the continuing test program, became of more immediate concern to the Northrop company when their competitor, Consolidated Vultee, rolled out their own Air Corps bomber candidate in mid-1946. This was the very conventional XB–36, with six pusher engines, undoubtedly the largest airplane ever built. The huge aircraft, with a 162-foot long fuselage, weighed 200 tons, unmatched by anything built up to that time, at least in weight and size. It was almost as long as the wing span of the XB–35, which had no fuselage at all to measure. It remained to be seen how the performance compared. As the flying wing test program proceeded, in fits and new starts, overcoming one mechanical problem after the other, it was increasingly apparent to all concerned that only one of the two bombers would survive the postwar budget crunch. There was talk about possible co-production of the two very dissimilar aircraft, but Northrop considered that questionable. Testing continued, constantly frustrated by equipment failures. The basic flying wing concept, even the internal structural engineering work by Otis Elevator Company, was unchallenged, but aircraft parts and operating accessories were mostly a failure, particularly the engine gearboxes and complicated contra-rotating fifteen feet diameter propellers supplied by the government.

The Air Corps Air Material Command, in their flight test reports, were discouraging in their cold recital of the incidents:

On the second flight, erratic operation of propeller governor #2 was experienced when the airplane flew at 250 mph. Also, propeller governor #3 hunted with a variation of about plus or minus 100 rpm; the pilot had difficulty feathering the propellers during the third flight. The airplane was then grounded because of propeller and gearbox difficulties. During the ninth flight, the gearbox in #4 engine failed. The #4 propeller was then feathered and the airplane landed. There were governor troubles and two propeller malfunctions on flight number 10. An emergency landing was made on the 11th flight after the #4 gear box failed partially.

After that incident, Jack Northrop reluctantly suspended all "further XB–35 flight testing until the government could supply more reliable power plant elements." The dual-rotating systems were removed and flight testing resumed when single-rotating propellers were installed, but other problems persisted to plague the flying wing. There were problems with engine exhaust leaks and failure of the 208 volt auxiliary power unit. Occasionally one of the eight hydraulic pumps acted up. None of the problems were considered serious enough to permanently ground the airplane, although each caused significant delays in the flight test program.

A year after delivery of the first flying wing to Muroc, Air Corps Major Robert Cardenas was at Northrop's Hawthorne Airport conducting final high speed taxi tests of the second flying wing. An unexpected headwind caught the airplane as it approached takeoff speed, causing the plane to become airborne. Cardenas stayed in the air and continued on to Muroc with his crew.

The second aircraft also suffered from a wide variety of counter-rotating propeller problems. Replacing the troublesome units with less complex four-blade single-rotation propellers was no panacea for the XB–35. Performance decreased seriously, vibration problems associated with propeller interference with the wing slipstream became a new problem, and instability became a matter of serious concern. Things were not going well for the XB–35. Consolidated Vultee's testing program, underway at Texas, while not without glitches of its own, was proceeding on schedule. The only consolation to Jack Northrop was his conviction that the competition's XB–36 would ultimately prove to be what it was, an old-fashioned airplane with no redeeming features.

Stanley confirmed redline speeds, stalled the flying wing in every conceivable attitude, and learned to recover promptly. While absorbing the plane's unique characteristics, he worried about the constant speed propellers' "searching" for the proper pitch, which shoved the plane forward in subtle surges like waves against a beach. It was difficult to maintain a straight course, because the transverse yaw movement tended, along with the propeller-induced surge, to give a slight twist to a straight ahead course, as if the flying wing wanted to search the skies on its own. It was a gentle aberration that Stanley respected. The flying wing was a flyer's airplane.

While not a pilot of great experience and many flight hours, Max Stanley had been chosen to make the initial tests of the big wing after showing unusual aptitude in flying a scale model of the XB–35. Four of these flying models, with 60-foot wing spans, had been built since 1943, and they served their purpose well. Both Northrop and military pilots, before flying the full-size wing, first served their apprentice hours training in the aerodynamic XB–35 equivalent, the N–9M, learning the difference between piloting conventional aircraft and the flying wing. N–9M flights also provided useful data for the engineers developing new control systems, data not easily obtainable from wind tunnel testing of smaller, nonflying models.

"Flying wings are easy to fly," says Max Stanley, "with flight characteristics not too different from conventional airplanes. It's just that they fly better than other airplanes. They go faster quicker." Stanley soon learned that a flying wing gains altitude at a much higher rate of climb and at a greater angle of attack than other planes of the same weight and size. On takeoff, the nose-high attitude assumed by flying wings was alarming to some pilots. Landing approaches must be at a low angle, almost like a Cessna light plane. The inherent tendency of the flying wing is to rapidly accelerate as soon as the nose is pointed toward the ground. The flying wing, with its aerodynamically clean, efficient wings, and without encumbering and drag-producing fuselage and tail, does not want to slow up.

This trait of the aircraft is what may have caused the death of Northrop test pilot Max Constant, who crashed in one of the small N–9Ms. Constant was conducting aft center of gravity and control tests, including stalls, tests that can sometimes push any aircraft beyond its ability to fly. A farmer north of Rosamond Dry Lake in the Mojave witnessed the crash; he saw the aluminum wings alternately flashing in the sun from an apparent spin or tumbling motion. Investigation after the accident indicated that strong aerodynamic forces had been generated, sufficient to push back on the control column with enough force to exceed Constant's strength, preventing him from regaining control of the aircraft. He was trapped in the cockpit and unable to bail out.

Subsequent engineering checks found all stall-spin characteristics within acceptable limits. However, to prevent unanticipated forces from overpowering the pilot in the full-size flying wing, a hydraulic boost device was installed to push the control wheel forward in an emergency.

Occasionally an Air Corps test pilot would be critical of the flying wing because he failed to recognize these typical peculiarities for what they were—not understanding it was the unique ability of the flying wing to accelerate rapidly in all flying attitudes that made the XB–35 a superior flying machine. At other times, military test pilots did not believe what they experienced, stating in one flight test report, "Climbs were fairly flat, but, owing to the position of the pilot, they seemed steeper than they actually were." In the same report, the pilot also wrote, "Initial climb attitude seemed rather steep, but this might have been due to the position of the pilot on the wing surface." The aircraft's performance was not to be believed.

While Northrop representatives at Muroc attempted to solve the XB–35 propeller problems, Jack's engineers at Hawthorne worked on installation of newly available General Electric jet engines in a modified, jet-powered version of the flying wing to be designated YB–49. The new engine was admirably suited for powering the flying wing, presented few modification problems, and overnight moved Northrop's flying wing into the jet age. Northrop had originally intended his aircraft to be powered by his company's own Turbodyne jet turbine engine, using propellers. Now his plane took a gigantic technological leap forward with modern jet power. As far as Jack was concerned, the flying wing was now unbeatable.

Other than redesigned engine mounts, fuel lines, and instrumentation for the eight jet engines, no internal structural changes were needed. Four small trailing edge fins were added to compensate for the loss of directional stability when the propeller shaft housings and propellers were eliminated. Four long wing fences were added, with a reconfigured wing leading edge offering a clean, low drag intake slot for each set of four jet engines. The finished aircraft looked exactly as Jack had felt a successful airplane should —beautiful. The YB–49 was a sleek, low drag all-wing airplane offering spectacular performance far beyond anything of its size. The plane was to quickly prove its capability, with a cruising speed of 400 mph at 40,000 feet and a range of nearly 4,000 miles, unprecedented for its day. For many years it was the longest range, jet-powered airplane in the world.

11

BREAKING RECORDS WITH THE FLYING WING

The year 1947 was an exciting one for Jack. His flying wing XB–35 was redesignated the YB–49 and was in the process of being modified for jet power, a development he had long desired. The acceptance program at Muroc Army Air Base was continuing without a hitch. He was confident the problems caused by piston engine gearboxes and propellers would quickly disappear when the jet powered YB–49 was delivered. He would have time for a flight to London to deliver the 35th Wilbur Wright Memorial Lecture on the development of all-wing aircraft before the prestigious Royal Aeronautical Society. He was received with honor by the great aeronautical names of England, including Sir Frederick Handley Page, Air Marshal Sir Hugh Saunders, and Sir Richard Fairey. Northrop was personally thanked by Handley Page, who remarked, "There is nothing more inspiring than the record of high endeavor; nothing more impressive than the logical development of a great thought."

Northrop was not the first to have the vision of an all-wing airplane. Stephenson was not the first to have the vision of a steam locomotive. But they both had a gift perhaps more precious than simple vision—the gift of being in the right place at the right time, enabling them to transform a vision into reality. Jack heard from all sides that an airplane should have the maximum size body with the mere sliver of a wing—a projectile with fins. Northrop saw things differently. He believed airplanes should have a maximum of wings and a minimum of body. "Better, no body at all. To concentrate on the body is gross, unsightly, and inefficient. To focus on the wings is to be on the side of birds in their graceful, seemingly effortless flight—to be on the side of the angels."

Northrop's timing in developing the flying wing was, in fact, almost uncanny. Not only did he design his plane with swept-back wings at a time when aeronautical engineers agreed that future high performance aircraft would all be designed with swept-back wings; he designed a plane best suited for jet power before jet engines were manufactured; he brought his lifelong vision to maturity at a time when the only power plant—jet turbines—that would give his aircraft aesthetic beauty with a minimum of drag, also reached maturity.

The flying wing's tremendous capabilities were still to be fully revealed when Max Stanley flew the jet-powered YB–49 aircraft, the newest of the line, from Hawthorne to Muroc on October 21, 1947. The designation from XB–35 to YB–49 had been made when the four piston engines and propellers were replaced with eight of the new General Electric Y–35–A–5 jet engines, developing a total of 32,000 pounds of thrust, capable of flying the YB–49 at a top speed of 520 miles per hour. Northrop's flying wing had entered the jet age. Three months later Jack Northrop made his first flight in the large flying wing bomber, joining Max Stanley and the crew in a routine flight from Muroc. Stanley's only concern when flying the new jet-powered YB–49 was the typical rapid acceleration after takeoff, now multiplied by jet engine thrust. Because of the slow rate at which the landing gear retracted, it was necessary to begin the operation only a few hundred feet above the ground. Otherwise the maximum speed with gear down would be quickly exceeded, blowing off the wheel covers.

A second YB–49 soon arrived at Muroc, and continued flight testing consistently exceeded performance forecasts and Air Corps' contract specifications. There was continued grumbling by military test pilots about uncomfortable seats, limited vision for the copilot, and an instrument panel awkward to view because of its low position. The panel extended halfway over on the copilot's side, making it easy for the copilot but difficult for the pilot to see the right side of the panel. The XB–36 also had its problems, but in comparing the two aircraft, project officers declared the new jet powered YB–49 to be the cleanest, most trouble-free, and most ready-to-fly bomber ever received from aircraft contractors. General Roger Ramey, commander of the 8th Air Force and the country's leading heavy bombardment expert, told friends after returning from a flight in 1948, "The YB–49 is the fastest bomber I have ever flown—a fine ship with a real future."

The flying wing was capable of flying the longest distance at the fastest speed with the heaviest payload of any jet powered airplane flying in the world in 1948. General Ramey was the only general officer to fly a Northrop flying wing. He continued to support the project, in spite of the growing skepticism of General Curtis LeMay and the general staff.

Northrop test pilot John Myers had driven General Ramey to Muroc, and expressed his appreciation of the general being sufficiently interested in the flying wing to make the long trip out to California to fly the YB–49. The general told him, "Myers, let's get something straight. This wasn't my idea. The boss (General LeMay) told me to come out here and get my ass in that damned flying wing. My superiors in Washington think that because a bird has a tail, kites have tails, and the Wright Brothers had a tail, that you are never going to fly without a tail!"

Many new records for both speed and range were set during 1948 and 1949. The first YB–49 was flown nonstop from Muroc to Andrews Air Force Base in Washington D.C., a distance of 2,258 miles, in 4 hours and 25 minutes at a speed of 511 miles per hour, a new record for the distance. On orders from Air Force General Ben Funk, the YB–49 was flown to Andrews for a forthcoming military air display with Major Robert Cardenas in command of a regular Air Force crew. Cardenas had replaced Captain Glen Edwards as Chief of Flight Test for the Northrop flying wing program at Muroc Air Field. Northrop's test pilot, Max Stanley, went along on the flight as an observer.

Max was flying the YB–49 during an instrument letdown through the overcast above Washington, D.C., when the entire crew was reminded of the flying wings penchant to accelerate rapidly when in other than a normal flight attitude. Since the copilot, who would ordinarily be doing the radio work, could not reach across to the radio compass controls at the pilot's left, Max was flying and navigating for the moment. In the process of making radio contact with Washington Approach Control, he inadvertently increased forward pressure on the control yoke, pushing the flying wing into an incipient dive, where its speed rapidly increased at an alarming rate. His copilot at the time, Major Cardenas, grabbed the controls away from Max, pulling the plane up into a normal descent. The sudden maneuvers frightened everyone aboard. On the return flight, Max was banished to crew quarters in the rear of the plane and Cardenas moved over to the pilot's seat.

After breaking through the overcast, before landing at Andrews

Air Force Base and participating in the military air show, Major Cardenas was authorized to make a low altitude pass over the city. Cardenas interpreted his orders quite literally and proceeded to fly up Pennsylvania Avenue toward the capitol at 350 mph, 500 feet above afternoon traffic, to buzz the capitol building. As Cardenas put it, "100 feet over the dome." He landed at Andrews to a bemused welcome from the commanding officer. But then, what was to be expected from a man flying the huge bomber who also considered himself a fighter pilot.

During the air show at Andrews on February 15, 1949, President Harry Truman looked over the flying wing with considerable interest. Upon emerging from the interior, climbing down the exit ladder, he was overheard to say, "This looks like one hell of an airplane. Maybe we should buy some of these." Northrop's jet powered YB–49 was the hit of the air show along with the brand new Boeing sweptwing XB–47. The two modern jet bombers were the talk of Washington military aviation brass for weeks afterward.

On the return trip, a scheduled stop was made at Air Defense Command Headquarters at Wright Field, in Dayton, Ohio, where the aircraft was again shown off by the Air Force. The YB–49 flight crew spent the night at the bachelor officers quarters. When the crew assembled the following morning to board the flight onward to California, one important crew member was missing. Flight Commander Major Cardenas was informed that a crewman was sick and had asked the flight go on without him. Cardenas ordered the Air Crewman to report to him at once. A short time later, the somewhat nervous crewman arrived at plane side as ordered, a little jumpy, but otherwise apparently healthy. As far as Cardenas was concerned, the plane was not going to leave without him. Everyone was ordered aboard the aircraft to prepare for takeoff.

The takeoff was routine for the nonstop flight to Muroc, until some distance west of Ohio, when the flying wing began to experience serious inflight engine problems and onboard engine fires, more than any bomber had ever encountered in peacetime. After 4 hours and 10 minutes, three of the J–35 turbojet engines on the left side caught fire and one on the right side was burning. All had to be shut down. Fifty percent of the power of the aircraft was lost. Major Cardenas still had four engines running but no way of knowing how long before the remaining engines would also develop excessive vibrations and have to be shut down.

The incident provided an excellent demonstration of the ability of the flying wing to fly on only half its engines. Concerned over possible failure of the remaining engines at any time, Cardenas deemed it wise to land as soon as possible. The navigator located on his map the nearest airport with a sufficiently long runway, Winslow Municipal Airport in Arizona. Advising the airport tower controller to clear the area of all aircraft, the YB–49 made a straight in approach to land on the narrow runway. Because the huge flying was too large to taxi off onto the adjacent taxi way, the aircraft rolled out to the end of the main runway and shut down, much to the consternation of several people quietly enjoying coffee in the airport restaurant. It was 4 hours and 14 minutes after takeoff and the only YB–49 in the world was an unexpected visitor to the small Arizona airport.

The heavy aircraft broke through the soft runway shoulder and had to be pulled out by the crew. Air Force headquarters and the FBI were notified to begin an investigation. It was soon discovered that bearings on the offending jet engines had burned out and caught fire because of a total absence of lubricating oil. Upon inspection, the oil tanks for each engine were found to be empty. The startled crew determined very quickly that in only fifteen more flying minutes all of the remaining engines would have also run out of oil. New replacement engines, along with mechanics and tools were trucked in from Hawthorne. There were no repair facilities for flying wings in Arizona, and it was a month before the crew was able to fly the YB–49 back to California.

Investigation revealed that on the flight from Washington, at the last stop in Dayton, a crew member had forgotten or deliberately neglected to fill the tanks with engine oil. A crew member might forget to fill one engine, possibly two, but, not all eight oil tanks. The J–35 engine lubricating system consisted of an oil reservoir from which lubricating oil was pumped through the engine and then discharged overboard, making it necessary to replenish oil reservoirs each time the YB–49 was refueled. It was standard preflight procedure to check that the amount of fuel and oil was consistent with the anticipated duration of the flight.

Major Cardenas insisted that all of the original flight crew return to California on the YB–49 after new engines had been installed, including the crewman who had claimed he was sick at Wright Field. Cardenas had reason to mistrust the crew member, but it was not until they arrived back at Muroc that he seriously suspected that this particular person must have known that the oil tanks for each engine

had not been filled since the plane left Washington. It was undoubtedly why he wanted to be left behind. Most personnel on the YB–49
considered the incident sabotage, as did Major Cardenas. The reason
for the failure to fill the engine oil tanks in Dayton remained a
mystery. The FBI investigated, but their conclusions were never
released to the public. Details of the incident were kept secret.

After the plane's return from Arizona, another flight was entered
in the record books when the repaired YB–49 stayed aloft for more
than 9 hours, covering over 3,000 miles without refueling. The YB–49
was then reconditioned and returned to Hawthorne for the promised
flyby of the Northrop plant on Visitors' Day. The several thousand
employees and their guests who turned out for the event on a clear
southern California day saw another flight characteristic common to
the flying wings, but impossible with other large conventional aircraft. After completing a low pass along the length of the runway at
1,000 feet, the pilot pulled the flying wing into a turn for a repeat of
the low-level pass. The YB–49 was capable of flying such a tight
turning radius that the much smaller P–80 *Shooting Star* chase plane
was unable to stay with the much larger bomber. As the YB–49
climbed away from Hawthorne, the rapid rate of climb again left the
P–80 pursuit far behind. The flying wing was definitely not a fighter,
nor were acrobatic maneuvers permitted, but the YB–49 always demonstrated capabilities far beyond any contemporary aircraft. They
were the characteristics Northrop expected of his airplanes.

In the postwar years, Northrop Aircraft was anxiously searching
for a future with the flying wing, still being dependent on the military
for most of their business. The company needed to complete qualifica-
tion testing for the first two YB–49 bombers and eleven other service
model YB–35s being converted to jet power at the Northrop factory
before receiving production contracts for a larger number of flying
wings. One of the original XB–35s was being modified to provide a
flight test vehicle for Northrop's Turbodyne gas turbine engine when
the Turbodyne engine contract was cancelled. That airplane was later
changed again. It became the YRB–49, which was completed and
delivered in May 1950, destined to be the last of the large flying wings.
A second YB–49 was lost with no fatalities when it flipped over on the
ground during a high speed taxi run.

Consolidated Vultee was counting heavily on their own candidate,
the B–36 bomber, to replace the now outmoded wartime B–29, B–17,
and B–24 bombers. Their plane still faced completion of its own test

program, demonstrating inferior performance to the YB–49. But conservative military test pilots were always more comfortable flying the conventionally designed B–36 that looked like an airplane should—with a tail and propellers.

After the end of the war, the huge government-owned bomber plant in Fort Worth, Texas, used for mass production of B–24 bombers, remained empty. It was available for building the B–36 if Consolidated Vultee was awarded the contract for the new postwar bomber. Should this come about, Northrop's YB–49 would be eliminated from consideration as the U.S. strategic bomber for the next decade, and the Northrop company would be in serious financial trouble. The exciting, record-breaking flights of the jet-powered YB–49, an advanced aircraft difficult for anyone except Jack Northrop to imagine in 1941, were, in 1948, no longer as meaningful to the military. The war had ended with an Allied victory. Long-range bomber development by Northrop, Consolidated Vultee, Boeing, and Martin was considered redundant and less important than other projects as congressionally budgeted funds for the military became increasingly scarce.

Consolidated Vultee had been having difficulties leaving the war behind and development of their B–36 bomber was not proceeding on schedule. Flight experience had demonstrated that the six Pratt & Whitney piston engines with propellers, originally intended to fly the B–36, were not powerful enough to give their bomber the range and cruising speed specified by the Air Force. It would not be a successful competitor to Northrop's YB–49. By adding four jet engines, two hung under each wing in pods, performance was improved but at considerable sacrifice in range. Consolidated Vultee engineers found it difficult to surpass Northrop's aerodynamically clean YB–49 in speed and maneuverability in their cumbersome B–36, designed on an already obsolete airframe.

The Northrop company continued work on their first production flying wings. When the Consolidated Vultee B–36 failed to demonstrate acceptable performance, a number of the B–36 aircraft, previously scheduled for production as bombers, had, by orders of the Air Force, been converted to cargo carriers. Orders for the B–36 bomber were reduced to ninety-five airplanes. Jack Northrop, learning of this change in procurement, began to feel increasingly confident that his all-wing, all-jet YB–49 would be the ultimate winner of the competition with Consolidated for the primary strategic bomber of the U.S. Air Force.

The company began exploring additional military uses of the YB–49 to convince the Air Force of the plane's practical superiority. One of the unusual advantages presented was the flying wing's inherent ability, because of its configuration, to fly into enemy territory undetected by radar. Max Stanley took the YB–49 on a several hundred mile flight out into the Pacific in 1948, and returned to the mainland of California on a direct route toward Coastal Command radar still in operation at Half Moon Bay south of San Francisco. The thin profile of the flying wing bomber, flying at over 500 miles per hour toward the target, was never detected by radar. The YB–49 was not seen by radar operators until the plane was almost overhead. It was another amazing ability of the flying wing. This unique characteristic was never understood by the Air Force to be a desirable attribute for a strategic bomber. Stealth aircraft was an idea that had not come to be accepted by the bureaucracy at the Pentagon.

The purpose of a stealth design in improving the ability of a bomber to penetrate the target area without being detected was not considered important by strategic bomber advocates of the day, although World War II fighter pilots knew better. Pilots who scored highest did so not so much in close-in combat and high speed aerial chases as they did in exploiting their ability to close the attack without being seen. They often used the classic maneuver of diving toward an enemy plane with the sun behind them—a universal blindspot, where not even a silhouette could be seen in the blinding sun.

In the years before air-to-air missiles, observability was a neglected science, largely because air warfare was thought of as being little different than ground combat. It was assumed that opposing forces would always see each other. Even the possibility of ambush by unseen opponents was seldom considered by the generals in charge, an outdated military philosophy to be later revealed as folly in Vietnam. This attitude was unconsciously carried over into airpower and the procurement of aircraft.

Bombers grew increasingly larger as a solution to longer range and heavier payload requirements. The Consolidated-Vultee B–36 was four times the size of World War II B–29s. Few strategic bombing theorists pointed out that these larger aircraft were not the best way to go, that smaller, more efficient bombers should be acquired if strategic planning were to be successful when hostilities occurred. The larger aircraft were more expensive and made bigger targets, easily seen by radar at greater and greater range. Few paid much attention to the disadvantages of these huge, clumsy aircraft. Emphasis was placed on defeating radar by evasive tactics, electronic jamming, and throwing aluminum confetti into the air ahead of bombers to confuse airmen at their radar scopes.

Northrop had not initially designed the YB–49 to make his flying wing less detectable to radar but his aerodynamically efficient craft did incorporate advance stealth concepts. While being ignored by military traditionalists, these concepts were without a doubt the forerunner of a radical change in future war by radar and missile.

When the second YB–49 was delivered to Muroc, only one problem remained to be solved. The new jet, like the first, still had a tendency to yaw, to fly a zigzag in straight flight. This oscillation would need to be corrected if the flying wing was to be a suitable bombing platform. The Norden bomb sight required a straight course when approaching the target. The YB–49s yawing made this impossible.

It was not unusual for high performance aircraft to require control assists and augmentive devices, hydraulic and electronic. These airplanes, because of their inherent instability and control limitations, required automatic-pilots if the plane was to perform properly in flight. Northrop had anticipated this problem and installed a rudimentary, off-the-shelf autopilot in the scale model N–9M. Commenting on its application in his lecture before the Royal Aeronautical Society, he said the, "automatic pilot was flown on the N–9M with complete success . . . when modified to respond to a yaw-vane signal at zero sideslip." In non-aviation terms, this meant the plane was then able to fly straight without the pilot overcompensating for the zigzags.

A more recent airplane with control problems, also flight tested in the desert at Muroc, was the original Lockheed U–2 spy plane. At high altitudes this plane required very precise flying beyond the ability of a pilot to maintain for any length of time. The stalling speed of the U–2 at maximum altitude and the speed at which supersonic destruction occurred was separated by only 4 or 5 miles an hour. Should the pilot fly too fast, the U–2 would break up in flight; should the plane be flown too slow at high altitudes, a stall and spin would result. In both cases the plane would fall from the sky. Pilot Gary Powers said that flying the original U–2 manually without an autopilot was like "walking a tightrope" and difficult to maintain in straight and level flight at high altitudes. When the autopilot malfunctioned on his ill-fated last flight over the Soviet Union, he descended to a lower altitude where the airplane would be easier to fly. It was also easier for Soviet missiles to shoot him down, to the embarrassment of President Eisenhower who had said the plane was lost on a weather flight over Turkey.

To make flying his YB–49 more pleasant and easier to keep on a straight course, Jack conferred with the Honeywell people who designed an autopilot adapted to a yaw damper in series, powered by four servo motors. This effectively eliminated the yawing problem and made piloting the flying wing an easy afternoon drive. It was the first time an autopilot designed especially for the plane was used to power aircraft controls, to augment directional stability by artificial means. The use of "Little Herbert," an autopilot to help fly the YB–49 was but another innovative application of new technology by Jack Northrop. This feature would lead critics to say the flying wing was uncontrollable by the pilot and therefore impractical. In later years, instability would be deliberately designed into airplanes to reduce surface controls and drag, as augmentive autopilots in high performance supersonic jet aircraft became the norm. In the forward-swept wing X–29 experimental fighter of 1987, a design that makes the plane inherently unstable to a point where the pilot's physical responses are not fast enough no matter how skilled he is, the plane is impossible to fly without the six computers on board. All of the computers must be used to control flight attitudes requiring microsecond responses to prevent the airplane from tumbling and breaking apart.

Two years of testing the XB–35 and YB–49 at Muroc convinced Air Force flight officers of the advantages of the all-wing bomber configuration. The YB–49 demonstrated outstanding performance capabilities in speed, range, and payload, although, when jet engines replaced the piston power plant, the range was substantially reduced below the originally specified 10,000 miles. The Air Force was pleased in any case, and in January 1948, publicly announced that the YB–49 was the longest range jet aircraft in the world.

Four months later, the second YB–49 flying wing bomber was flown from the ramp at Hawthorne to the desert military base for acceptance testing. Everyone at Northrop was satisfied that the YB–49 was a winner. Jack Northrop's confidence was never greater. He was exuberant and smiling in every conversation as he made his usual rounds of plant departments, shaking hands and joking with Hawthorne employees.

On June 5, 1948, the YB–49 flying wing crashed in the Mojave

Desert killing everyone aboard. A series of Phase 2 Air Force acceptance tests were being conducted with the second YB–49. These tests involved stability of the aircraft at differing locations of the center of gravity. Performance of the flying wing under these circumstances was of particular importance. Faulty management of the fuel systems in flight could easily shift the center of gravity adversely if inboard fuel tanks emptied before those in the outer wing panels. Under these circumstances, behavior of the aircraft in erratic stall attitudes and subsequent recovery procedures would change considerably.

Since its arrival at Muroc, the YB–49 had been flying without incident for nearly 5 months, for a total of about 66 flying hours. Northrop test pilots had flown the aircraft during the first twenty-four flights. On the day before the June 5 flight, Air Force orders transferred the plane to military control. On the same day, three flights were made for the first time with military pilots. The Air Force pilots assigned to the YB–49 had never flown the plane before, nor had they been checked out in the aircraft by more experienced Northrop pilots. Captain Glen Edwards and command pilot Major Dan Forbes had both previously flown the scale-model N–9M, which was relatively easy to fly. They did not consider it necessary to first fly the full-size YB–49 with a Northrop pilot. It was now exclusively an Air Force operation and they felt that a check-out flight with Northrop pilots might compromise their objectivity in evaluating the aircraft.

The apparent adversarial feelings toward corporate civilian test pilots by military test pilots was always evident at Muroc, where test flying of the YB–49, and other aircraft was underway. A feeling of superiority prevailed in both civilian and military ranks, exaggerated by competitive jealousy. Close cooperation between military and corporate test pilots would have greatly benefited the test programs and tempered professional relationships. Advice offered by Northrop test pilots was routinely refused by military pilots, who accepted the idea that Northrop pilots would be prejudiced in favor of their employer's radical aircraft. Air Force test pilots were convinced that they were the only pilots writing test flight reports who would be objective. To compare notes might have prevented this.

Perhaps Max Stanley could have saved the life of Captain Edwards and the crew, if Edwards and Forbes had accepted the offer of a check-out flight. Edwards had privately expressed doubts about the plane's stability, and had a concern over the YB–49's tendency to stall. Max Stanley had recovered from properly executed stalls many times. Edwards and Forbes declined his help.

Glen Edwards left a personal diary containing his impressions after a day of flying. On June 22, 1948, he wrote, "Flew the YB–49 again today, too rough to get any data. Darnedest airplane I've ever tried to do anything with. Quite uncontrollable at times." The next day he wrote, "Col. Boyd flew the YB–49 for the first time today and wasn't too impressed. We all share the same view—a passable airplane under ideal conditions." Edwards had previously flight tested two other military aircraft in the desert, the North American XB–45 and the Convair XB–46, which lost out to rival Boeing B–47. The original piston engine powered Consolidated Vultee XB–36 was never flight tested at Muroc.

Major Cardenas and the other Air Force pilots, including Captain Edwards and Major Forbes, neither asked questions nor went near Max Stanley and other Northrop crew members. They even kept their distance from the Northrop project engineer when they took over responsibility for the YB–49. After only about 11 hours of flight time in the YB–49, the fourth flight by the Air Force, with the military crew aboard (Edwards, Forbes, Flight Engineer Lt. E.L. Swindell, and two civilian text observers, C.C. Leser and C.H. LaFountain), took off from Muroc at dawn, routinely reporting back to base twenty-six minutes later over Bakersfield in the San Joaquin Valley. According to a Northrop memorandum, the test flight agenda called for a climb to 40,000 feet, where "speed power runs" were to be conducted to determine how much power was needed to reach a specific airspeed. The crew also was to record data on engine operating temperatures before shutting down and restarting two engines in flight. The pilot, Dan Forbes, was scheduled to initiate a series of stalls at progressively higher power settings while flying at 10,000 to 15,000 feet. Over the Antelope Valley near Mojave, the YB–49 radio operator made another position report, advising of their descent through 15,000 feet. They were never heard from again.

No one witnessed the actual crash. Both Northrop pilot Fred Bretcher and Air Force Major Russ Schleen, a fighter test pilot who was driving on the highway north of Muroc, saw the bomber in an apparent tumble from the sky, out of control. Commenting about the event in a letter to the National Air & Space Museum, Schleen wrote,

At first it appeared to be falling pieces of metal. Probably it was the outer wing panels or control surfaces that caught my eye. I then glanced north and noticed the main section of the airplane tumbling and later contacting the ground just north of the Mojave-Victorville highway. I rushed to the scene after scanning the sky for parachutes and rummaged around the wreckage, but could not identify anything of consequence due to the impact damage and resulting fire and total destruction of the aircraft.

The two outer wing panels, torn in flight from the main wing structure, were found several miles from the crash site near the Mojave community.

Shorn of its outer wing panels, the uncontrollable aircraft had fluttered from the sky like a mortally wounded bird. There were no ejection seats. Pilots were not able to jettison the bubble. Escape for the five man crew was impossible. All were killed. Muroc was later named Edwards Air Force Base in honor of Captain Glen Edwards of the destroyed YB–49 flying wing.

Exactly what happened on that morning over the Mojave Desert is conjectural, but evidence indicates the aircraft may have inadvertently exceeded the speed at which the plane's structure could withstand the excessive stresses imposed on the wing during a high-speed pull out of a dive in recovering from a stall. The YB–49 with eight jet engines was the same basic structure as the XB–35 with four piston engines. While the design weight was 213,975 pounds, all test flights were arbitrarily limited to 170,000 pounds takeoff weight, because no static stress test had been conducted on the YB–49 airframe. The aircraft was not designed for supersonic flight, a speed that could easily be exceeded in a dive. No instruments indicated maximum speeds permitted in specific maneuvers, but test pilots had been made aware of the flying wing's aerodynamic efficiency and tendency to accelerate rapidly when descending in nose-down attitudes. Maximum indicated permissible airspeed was "redlined" at 650 miles per hour—faster than the speed of sound at 15,000 feet.

Max Stanley later commented, "The stall characteristics of the flying wing loaded in a normal configuration are not very different from conventional aircraft. Any professional pilot could recover from them easily. The flying wing exhibits no unusual behavior in approaching a power stall, and recovery is routine. Its reputation as an airplane with unacceptable stall characteristics is not deserved." Wind tunnel tests demonstrated that none of the flying wing bombers, including the YB–49, could possibly tumble from stalls at any conceivable flight attitude. However, stalls were not an activity that Captain Edwards wanted to engage in. He was particularly reluctant, according to Air Force records, to even attempt power stalls in the YB–49.

Anxiously awaiting news that his second YB–49 had been accepted by the Air Force, Jack Northrop was shocked upon hearing of the crash in the desert. His light-skinned face became paler and his hands shook as he returned the telephone receiver to its place on the desk. He was totally perplexed, dumbfounded. The airplane had performed so well on all previous flights. Jack explained the accident to his associates, "The YB–49 had been flown at altitude, and on the way down the pilot apparently decided to carry on some stall tests. He made several stalls at an altitude of about 10,000 feet which gave him clearance of only about 7,500 feet over the surrounding terrain. In one of the stalls, he didn't catch the airplane quickly enough, he started to nose-down and apparently felt that he was losing altitude so rapidly that he had to pull the airplane violently out of a dive. The result was a symmetrical wing failure in bending—both sides of the airplane, the outer wing, folded upwardly, and the center section, of course, crashed and killed everyone on board instantly. However, the airplane had previously been static-tested and we knew that it was strong enough to withstand the loads that a bomber was required to sustain."

Walt Cerney, Jack's loyal veteran assistant chief engineer, tried to cheer him, but could not. Jack ordinarily did not display his feelings, but this day he became obviously discouraged. His disappointment spread throughout the entire organization. The associates of Jack Northrop were well aware that, not only had the Air Force lost a plane and a crew, but that Consolidated Vultee and their supporters in the Pentagon would be expected to take full advantage of the accident at Northrop's expense.

A little known coincidence remains to beg the question of possible sabotage. On the morning of the fateful flight by Captain Glen Edwards, an Air Force crewman assigned to the aircraft reported in sick at the base hospital, and was excused from taking the flight. This was the same crewman who was to report in sick again before takeoff of the YB–49 from Wright Field—a flight that resulted in an emergency landing when four engines of the flying wing caught fire because the engine oil tanks had not been filled during a refueling stop. On the flight from Wright Field, the aircraft commander ordered the crewman to climb aboard, sick or not. A week after returning to Muroc—before any proof of sabotage could be found and the investigation of the aborted flight completed—the airman was killed in a mysterious motorcycle accident in the Mojave Desert.

12

THE POLITICS OF FLYING WINGS

A few days after the tragic accident at Muroc, when all seemed to be lost, Jack Northrop received a telephone call from General Joseph McNarney in Washington. The General wished to see him immediately and would be in California the next day.

General McNarney was a likeable officer, balding with bushy eyebrows and a ski-slope nose. He wore the wings received at his army flying school without the usual rows of active duty ribbons. McNarney had been Deputy Chief of Staff under General George Marshall and was now Commanding General of the Air Force Air Material Command. It was McNarney who actually signed purchase orders for Air Force aircraft, and his visit to Northrop was not considered an ordinary event. Jack was still somewhat depressed from the loss of the YB–49 at Muroc and wondered what other bad news was on the way.

He welcomed General McNarney at the door of his office, and McNarney continued inside with a wide grin on his square-jawed face, greeting Jack with unrestrained enthusiasm. Without ceremony he handed Northrop a sheaf of papers pulled from his attache case. Jack shuffled through them rapidly, returning again and again to one particular page, before looking up and returning the General's grin. Jack's smile was even bigger. The papers were a signed contract ordering thirty RB–49 flying wing bombers, with production to begin immediately. The general explained they were designated RB–49s, to be used by the Air Force for photo reconnaissance. He added, "The order is only a drop in the bucket. Consolidated Vultee's Fort Worth bomber plant, owned by the government, will be made available to you for production of the RB–49. In large numbers."

Jack could hardly believe what was happening. The production contract answered the lingering question of who was to blame for Captain Edwards' fatal accident—it was not Northrop's design of the flying wing. The Northrop YB–49 was the superior aircraft and the Air Force was now prepared to substitute the YB–49 for the Consolidated Vultee B–36. Northrop was elated, and as he later said, "I felt we had at last won the battle." At home that evening, Jack was more than the usual happy family man. He was relaxed with his children, and told stories with them long after their bedtime. He even brought out the accordion to play, something he had not done for several months.

Washington had finally awakened to the fact that the Northrop flying wing bomber was a viable weapons delivery system—a plane that was not just an unorthodox experimental design of a visionary. The Air Force orders were proof of the plane's ability to outperform its B–36 competition. The YB–49 could climb at a higher rate to a higher altitude, and protect itself with an array of defensive armament that was quite impressive. There would be twenty 50-caliber machine guns in four outer wing mounted turrets plus a tail cone cluster, all remotely controlled units operated electrically from four remote gunner blisters.

Perhaps the most important attribute in favor of the YB–49, when compared to the B–36, was its lower maintenance requirements. It had two fewer engines, all of the same type, not the B–36s awkward mix of piston and jet. Two different kinds of fuel must be carried by the B–36 with complex engine related subsystems. None of this was required on the Northrop YB–49. The flying wing required less fuel to operate and, most importantly from a maintenance point of view during war, it was simply less airplane. The flying wing would be easy to keep flying.

The next morning, Jack prepared an announcement of the new contract for distribution to Northrop employees. The engineering staff had difficulty keeping their congratulatory tours around the plant in check, knowing that hard work must now begin, the preparation for actual production in quantity of the flying wing. Two weeks later, General McNarney notified both Northrop and Consolidated Vultee of the production decision by letter:

It is the desire of the Air Force to retain the production facilities at Fort Worth which is now employed in the construction of B–36 airplanes. Since it is not intended to buy more than the ninety-five B–36 airplanes presently on contract, it is desired that the production of RB–49s be moved to that facility at the earliest possible date. An absolute minimum number of RB–49s will be built in the present Northrop facility at Hawthorne . . . It is requested that representatives of Northrop Aircraft and Consolidated Vultee Aircraft arrange the necessary plans for carrying out this program with the least possible delay.

The Northrop organization began to plan for the production of thirty RB–49 flying wing airplanes soon after the letter was received. Eleven huge airframes remained at the Hawthorne plant, representing the unfinished portion of the original fifteen airplane order for XB–35 and YB–49 bombers. Most of these could be modified for use in the new reconnaissance configuration. The majority of the new RB–49s, responding to the suggestion by General McNarney, would be built in the plant at Fort Worth, under a subcontract with Consolidated Vultee. Northrop's Hawthorne plant did not have space available at the time to produce thirty of the large flying wings, although engineering work on production jigs and tools had already been completed. Most of the final assembly work on present aircraft could be completed outside the plant, on the adjacent paved airport ramp.

Jack savored his personal pleasure at the prospect of subcontracting out work on the flying wing to his biggest competitor, Consolidated Vultee. He remembered the prewar year of his new company, struggling to get started in the business of building airplanes, when the contract was received by Northrop to manufacture Vultee's *Vengeance* bombers. Northrop was begging then. Now Northrop was the big boy on the block. The flying wing that he had worked on for so long, overcoming so many business and bureaucratic obstacles, had finally proven its superiority against all competition. Aviation was making a quantum leap into the future with Northrop leading the way. General Manager Claude Monson announced to Northrop employees that a subcontract would be negotiated with Consolidated Vultee to built the RB–49 in Fort Worth. Northrop employees would not have all the work, but they would have all the glory.

Northrop's project engineer, Warren Kneriam, was sent to Fort Worth to inspect the extensive production facilities available. The Fort

Worth facility was one of the largest government-owned plants in the country, and there would be ample room to begin B–49 production while phasing out the B–36. At first, relations between the Northrop representatives and Consolidated Vultee proceeded in a friendly and cooperative fashion. Word quickly spread through the Consolidated Vultee organization that production of B–36s in the plant would end when the current contract was completed, and Northrop's B–49 built in their place. From then on relations were cool. John Myers and Gilbert Nettleton, John's assistant in Northrop sales, had already arrived in Texas to negotiate the subcontract.

The bad news was not long in reaching Floyd Odlum, Atlas Corporation Chairman, and a major Consolidated Vultee shareholder. He was the same investor who had purchased Northrop securities at a critical time when seed capital was needed for the nascent Northrop company. In some respects it was Floyd Odlum who may be credited with making the first security underwriting program for Northrop a success, although his investment company was no longer a shareholder in Northrop, having sold all of its stock in 1939. Odlum was well aware of Jack's design capabilities and was deeply concerned over Consolidated Vultee's position as a major military aircraft supplier being challenged by upstart Northrop.

The test program with the one remaining YB–49 aircraft continued at the desert air base, now called Edwards Air Force Base. There was nothing to indicate there would be any problem with the Air Force contract, as Northrop engineers preceded with plans for moving production to Fort Worth.

On the evening of July 16, 1948, Jack Northrop was invited to meet with Secretary of the Air Force, Stuart Symington at the home of John McComb in San Marino, and to bring Northrop board chairman, Richard Millar, with him. The invitation sounded more like a summons than an invitation to a festive occasion. Symington was in town to address a meeting of the Institute of Aeronautical Sciences. He wanted to talk with Northrop about the B–49 flying wing. McComb had been a member of President Truman's Air Policy Commission. He was now the secretary's assistant and had invited Symington to stay at his house while in southern California. Northrop knew McComb, as he had previously been a member of the Joshua-Hendy firm with whom Jack had formed an ill-fated partnership to develop the Turbodyne turbine engine.

Dick Millar had joined Northrop's board of directors and was elected chairman after the colorful La Motte Cohu resigned to become president of TWA. This association did not last long, as La Motte was unable to get along with Hughes. Cohu was then hired by Floyd Odlum as President of Consolidated Vultee in San Diego. LaMotte persuaded a number of former Northrop executives to join him, including Bob Byron, Director of Public Relations; Jack Naish, who became Director of Sales for Consolidated Vultee; and B. G. Reed, who advanced to General Manager of the Fort Worth production line. Cohu did not last long in San Diego but, during his tenure the Consolidated Vultee firm inherited much of Northrop's management. This was typical of aircraft company relationships at the time, somewhat like musical chairs. Loyalties were more associated with individual executives rather than a company. It was Dick Millar who had persuaded Donald Douglas to buy Jack's company from United Aircraft in the 1930s when Millar learned Jack was leaving. Dick had been president of Vultee aircraft at the time Northrop arranged the Vultee *Vengeance* contract with the British. Both companies benefited financially from having Northrop build 400 of the Vultee-designed dive bombers. Millar had left Vultee when the company merged with Consolidated in San Diego, forming Odlum's Consolidated Vultee. Many of these personal relationships had developed before the war, when the aircraft industry was small and built around a group of close friends and individuals who often became business associates. With large holding companies setting up diversified corporations, past individual friendships were often strained, and allegiances confused.

When Jack Northrop and Dick Millar arrived at John McComb's beautiful home in the late afternoon, they were surprised to find that Floyd Odlum had also been invited. General McNarney, who had personally brought the RB-49 contracts to Jack, was also in attendance, sitting in an easy chair on the far side of the room. Millar sat in the empty chair alongside McNarney, Jack beside him. Symington and Odlum sat apart, on a raised portion of the living room, the guests below looking up at the two above. It appeared to Jack that the Northrop people were to be the audience.

The conversation began abruptly, without much talk beyond the usual opening banter. Secretary Symington began by baldly announcing, "There are too many aircraft companies. The Air Force cannot afford to support another large aircraft manufacturer. We're going to have to cut one down." He looked directly at Jack. Millar felt that Northrop had already been nominated to be eliminated. Symington followed with a request spoken in the form of a demand, "I want Northrop combined with Consolidated."

Jack Northrop was stunned. He replied in a formal tone of voice, trying to be level-headed and unemotional, as he listened to an attempt to destroy his company before his eyes. He asked, "Mr. Secretary, what are our alternatives to this move?"

Symington was unequivocal and blunt in his reply, spoken in the language of a production line worker, "You will be goddamned sorry if you don't." At this, General McNarney half rose from his chair to say, very concerned, "Oh, Mr. Secretary, you don't mean that?" To which the Secretary of the Air Force immediately replied, "You're goddamned right I do!"

There was little to say in response. Both Jack Northrop and Dick Millar were shocked by the Secretary's abrupt and demanding manner. It sounded to them as if Symington was ordering the Northrop company to be taken over by its principal competitor for the long-range bomber contract. Floyd Odlum had been silent throughout the meeting. However, the particular combination of people, most with a substantial financial stake in the outcome of the bomber contract, made Jack very uncomfortable. He asked for time to consider the implications of such an important step, explaining that any decision must be referred to their board of directors, as Northrop had a majority of public shareholders. They agreed to meet again at Floyd Odlum's Indio home to discuss terms of the proposed merger in detail.

As Millar and Northrop were leaving the McComb house, walking to their car, Odlum came running up as fast as his arthritic legs would allow, calling out, "Hey, hey!" As he caught up with them, he said anxiously to his old friends, "I want you to know that I never knew what this meeting was going to be about." Symington later denied that he had arranged a meeting at all, saying he thought Northrop had called him to arrange a meeting while he was in Los Angeles. He was on the defensive, defending his actions for reasons unknown, offering no explanations, only denials. He said he couldn't remember ever saying anything about making trouble for Northrop. In later years, when Los Angeles public television commentator Clete Roberts had prepared a documentary for KCET-Channel 28 on the flying wing controversy, Symington, through his attorney, Clark Clifford, threatened the station with a lawsuit if the program was aired. The documentary was finally presented after considerable delay and no suit was filed.

Northrop clearly remembered Symington's threats at the San Marino meeting, and remained perplexed by Symington and Odlum's behavior. Jack and Dick Millar were deeply offended by the demand proposed by Secretary Symington, a government official. As far as they were concerned, Symington should not be making demands for corporate mergers that would affect competitive bidding on military contracts. Nothing sounded right about the proposed deal, but Northrop and Millar swallowed their pride and decided to keep the appointment to meet with Floyd Odlum at his Indio home. They agreed that, on the basis of the few words exchanged at San Marino, it was evident that much had gone on before they arrived. Millar said that he left the meeting, "Feeling like he'd been hit on the head by a baseball bat."

As Northrop and Millar entered Floyd Odlum's Indio home, the two aviation pioneers were not unaware of the aircraft personalities that preceded them on the sacrificial altar of corporate mergers, and of the predatory acquisitiveness of Consolidated Vultee and its major shareholder Odlum's Atlas Corporation. It was quite obvious to Jack, and history had been his mentor, that Northrop was next on Odlum's list for corporate assimilation. He didn't like the idea at all.

Northrop remembered his old friend, Major Reuben Fleet, talking many years before about Consolidated Aircraft when it was his company, boasting, "No holding company owns or controls us." When Jack's own Northrop company was organized, he insisted that there be general public ownership of the stock so no individual or corporation could dictate what he must do. Fleet's company had remained independent, a proud "airman's outfit," for twenty years, until the company was drawn, struggling, into Aviation Corporations orbit. Consolidated was one of the largest aircraft manufacturers in the country when assertions by government officials alluded to a "one man" operation by Fleet that was causing serious production difficulties. The rumors continued, saying delivery of Navy PBY flying boats on order would not be delayed if someone would buy Consolidated. Fortuitously enough, Aviation Corporation said they would be able to take over the company and solve the government's supposed problem. Working through its recently purchased Vultee subsidiary, Odlum's Aviation Corporation bought Fleet's controlling interest in Consolidated, 34 percent of the common stock. Executives of Republic Steel were put in charge of the aircraft company, amidst much controversy. In 1943, Consolidated and Vultee were merged to become Consolidated Vultee Aircraft Corporation—Convair. At the time, a commentator described the merger as, "Jonah has swallowed his second whale," alluding to a previous acquisition by the holding company of the submarine builder, Electric Boat, as the corporate groundwork was being laid for the creation of General Dynamics. Jack wondered if there had been a meeting between Fleet and Odlum before that merger.

Declassified records of the War Production Board make clear the federal government's dissatisfaction with Fleet's management of Consolidated as World War II approached. George Mead of the National Defense Advisory Commission said in a blunt letter to Fleet in 1940, "Frankly, you have a one-man show and you are the man. . . . Capable as you are, you cannot possibly keep your fingers on everything in an operation as large as you now have." A year later Vultee Aircraft finalized the deal with Fleet to buy him out. Vultee's president said of Fleet, "We have the benefit of his advice if we want it. If we don't ask for it, it isn't to be proffered."

Aviation Corporation had been organized by W. Averill Harriman in 1929, when control of half of the government-authorized airmail routes were obtained by "effectively excluding the majority of smaller independent operators," as a General Dynamics company history describes the procedure. Among the early aircraft companies to be absorbed into the growing conglomerate were the remnants of Thomas-Morse, Gallaudet, and Dayton-Wright that were acquired by Consolidated before their merger. Barkley-Grow Aircraft and Stinson disappeared when acquired by Vultee before being absorbed into Consolidated and Aviation Corporation by E. L. Cord, the motor magnate. Consolidated and Vultee-Convair was sold to the Atlas Corporation, controlled by Odlum, in 1947, when La Motte Cohu, formerly of Northrop, became president.

As far as Northrop was concerned, Odlum was looking for another aircraft company to enhance his collection. It was obvious that Northrop and the RB–49 contract would be a worthy acquisition. The Air Force had let it be known that the RB–49 was the better aircraft, and had already said that contracts for additional RB–49s were on the way. The military budget made it obvious that only one company's aircraft would be ordered in quantity. Odlum wanted that company to be Convair, as Symington had made clear at the San Marino meeting, even if it meant that Convair would be manufacturing Northrop's RB–49.

At Odlum's home in California, the matter-of-fact, uncompromising tone of the conversation made it clear to Northrop and Millar that Odlum knew he had the backing of the Secretary of the Air Force and that President Truman's new budget did not provide for money to buy both the B–36 and the RB–49. He would drive a hard bargain in order to gain the entire strategic bomber contract by default, perhaps to deliberately make any corporate merger impossible. The precise terms of the proposed exchange of shares in the two companies was not recorded, but Northrop and Millar both recalled that Northrop shareholders were to get less than one-fourth of the total shares in the merged companies. Consolidated Vultee shareholders would end up with the Northrop-developed flying wing design, all the aerodynamic and production knowledge that was the result of years of work by Jack, the RB–49 Air Force contracts, and all the other Northrop business, including the Northrop organization and company-owned facilities. According to Millar, Odlum never came up with any kind of an offer they could even pass on to Northrop stockholders for consideration. "We had to turn it down."

When the two Northrop executives objected, Odlum became adamant, but offered no possible alternatives. Jack shook his head in amazement at this uncompromising demand from his competitor, an outrageous offer by any measure—an offer that could destroy his company. The answer was predictable. After talking the deal over the next day with fellow Northrop directors, all voted to reject the offer, even if it resulted in the loss of the coveted YB–49 flying wing bomber contract.

Floyd Odlum and his wife, famed aviatrix Jackie Cochran, owner of one of Northrop's famous Lockheed designs, the *Gamma*, and a longtime friend of Jack, often entertained Air Force Secretary Stuart Symington at their desert home in Indio, near Palm Springs. It was a friendly relationship that was helpful to Consolidated Vultee in winning and keeping Air Force contracts. Consolidated Vultee may have learned of Northrop's being awarded the B–49 bomber contract before Northrop himself knew.

Six months after Jack Northrop said "no" to Floyd Odlum's demand that Northrop merge with Consolidated Vultee and give the flying wing to his competitor, the Air Force notified Northrop that the production contract for thirty RB–49 flying wing bombers was cancelled. At the same time, Jack learned that production by Consolidated Vultee of the B–36 would continue. Work on all but one of the eleven YB–49 airframes was terminated, including the single YB–49 flying wing that was to have been used as a test bed for the powerful Northrop developed XT–37 Turbodyne engine. This project had been stopped by the Air Force earlier when Northrop was ordered to divest itself of the manufacture of the jet turbine engine. A single YB–49 was converted to the YRB–49 photo reconnaissance version, which was delivered to the Air Force in early 1951.

Major Robert Cardenas, command pilot of the YB–49 flying wing on its record-breaking crosscountry hop to Washington D.C., had submitted a very favorable report on his flight, evaluating the excellent performance of the flying wing under very trying conditions, including flight with four engines out. Cardenas immediately flew to California to confer with Jack about the cancellation, worried that something he might have said in his report had caused the change in mind by the Air Force. Jack said, "No, there had not been as far as he knew. There were other reasons." Jack continued, cautioning Cardenas, "Please do not talk about the flying wing or the cancellation to anyone. Reporters will be asking you all kinds of questions. But say nothing. It would be detrimental to my company and to you."

Jack was bitter in private comments to his friends, saying,

Two of the flying wings had been redesigned to accommodate a big gas turbine engine that we had developed as one of the original projects at Northrop. We had a good gas turbine and it had passed through the required 50 hour tests at 10,000 horsepower. The turboprop and flying wing combination would have given us an airplane that would have carried a 10,000-pound bomb load 11,500 miles nonstop at 400 miles per hour, which was quite a performance in those days.

Mr. Symington said we had no business being in the gas turbine business and he stripped our plant of our gas turbine war work and turned it over to General Electric. Our project was washed out lock, stock, and barrel. The only thing that preserved the company was that, for some reason or other, he didn't cancel our order for F–89 fighters, and that production went on for some time and sustained the life of the company . . . This, to my knowledge, was the first time in Air Force history when something that was absolutely pure politics and dirty politics, determined the decision of where and which airplanes should be built. Of course, to me it was a heartbreaker, because the airplane was unique. Its ratio of lift to drag was better than any contemporary aircraft of its time, and its ratio of payload to weight empty was far better than any plane ever built, to the best of my knowledge. But, naturally, we were unwilling to merge on terms that we considered unfair to Northrop stockholders, and we suffered the vicious bureaucratic consequences.

Cardenas later learned that his report had been tampered with, and excerpts from his comments about the YB–49 quoted out of context for use in other, critical documents. Comparing the quoted criticism with his original document is quite revealing. It is easily seen that, if the fabricated quotes were taken as fact, there would be sufficient reasons to convince politicians that no YB–49s should be built. In the purported Cardenas test report distributed in Washington, Cardenas, who had thirty-five to forty hours in the bomber, was quoted as having said,

> The YB–49 was extremely unstable and very difficult to fly on a bombing mission because of continual yawing and pitching caused by the control arrangement. Also, the bomb bay doors could not be closed in flight. It was concluded that this bomber was not a good bombing platform—its directional stability was a little better but still not perfect, and its lateral stability was neutral. Additionally, the airplane suffered from "flap flutter."

Unfortunately for Northrop, critical comments such as these were taken at face value without attempt at verification. In the actual Cardenas test flight report, none of these adverse comments were made. It is not known who wrote the "revised" report.

The Air Force also received an adverse report from Joseph Foa, head of the propulsion branch of the Cornell Aeronautical Laboratory in Buffalo. Foa and his colleagues did analyses that differed quite considerably from those of Sears and Von Karman, that showed flying wings to be the worst possible aerodynamic configuration for jet-propelled long-range bombers. Cardenas' crosscountry flight would seem to have proven otherwise.

News of cancellation by the Air Force of all work on the remaining YB–49 flying wings was received with considerable emotion by the hundreds of factory workers who looked up to Jack Northrop, and shared his personal grief and sense of loss. The cancellation represented much more than possible loss of their jobs—every individual had placed great faith and hope in the graceful flying giant, and now took the cancellation as a personal affront to their boss and his inspiration, to their sense of accomplishment, and their pride in skilled workmanship down to the last flush rivet.

Without contacting management, acting spontaneously as the dread news spread, a group of employees on the production line circulated a petition quickly signed by several hundred fellow workers. A petition urging the company to allow them to complete work on the last YB–49 flying wing, then in the last stage of completion on the production line, in the process of final assembly. They proposed to finish the work required by volunteering their own time, without pay, on Saturdays, Sundays, and holidays, until their airplane was ready to fly.

Jack was deeply moved by this gesture of loyalty and faith in his flying wing, but could find no way of agreeing with their desire. He tearfully advised them that there was no way the company could assume the liability of completing work on the unfinished YB–49 which was actually owned, and had been financed, by the Air Force. He had to urge them to forget the idea, for it would have offended the company's principal customer, who expected the same loyal employees to continue building the F–89 *Scorpion* all-weather fighter and the *Snark* long-range cruise missile, also on the production line.

The most dramatic incident following the Odlum demand on behalf of Consolidated Vultee and cancellation of the contract, was the order from the Air Force to scrap all unfinished YB–49 flying wing bombers at the Northrop plant. Having been built on a cost plus fixed fee contract, the bombers were the property of the government. The Air Force had title and could do what they wished. Northrop employees to the last man and woman were appalled at the decision to destroy the flying wings, in the final stages of assembly, parked on the Northrop airport ramp ready for flying away to the Air Force. Apparently not trusting Northrop employees to destroy their own planes, the Air Force trucked in outside crews to reduce the flying wings to junk.

First to be removed were the government furnished components such as flight instruments, radios, and landing gear. Then the engines came out. Over a period of three months, the hundreds of loyal Northrop employees who had worked on the YB–49 over the years now saw a bunch of strangers swarming over their creation, carving the eleven aircraft up like so many turkeys. Riding the shuttle bus moving by the carnage on the run from Plant #1 to Plant #3, employees passed the shambles of what were once proud aircraft, weeping as the Air Force crew continued to cut, slice, and carve the historic aircraft into pieces small enough to throw into dump trucks. The Northrop employees could not believe such wanton destruction, without apparent reason, could actually be occurring to the glorious machines they had built, that they had seen fly so gracefully over Hawthorne. Company morale sank to a level where it could go no lower. Said one employee, describing the sad affair, "We shuddered every time we went by the ramp. The utter mayhem, utter destruction of airplanes we all loved, was absolutely incomprehensible. They were the worst days of my life."

Using cutting torches, an occasional axe, and whatever destructive tool was available, they dismembered and cut up Jack Northrop's flying wings into scrap, destroying the dreams he had conceived and nurtured into the most advanced aircraft in the world. The Air Force, without apparent remorse, hauled the scrap away for disposal and meltdown in an unmarked junkyard. The Air Force had paid many millions to build and develop the flying wings. Now the generals said they had no further use for the plane and could not afford to keep them in storage. The Air Force paid Northrop a final contract termination fee to end production. Some 2,000 employees were laid off overnight, as the company staggered around trying to recover its equilibrium. Chairman Millar said, "By destroying the wing you take a good crack at destroying Northrop." This may have been what someone had in mind.

Not even the Smithsonian museum was permitted to receive a YB–49 for exhibition; it was as if the Air Force wanted to wipe out all trace of the flying wing, erase all memory of its existence. To be absolutely positive that the flying wing would never be revived, the Air Force also ordered all production jigs and dies destroyed. Gilbert Nettleton, former Northrop pilot and sales representative, made a special trip to Edwards Air Force Base to procure copies of the official Air Force reports on YB–49 flight test programs, including the report by Major Cardenas. He was too late. The YB–49 test reports had been removed from the files before he arrived, and were unavailable. As far as the Air Force was concerned, the flying wing no longer existed.

As if vindictiveness was a virtue, and total destruction a goal, when one intact YRB–49 reconnaissance version, the only flying wing escaping the Hawthorne massacre, was discovered two years later, parked in a old vineyard next to Northrop's P–89 *Scorpion* flight test facility in Ontario, the Air Force promptly reassembled its scrapping crew. Relighting their cutting torches they reduced the somehow overlooked flying wing to unrecognizable pieces. The Air Force was now finally sure of receiving Symington and Odlum's official approbation. What the Air Force did not destroy, the Northrop Corporation itself did away with. New management decided that possible discussion of the controversial YB–49 project would be detrimental to being awarded future government business. It was determined there was no value in having flying wing engineering drawings and notes around for some inquiring journalist to paw over and write about in a manner that might be critical of the Air Force. No known photographs exist of the actual break-up of the YB–49s, on orders of the Air Force, who prohibited any photography of the destruction. Even the Northrop company photographer was banned from the scene of the crime.

The Consolidated Vultee B–36 was not forgotten, however. While no museum possessed a YB–49, the Strategic Air Command's favorite bomber, the B–36, upon retirement from active service and was enshrined for perpetuity in the Air Force museum at Wright-Patterson Air Force Base. Museum trustees decided against displaying the plane outside on the ramp with the other large planes on exhibit. Eight-million dollars was spent on building a special exhibition hanger with a clear span great enough to enclose completely the giant B–36, thus protecting it from the controversial world outside. At the Dayton museum, what may be the most gracefully beautiful airplane ever built, the delta-wing North American XB–70 *Valkyrie*, was parked in the weather outside the B–36 hanger.

Destroying aircraft they had paid to have built was a most unusual and bewildering procedure that the federal government would repeat in later years. About twenty years later, Robert McNamara gave the order to scrap production jigs and tools for the fastest airplane in the world at the time, the high-flying Lockheed YF–12A, apparently to prevent building any aircraft of the same design again. The designer of the airplane, Lockheed's genius engineer, Kelly Johnson, was incredulous at the order and decided to hide the irreplaceable manufacturing equipment, but to no avail. When McNamara learned that Kelly was attempting to get around his orders, McNamara personally oversaw the destruction of the tools. Reason for the unwarranted destruction was never divulged to the public or to Lockheed. George Larson, writing later in the Smithsonian's *Air & Space* magazine, commented on how Lockheed test pilot Ken Weir, telling of the incident in a dinner speech, "could scarcely conceal his bitterness at how the tangible achievements of engineers and pilots were so easily erased by a political penstroke."

Jack Northrop tried desperately to stop the desecration of his flying wing. When he finally reached Secretary Symington on the telephone, asking for an explanation, all the secretary would say was, "I have an adverse report on the airplane." Jack had never received any such report. Shortly after Symington's statement, Dick Millar received anonymously a photographic copy of the Air Force tests of simulated bombing runs of both the Y–49 and B–36. The recorded results in the document, showed the YB–49 to be on a par with the B–36, and, in some respects, superior bombing platform. Millar never learned the identity of the sender, nor did he have any way of verifying the recorded results, since the YB–49 files at Edwards were now missing. It did appear to him that a friend at Edwards Air Force Base wanted Jack to know that the excuse regarding the YB–49s purported poor bombing performance was false.

"Nobody seems to know what the Secretary's reasons were for this incredible destruction of public property," said Northrop's scientist consultant, Dick Sears. "Anger? To punish Northrop? To destroy the evidence? Whatever it was, it succeeded in wiping out the results of the nation's multimillion dollar experiment, the world's first serious effort to prove or disprove the "span-load" theory of the design of big airplanes."

When Northrop sales representative Nettleton asked Senator Carl Hayden, chairman of the Senate Armed Services Committee, for an explanation of the flying wing contract cancellation, he was told that President Truman had personally ordered cancellation of Northrop's YB–49 bomber contract because of a shortage of funds. Hayden said it was Truman's understanding that Northrop's flying wing bomber still needed additional expensive development, and had to be dropped in favor of the B–36. The bomber command would then receive operational B–36s before the flying wing B–49 could be accepted. Apparently Secretary of the Air Force Symington had spoken to the President before flight test reports were completed, and convinced him that the B–36 was the plane the Air Force preferred. President Truman had been apparently misinformed about the successful YB–49 flight testing program at Edwards, and corroborating files then removed to prevent anyone else from knowing the true facts about Northrop's flying wing.

In addition to the Secretary's close association with Odlum and his conflict of interest regarding the B–36 vs B–49, there is little doubt that another factor played an important role in predisposing the Secretary in favor of the B–36 in its competition with Northrop's B–

49. A dispute had arisen between the Air Force and the Navy over allocation of scarce defense dollars appropriated for the two services. Secretary Symington had apparently found it quite easy to persuade Louis Johnson, President Truman's Secretary of Defense and a former director of Consolidated Vultee, to terminate construction of the large supercarrier *United States*, because the budget would not permit both the completion of the aircraft carrier and production of the number of bombers desired by the Strategic Air Command.

Symington's action had angered the Navy. In a hearing before the House Armed Services Committee, Admiral Arthur Radford, a thirty year Navy flyer and commander of the Pacific Fleet, supported by a panel of expert witnesses, testified, "The unescorted B–36 is unacceptably vulnerable, and the plane could not hit precision targets from very high altitudes under battle conditions." Admiral Radford denounced the B–36 as a "symbol of a theory of warfare—the atomic blitz—which promises a cheap and easy victory." The Navy appeared to be fighting the Air Force, not so much because they felt their program of supercarriers was being unduly proscribed, but because it was their conviction that conventional warfare, not atomic bombing, was more likely to occur in the future. In view of this interdepartmental wrangling, which directly involved Secretaries Symington and Johnson in 1948 and 1949, it would have been difficult for them to be objective in choosing the YB–49 over the B–36. They were already firmly committed to the B–36, even if they had not had any conflict of interest outside their official cabinet positions.

Symington revived the matter with General Curtis LeMay, who had become commander of the SAC. He replaced General George C. Kenney, an enthusiastic booster of Northrop's YB–49 flying wing, who at one time expressed serious misgivings about Consolidated's B–36, even suggesting in 1946 that the B–36 contract be cancelled. LeMay readily admitted that he had never wanted the Northrop flying wing, as it was designed before the atomic bomb had been thought of, wasn't large enough, and could not accommodate the number and size of bombs required by the SAC to mount an effective strategic deterrent. He was wrong about the atomic bomb-carrying capacity of the B–49, but there was no one at the time with adequate knowledge of the highly secret atomic bomb to challenge him. LeMay had never expressed an interest in Northrop's radical flying wing concepts, preferring traditional aircraft. He had convinced himself that the conventional Consolidated B–36 could do the job better. When he appeared before a review board of senior Air Force officers to give them his opinion, he found vocal support for his views. None of the generals were particularly interested in advancing the "state of the art" in aircraft design. They thought only of immediate requirements, of aircraft that would be flown while they were still in command.

Several years later, General LeMay said he did not recall having taken part in any conference in which cancellation of the flying wing was decided upon,

> But we had a shortage of funds, and were in the hands of Congress as to what we could afford. Because the B–36 was further along and more conventional, which required less costly further development work, we preferred to buy it rather than the YB–49 bomber. Also, I remember hearing that a YB–49 had crashed at Edwards, killing Captain Edwards and his crew, and this played a part in my opinion. I had not heard of any plan to merge Northrop with Convair at the time a decision to cancel the big wing was made. At this time jet engines were being introduced, and I thought that to make the best use of jet engines, a thin wing would be necessary. The YB–49 had a very thick wing to carry the crew and bomb load, and therefore it would not be suitable for supersonic speeds when equipped with jet engines.

Former Secretary of the Air Force, Stuart Symington, wrote the author in 1987 that the person who was most involved in choosing the B–36 over the other planes was the former Chief of Staff of the Air Force, General Curtis LeMay. Symington wrote that

> During my time as Secretary, I never once chose any military equipment that was not recommended to me by the Air Staff. When I was told by the military that the B–36 was their choice, it was up to me to so inform Mr. Northrop. As you know, he did not like their decision. But it is, and always was, my conviction that the men who fight and die in military planes, if so expressed by such people as General LeMay, should have a decisive voice in the decision.

At a Washington meeting organized by Secretary Symington, invited executives of military aircraft manufacturers such as Douglas, Boeing, Lockheed, and others, testified to what they took to be the probable superiority of the Consolidated Vultee B–36 bomber. Chairman Millar of Northrop said they could say little else. "You don't fight the Secretary of the Air Force. You're fighting a losing game. What company with only one customer will help you?"

At this juncture the Air Force made a sudden discovery. It announced the finding that jet fighters were unable to intercept the B–36 at altitudes above 40,000 feet. The Air Force allegedly learned of this new ability of the B–36 in extensive interception tests conducted at Edwards Air Force Base in California. The timing of the "discovery" was interesting. The Air Force had already "finalized" its procurement program for fiscal 1949 in early May of the previous year, and not a single B–36 was included in the program. The B–36 had been considered a "dead duck" in military circles. Now, the Secretary was informed that interception tests proving the "invulnerability" of the B–36 had been going on for about three months. At the same time the Air Force was awarding contracts for construction of the flying wing YB–49 to Northrop and also buying more of Northrop's deadly night fighter, the jet powered P–89 *Scorpion*. This was a fighter with a service ceiling of 51,000 feet, leaving some critics to wonder what kind of intercepting aircraft they were flying at Edwards that could not fly higher than 40,000 feet? No one publicly doubted the Soviet's ability to build an aircraft of capability equivalent to the *Scorpion* eventually.

Even then the Air Force had not yet allocated all its appropriated monies. In fact it still had $197 million left, but it still awarded no B–36 contracts. At this late date, and with newly discovered, if somewhat questionable, information in hand, the Air Force wanted to change their mind. Toward the end of the year they decided to "finalize" themselves again, this time reviving the Consolidated B–36 program.

The semiannual Washington economy drive, then in full swing in 1949, threatened to knock $800 million out of the Air Force budget for the coming year. Faced with the multi-billion dollar federal deficit, the Truman administration and Congress had three alternatives: lapsing into deficit financing, increasing taxes, or slashing expenditures. The last was apparently the least distasteful to Congress and it was the Air Force that would be the principal victim. The reason given at the time was that the President's budget, which called for a forty-eight group Air Force, was now placing emphasis on long-range bombing, a somewhat weak explanation. Anyone who has ever been exposed to Air Force publicity knows that strategic bombing has never been subordinated by the United States Air Force. If the seventy-five B–

36s they now wanted to buy from Consolidated had been included in the program at the outset, or if money had been reserved for them, pending complete evaluation of the interception tests, the Air Force would have saved about 90 percent of its termination reserve monies. The puzzling question remains; Why did they find out in December what wasn't known in May? Why was the Consolidated B–36 suddenly the best airplane?

There was no money to buy the seventy-five expensive Consolidated B–36 bombers unless practically everything else was cancelled. Symington issued the orders to do so, cancelling contracts in force for aircraft already being constructed at a loss of $71 million in contract termination costs.

The eight cancelled contracts involved 480 fighters and bombers and ten transport helicopters, including orders for the last 100 Republic F–84s not yet delivered, 51 North American B–45C four-jet bombers, 88 Curtiss-Wright F–87 night fighters, 118 North American F–93–1 jet fighters (a modified F–86 powered by an advanced model of the British Nene engine), 43 of the Boeing B–54 bombers, an advanced type *Superfortress* powered with piston engines, 10 Kellett H–10 helicopters, 30 Northrop C–125B *Raider* trimotor assault transports, and 30 Northrop RB–49 reconnaissance flying wings. All these contract cancellations were issued in order to buy 75 B–36 bombers from Consolidated Vultee, including modification costs to add four turbojet engines to each plane in addition to the six piston engines for which the bomber was designed. The remainder of the funds available were allocated to purchase Northrop F–89 *Scorpion* jet night fighters, Boeing B–47 *Stratojet* bombers, Lockheed F–94 jet night fighters, and Fairchild T–31 trainers, in addition to the modification of Boeing B–50s for aerial refueling.

The Secretary of the Air Force, having decided the Air Force wanted seventy-five B–36s, and having spent all its money, was forced to chop the other contracts. It was a very strange way to run an Air Force, and was hardly calculated to bring credibility to the military planners and politicians involved. It would not be until 10 years later, when the giant Boeing B–52 strategic bomber was operational, that it could be said the Strategic Air Command was in a position to defend the United States adequately. Politics and corporate machinations had taken their toll of professional soldiers and airmen.

The official reason for cancellation of Northrop's RB–49 was that a shortage of funds prevented the Air Force from supporting both the

B–36 and the RB–49 programs. By implication the public was allowed to assume that the B–36 was a much better strategic bomber, even though B–36 maintenance reports show otherwise. The six B–36 engines were always overheating, often catching fire in flight. A retired mechanic commented, "One week maintenance was routine for each hour of flight." Even worse, fighter pilots said Soviet MiG's of the time would have had no trouble shooting down a B–36. The Air Force said the B–36 was successful because it kept the United States out of war.

No physical evidence, no files, no engineering drawings, few reports, remain to prove otherwise. The FBI report on Major Cardenas' accusation of sabotage on the cross-country YB–49 flight disappeared. The airman who failed to fill the oil tanks at Wright-Patterson was killed in an unexplained accident. The official report on Captain Glen Edwards' fatal crash in the YB–49 still remains classified after forty years. Only the first page can be seen in a display case of historical artifacts in the Edwards Air Force Base Officers' Club.

The Consolidated B–36 bomber, already obsolete when delivered, never reached full-scale production as anticipated by the Secretary, and Boeing's superior jet-powered B–52 eventually became the Strategic Air Command's firstline operational bomber. Even the transitional Boeing YB–47 had its problems with yawing on bomb runs, but the Air Force showed no hesitation in paying additional monies to design and install advanced automatic pilot equipment for the B–47, something Jack Northrop had also requested of the Air Force. Northrop was denied additional funding for design of an advanced auto-pilot for his YB–49. The Northrop YB–49 bomb-bay doors were the same as originally designed for the slower YB–35, yet when Jack requested additional monies to modify the twice-as-fast YB–49 bomb-bay doors so dropped bombs would not tumble, the Air Force refused his request. High speed taxi tests of the YB–49 were run by the Air Force with a full gas load, with the flying wing at maximum gross weight, across the dry lake beds of Muroc, carving ruts across the desert floor that can still be seen today. The unusual behavior was not unlike someone telling the pilot to drive the flying wing across the desert until it was destroyed—which it was, in a fiery collapse of the nose wheel, the second of two flying wings destroyed at Edwards Air Force Base. It was a strange way, indeed, to run taxi tests. It was almost as if the Air Force was insisting that the flying wing fail.

A few years later, Floyd Odlum made the first contribution,

$100,000 to Stuart Symington's abortive campaign to win the Democratic nomination for President. Odlum was the last chairman of Consolidated Vultee, then called Convair. When the newly organized General Dynamics Corporation assumed controlling interest in Convair from Odlum's Atlas Corporation, they reorganized the company into the Convair Division of General Dynamics, taking over the B–36 production contract. General McNarney, procurement officer for the Air Force, who offered no objection to the demands made of Northrop by Symington at the San Marino meeting, later retired from the Air Force to become president of Convair, with headquarters in San Diego.

Northrop's flying wing YB–49 slipped into history, a dream destroyed. Had it not been for political and budgetary considerations, military aircraft and commercial air travel today would be very different. Our airliners might have been flying wings. The demise of the Northrop flying wing was a step backward for the Air Force and the U.S. aerospace industry.

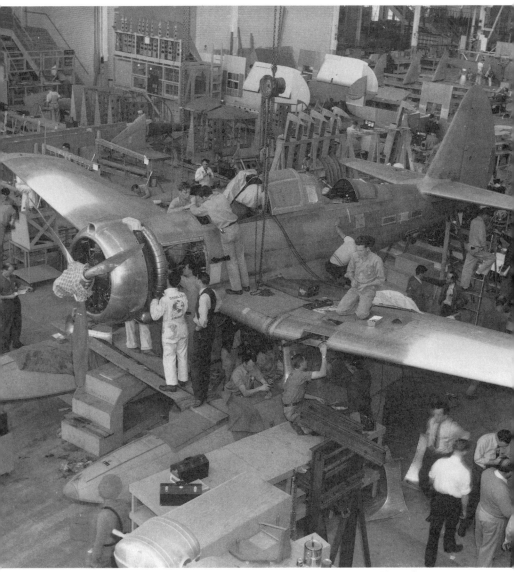

First Northrop patrol bomber N–3PB seaplane is finished in record-breaking nine months. First aircraft manufactured by the new Northrop company.

The Northrop N–3PB seaplane is tested at Lake Elsinor in California before delivery to the Norwegian government.

Jack Northrop, captain and pitcher of the company softball team, Northrop Recreation Club softball, 1942.

From left: Jack Northrop; General William Knudsen, Chairman of the War Production Board, and La Motte Cohu, at the Northrop Hawthorne plant, 1943.

From left: Paul Buckner, Factory Manager, Dick Nolan, Quality Control, and Jack Northrop, 1943.

Jack Northrop holding his weekly plant briefing in Plant 1.

Roy Wolford, Northrop Chief Photographer, 1940–1981. All of the Northrop company photography is by Wolford.

Claude Momsen, Vice President, 1939–1942, Vice President and General Manager 1947–1949, with Charlie McCarthy and Edgar Bergen on a Northrop plant visit during the war years.

Ted Coleman and Loretta Young during wartime visit at the Northrop Hawthorne plant, 1944.

Test pilot Max Stanley in N–9M flying wing prototype, 1944.

Northrop P–61 *Black Widow* night fighter, first plane equipped with radar. First flown in 1943.

Reading Air Force congratulations on delivery of the 700th P–61 *Black Widow* night fighter, 1945. From left: Dick Rinalde, test pilot; Moye Stephens, Corporate Secretary and Chief Test Pilot: Gage Irvine, Vice President and Assistant General Manager; Ted Coleman, Vice President-Sales.

P–61 *Black Widow* departs Hawthorne for war with Japan.

Consolidated Vultee XB–36 strategic bomber.

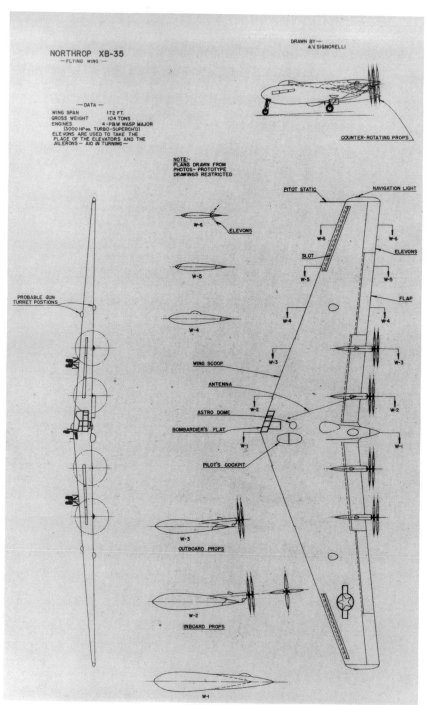

NORTHROP XB-35
— FLYING WING —

— DATA —
WING SPAN   172 FT.
GROSS WEIGHT   104 TONS
ENGINES   4 - P&W WASP MAJOR
(3000 HP ea. TURBO-SUPERCH'D)
ELEVONS ARE USED TO TAKE THE
PLACE OF THE ELEVATORS AND THE
AILERONS — AID IN TURNING —

COUNTER-ROTATING PROPS

NOTE:-
PLANS DRAWN FROM
PHOTOS- PROTOTYPE
DRAWINGS RESTRICTED

PITOT STATIC

NAVIGATION LIGHT

W-6

ELEVONS

W-6

W-6

ELEVONS

SLOT

W-5

W-5

W-5

FLAP

W-4

W-4

W-4

PROBABLE GUN
TURRET POSTIONS

WING SCOOP

W-3

W-3

ANTENNA

W-2

W-2

ASTRO DOME

BOMBARDIER'S FLAT

W-1

W-1

PILOT'S COCKPIT

W-3

OUTBOARD PROPS

W-2

INBOARD PROPS

W-1

Three view drawing of Northrop B–35 flying wing bomber.

Original Northrop XB–35 flying wing bomber, modified with jet power to be designated YB–49, Hawthorne, 1947.

Cockpit of the Northrop XB–35 flying wing bomber.

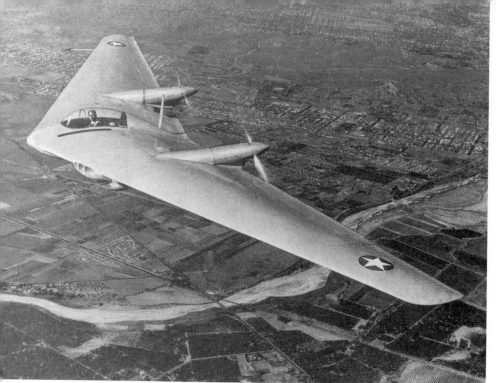

John Myers in the N–9M over Hawthorne, 1945. This aircraft is now being restored to flying condition by the Planes of Fame Aviation Museum in Chino, California.

Northrop XB–35 flying wing bomber on takeoff, with the Northrop *Buzz Bomb* flying chase, 1945.

John Myers warms up the radical Northrop fighter, the XP–56 *Silver Bullet*, 1945.

The 1945 Northrop flying wing *Buzz Bomb* with pulse jet engine.

Test pilot Harry Crosby preparing to fly the Northrop MX–334 at Muroc. Crosby was later killed flying another Northrop experimental aircraft, the XP–79B *Flying Ram*.

First flight of the Northrop YB–49 flying wing bomber from the company airfield at Hawthorne, 1947.

Northrop YB–49.

Northrop YB–49.

Jack Northrop (fourth from left) joins a routine test flight in the YB–49 with USAF crew, 1948. Northrop test pilot Max Stanley is at left.

Northrop N–123 *Pioneer* prototype, later converted into an army assault transport called the *Raider*. Originally developed as a post-war commercial product, 1947.

L. A. "Slim" Peret, test pilot killed in Northrop *Pioneer*.

Northrop company-designed gas turbine engine, the Turbodyne, on test installation at the Hawthorne plant, 1947.

Arthur Phelan, Chief Engineer of the Turbodyne program, 1942–1950.

Northrop *Snark* guided missile at Hawthorne, 1951.

13

The World's First Gas Turbine Aircraft Engine

A revolutionary new power plant for airplanes was conceived in 1940 by Vladimer Pavlecka, chief of research for Northrop. A Czechoslovakian, Pavlecka had been involved in development work in Europe, where the gas turbine engine was first adapted to a stationary power plant. Unlike the traditional gasoline-fueled piston engine in wide use by automobiles and airplanes in the 1940s, the gas turbine is most efficient when operating at full power. This difference, Pavlecka reasoned, would make the engine an ideal power source for airplanes. Little was then known about jet propulsion where, today, the gas turbine principle has its widest application.

Pavlecka proposed to Jack Northrop that an engine utilizing the gas turbine principle be developed for direct drive of an airplane propeller, thus its name, "turboprop." The idea appealed to Jack's creative mind. He made arrangements for Pavlecka to accompany me on a trip to Washington in 1941, where I had made an appointment with the head of the power plant division in the Navy's Bureau of Aeronautics. The Army Air Corps, at that time, had only a small budget for airplane engine research, most of which had already been allocated to Curtiss Wright and Pratt & Whitney for improvements in their conventional radial piston engines, the principal engines used in the 1940s.

Pavlecka had brought with him a large cutaway drawing of his proposal, allowing those present to visualize exactly how the engine would work. His drawing was of the first American axial flow gas turbine airplane engine, showing a cross-section of a compressor taking in air at one end and compressing it through rotating blades at very high speed. The drawing graphically depicted how the compressed air was fed into a combustion chamber, where it was mixed with fuel and ignited by a spark. The resulting explosion produced the power to run both the compressor and the turbine blades, which in turn rotated the propeller mounted on the same shaft. It was an amazingly simple engine in some respects—everything revolving around the same axis, with very few moving parts.

He pointed out to the experts present that, by eliminating the propeller shaft, the same type of engine could expel a jet of air traveling at high speed from its outlet, producing thrust to directly drive an aircraft forward through the air. Pavlecka had, for the first time, demonstrated the principle of the modern jet engine. Pavlecka, however, felt that the use of a propeller would provide a more efficient use of the energy being generated by the engine, and was a more practical application. He advised that use of the jet engine without a propeller would consume excessive fuel in developing the same thrust. Basically, they are both the same engine except that, when using a propeller, the thrust from the jet combustion chamber is diverted to spin turbine blades attached to a drive shaft turning the propeller.

Steam turbines generating power had been operating in electric power plants for many years, but the engineers assembled by the Navy for the Washington conference, were not familiar with the very different gas turbine type engine under discussion and had never considered their use. They expressed doubt, as bureaucrats generally do when presented with someone else's idea, that Pavlecka's engine could be made light enough to adapt for use in an airplane. Diesel engines first developed in Europe had been previously tried as aircraft engines. However, designers were never able to bring the weight down to a practical low pounds per horsepower.

Fortunately, not everyone present was a pessimist. One engineer with the group turned out to be well versed in all types of engines, particularly the use of stationary gas turbines. He expressed enthusiasm about the possibilities of Pavlecka's proposal. Those present were persuaded to recommend that Northrop be given a modest contract to complete *Turbodyne* studies (as Northrop called the engine) and design an experimental turbine engine suitable for powering an airplane. Pavlecka's detailed drawings and his knowledge of the gas turbine convinced those present that his new idea warranted the Navy's financial backing and, incidentally, gave the Navy all military design rights.

It was an historic occasion. The government's decision to support the Northrop *Turbodyne* engine project was a quantum leap in jet engine development. Nothing was then known in the United States about the pioneering gas turbine jet engine design work being done in England and Germany.

Returning to the plant in Hawthorne with the encouraging news that government financing was forthcoming, Pavlecka was placed in charge of a project team that included Arthur J. Phelan, an experienced power plant engineer, who had been chief of research for the design and development of automobile engines for the Chrysler Corporation in Detroit. Dr. Von Karman was asked to consult on the project, dividing his time at Northrop between the flying wing and the *Turbodyne*.

The first engine to be developed was designated the Alpha 1500. The objective was to design and build an engine that would produce the equivalent of 2,400 horsepower at 18,000 feet altitude at 375 miles per hour. The project did not proceed smoothly. Early in the design stage, differences of opinion arose between Pavlecka and Von Karman.

Pavlecka undertook a research program at Northrop intending to solve metallurgical problems involved in fabricating turbine blades able to withstand the high speed rotation and extreme operating temperatures of a jet engine without disintegrating and destroying the engine in flight. He felt this was critical if Northrop were to manufacture the engine. Progress in detailed design of the *Turbodyne* was slow, to the detriment of the development schedule. Von Karman reminded Pavlecka that considerable time and money would be saved if he worked closely with others experienced in the design of turbine blades, such as General Electric, who had been building steam turbine electric generators for years. Like most inventive geniuses, Pavlecka was convinced that Northrop must complete development and design on its own, and as directed by him, to be positive that the correct materials would be used. He strongly disagreed on subcontracting the work, and insisted on spending much of his personal time, and company hours as well, on what Von Karman and Northrop perceived as duplicating time-consuming research already done by others. Pavlecka soon resigned, and a more practical engineer, Arthur Phelan, took over the project.

With Phelan in charge, development work progressed rapidly. It also became apparent that the power required to test drive a separate turbine compressor at the Hawthorne plant would be in the neigh-

borhood of 7,000 horsepower. The only practical means of completing
the project was to test the compressor as a component of the completed engine. In July 1943, the *Turbodyne* contract was amended to
include fabrication and testing of all engine components, as well as
compressor parts.

Throughout the period from 1941 to 1943, numerous visitors
dropped by the *Turbodyne* research department, including Group
Captain Whittle from Great Britain, the man credited with invention
of the jet airplane engine. He made several suggestions that helped
speed up the *Turbodyne* development progress. The project also benefited when Phelan was invited by the Navy to become a member of the
U.S. mission to Great Britain in 1943, a mission that included such
prominent members as Leroy Grumman, president of Grumman Aircraft, and James McDonnell, president of McDonnell Aircraft Company of St. Louis. By this time the British were considerably
advanced in the development of turbine power plants, and the group
witnessed the first flight of a jet engine-powered aircraft at Barford
St. John's airfield.

Because the Northrop company was known as an airframe,
rather than an engine manufacturer, management had early on decided it might be to the company's advantage to join with another
experienced manufacturer to provide needed facilities and know-how
in the design of engines. When the General Electric Company of
Schenectady, New York, approached Jack Northrop and offered a
fifty-fifty partnership in a joint effort to produce *Turbodyne* aircraft
engines, it appeared to be a solution to many problems.

Jack called a special board meeting to discuss the offer from
General Electric. He was willing to exchange some engineering data
and research under certain conditions, but it was soon apparent to
those present that he did not favor a partnership with G.E. While he
did not speak about the matter, there had been some patent difficulty
with G.E. in the past. Typically, Jack decided that because of this,
they were not to be trusted. He never mentioned his adverse views,
never talked about the problems, he just pushed for an unfavorable
vote as President and Chief Engineer, and the directors accepted his
recommendation.

Jack argued that a West Coast engine plant was badly needed.
Why must all airplane engines be manufactured in the East? He
proposed that Northrop approach the Joshua-Hendy Company of Sun-
nyvale California, who were also interested in a joint venture. He did

not favor a partnership, under any circumstances, with General Electric. An acquaintance, John McComb, was connected with Joshua-Hendy, and undoubtedly had influenced Jack's interest in a West Coast collaboration, where engineering work would be done nearby with easier control over progress. Jack wanted to be involved in the decisions, in what was happening, and this was not possible, in Jack's view, if daily decisions were being made 2,000 miles away. He was never quite sure the parts would fit if they were made on the East Coast. Communications were poor. Design changes were impossible to implement with any degree of confidence. Modern methods of transmitting documents, and interoffice computers, were nonexistent.

The *Turbodyne* engine was still in the developmental stage, and the other directors were hesitant about overruling Jack Northrop on an issue over which his engineering department exercised control. To them, there was no comparison between the many advantages of association with General Electric, compared to being in partnership with a manufacturer of steam engines, even if that company was located on the West Coast. General Electric was the world leader in the manufacture of steam and electric turbines, and had prestige and experience in dealing with the Navy. Most members of the board could only see advantages in going with General Electric. However, to satisfy Jack, the majority went along with his proposal to form a joint venture with Joshua-Hendy rather then G.E. The Northrop-Hendy Company was formed to take over the Turbodyne project. Northrop continued all engineering work at Hawthorne with various turbine parts made by Joshua-Hendy in the San Francisco Bay area, where they were manufacturing steam turbines for Kaiser's Liberty ships.

On March 28, 1945, the first Northrop *Turbodyne* engine was ready for its maiden run in the Northrop test cell. It was the first actual jet engine operation in the United States, the engine running at 4,000 rpm at reduced power. No attempt was made to exceed the 500 horsepower developed at this low speed. After inspection of the components, additional progressive tests were made, gradually increasing power output. All went well until April 16, when, during a run at 10,000 rpm a compressor blade failure resulted in extensive damage to the engine. A second engine was rushed to completion, while metallurgists concentrated on finding the cause of the blade failure.

The Army Air Corps became interested in the development and gave Northrop-Handy a contract to design and develop a more powerful engine capable of delivering 4,000 horsepower at 35,000 feet in an aircraft flying 500 miles per hour. Work on this larger engine, called the XT–38 Turbodyne began in November 1944. Five years later the partnership with Joshua-Hendy was terminated. The Bay Area company had contributed little to the project, but had impeded progress because of late delivery of parts. Northrop-Hendy became the Turbodyne Corporation, a wholly-owned subsidiary of Northrop.

As parallel progress in the design and development of the full size flying wing bomber proceeded at Northrop, the Air Corps entered into a new contract with Northrop to modify an existing YB–49 flying wing to incorporate the T–38 Turbodyne engine. The T–38 was also designated as an alternate engine for the Wright T–35 engine being used by Boeing's eight engine B–52 bomber. *Turbodyne's* future seemed assured as the B–52s were being planned for volume production and the new version of the *Turbodyne* would have substantially greater power than the older Wright T–35 engine. The good news did not last long. Unfortunately for Northrop, this chain of events did not come to pass. The original design of the B–52, planned as a turboprop aircraft, was changed to a pure jet, and the opportunity was lost for installation of the *Turbodyne* engine in a large production aircraft.

In early 1950, the newer, larger *Turbodyne* engine was successfully flight tested. Again, Northrop thought the company would find customers for its engine. With the B–49 contract cancelled (the plane for which the engine was originally developed), an approach was made to Convair, suggesting use of the Turbodyne in the Convair B–36 bomber, now planned for production instead of the B–49. Performance of the B–36, with its conventional Pratt & Whitney 4360 piston engines, had not come up to design expectations. Northrop was sure that a full test with the Turbodyne would result in considerably improved speed and range for the new bomber, but to no avail. There was no opportunity ever given to the Turbodyne by the Air Force to prove the superiority in flight of the more efficient and powerful Northrop-designed engine.

Most unusual and, potentially the most practical of the several *Turbodyne* applications, was to have been on a modified flying wing designated EB–35B, planned as a flying test-bed for the *Turbodyne* turboprop engine after it had passed ground tests and was ready for flight trials. The EB–35B was to have the six jet engines as in the other jet-powered flying wings. In this particular aircraft a single *Turbodyne* engine was to be mounted to the left of the aircraft centerline, as a pusher power plant. The jet exhaust was to be discharged through the hubs of the large counter-rotating propellers. The plans were to takeoff and land using the six jet engines. Then, once the aircraft was airborne, the pilot would throttle the jet engines back and maintain flight on the *Turbodyne*.

Air Force planners were convinced that military strategy called for a large bomber with a 10,000 mile range for delivering the atomic bomb. With the B–36 in increasing favor, it was natural for Jack to consider all the alternatives possible to make his flying wing fly, and be powered by his *Turbodyne* engine. Jack's ultimate intention was to use twin 10,000 shp *Turbodynes* as the principal power source in the existing YB–49 airframe, with the further possibility of jet power boosting the performance in pods hanging from the wings like the B–36D.

Northrop engineers planned a *Turbodyne*-powered flying wing designed for ranges as great as 12,000 miles, cruising at 459 mph, with a maximum of 550 mph. Jack Northrop's firm conviction of the feasibility of such an aircraft was expressed in his observation, "In the extremely long-range category, the turboprop comes nearer to combining the speed of the jet with the range of the reciprocating engine than any other power plant and, theoretically at least, a turboprop flying wing has adequate range and operating speed, as well as high speed, equal to, if not better, than its turbojet sister."

But the decisions were not to be made on the basis of engineering calculations or on technical grounds. The financing of Northrop's flying wing was inextricably bound up with the military bureaucracy and what the generals thought was the best way to fight the next war. It depended on how bomber strategists evaluated speed–altitude–range–payload options, how future strategic bomber commands were expected to operate. It depended on what enemy interceptor performance was expected to be at the time the hypothetical turboprop bomber reached operational stage. And it depended on Congressional budgets.

With all these imponderables to consider, Northrop produced from his drawing board another possibility, a carrier-based, turboprop patrol bomber, with a crew of three, designed around the flying wing and powered by twin Turbodyne engines. It was never more than a sketch.

The Air Force withdrew further financial support from the Turbodyne engine project. Continued development by Northrop without definite sales prospects was too expensive for the company to continue on its own. The Turbodyne Corporation, all design rights and several completed engines—all that the company had built—were sold to General Electric. The same company that had offered Jack Northrop a fifty-fifty deal to join them in developing engines ten years earlier acquired all the valuable Northrop research and testing experience at a bargain price—with most of the jet engine problems already solved. General Electric became one of the nation's leading manufacturers of jet turbine power plants for commercial and military aircraft. Jack Northrop's insistence that the company needed a West Coast partner for this important engine development proved to be a costly mistake.

As if to prove once more the correctness of Jack's vision and his advanced ideas for flight and power plants, in October 1987 a McDonnell Douglas MD–80 took off from Long Beach airport, powered by an experimental 10,000 shp, geared, turboprop engine manufactured by the Allison Gas Turbine Division of General Motors, with counter-rotating propellers by Hamilton Standard. Pratt & Whitney and Allison Engines teamed together to pursue propfan engine development (a jet engine with propeller, in which exhaust gases are brought to a higher velocity within the engine by a turbine "fan"), aimed at the 100–160 passenger transport market. According to estimates made by the new company, 4,500 propfan engines will be needed between 1991 and 2001. The ultrahigh-bypass engines are expected to consume nearly 30 percent less fuel than current jet engines and reduce operating costs by about 10 percent. What would have made Pavlecka and Phelan most excited about the new program was the engine installation with exhaust vented through the pusher propeller blades, just as planned on Jack's flying wing with his *Turbodyne*.

The exciting dreams of Vladimer Pavlecka, Arthur Phelan, and Jack Northrop, in 1940, were not to be another Northrop success. It was apparently a government decision not to give Northrop the opportunity to capitalize on his firm's development of the jet engine. Others would reap the financial rewards.

14

PICKING UP THE PIECES

Without government financial support, Jack Northrop was unable to continue work on designing and building his ultimate flying wing, a large long-range passenger and freight-carrying version of the B–49 bomber. The company had paid a Hollywood film company to make a promotional film, utilizing a full size wood mock-up of a flying wing passenger transport cabin, but no airline could be found who was interested in the radical new design that the Air Force had summarily abandoned, leaving behind stories, unsubstantiated as they were, that Northrop's airplane couldn't fly properly. Under the circumstances an airline could hardly be expected to buy from a wooden mock-up.

The Northrop company had only two major contracts left with the Air Force. Production contracts continued in force for Jack's design for an all-weather fighter, the XP–89, and for the *Snark* long-range guided missile. These projects kept the company alive until war in Korea began two years later, and military budgets again substantially increased. Shortly after the flying wing contracts were cancelled, Dick Millar decided to return to his previous career as an investment banker. Retired General Oliver Echols, a former chief of Air Force procurement, became board chairman and replaced Claude Monson as general manager. Millar continued on as a Northrop director.

The new management of Northrop decided it was useless to oppose the Secretary of the Air Force and his friends in Washington by continuing to insist that it was a mistake for the government to cancel all work on the flying wings. The new management consisted of practical men and the company was still very dependent on the Air Force for much of its business. There was only one customer, as far as the newly constituted board of directors was concerned, and that was the United States. If the company was to thrive, it would be irresponsible to antagonize Washington. Jack Northrop was persuaded that he also should go along with this policy. Very reluctantly, he agreed to testify before the upcoming House Armed Services Committee hearings investigating the B–36 bomber program, and affirm that the YB–49 flying wing bomber did require considerably more development and modification before the bomber would be ready for production. From Jack's point of view, this would be committing perjury, but if it was necessary to save the company, which required continued Air Force financial support, he would do so.

Seated in the witness chair before the congressional committee, Jack acknowledged as agreed to with Dick Millar, that his firm did not have the production capacity to manufacture the increased purchases of the YB–49 being contemplated by the Air Force. When asked by Joseph Keenan, general counsel for the committee, to describe what occurred at the San Marino meeting where the demand to merge with Consolidated Vultee was made, Jack described only a lengthy discussion, concluding, ". . . that the best solution to the problem consisted in Northrop subcontracting the actual construction of a major portion of this contract to Convair who would continue to operate the Fort Worth facility." The questioning continued between the counsel and Northrop, with the counsel asking, ". . . Did you believe that was the best solution?" Northrop answered, "Considering all factors, yes. Considering Northrop, no. But we felt it was the right thing to do in view of all the circumstances that were presented to us . . ."

The committee counsel asked Northrop if there was, ". . . any evidence of any politics in that deal?" Northrop answered firmly, "No, sir . . . It appeared to us to be a logical solution to a difficult problem. No contractor gladly gives up the manufacture of his own product. We would have much preferred to have found a solution that would have prevented that result . . ." Counsel Keenan pressed further about possible political implications in the flying wing cancellations, and Northrop said, "I believe there were none. I can't conceive of there being any."

Counsel Keenan: And you make that statement under oath before this committee?

NORTHROP: I do, sir.
KEENAN: Genuinely believing it?
NORTHROP: I certainly do.
KEENAN: And not because you are in fear of reprisals?
NORTHROP: No sir, I am not in fear of reprisals.
KEENAN: Have you any knowledge that either yourself as president or any officer or anyone else connected with Northrop Corporation being informed that unless Northrop agreed to merge with Consolidated that business would be bad for Northrop?
NORTHROP: I have no such knowledge.
KEENAN: Has anyone ever said anything from which you could draw such an inference?
NORTHROP: No, sir.
KEENAN: Specifically, did Mr. Odlum ever say that?
NORTHROP: No, he did not.
KEENAN: Or Mr. Symington?
NORTHROP: No, sir.

It was a difficult day for Jack Northrop. Under pressure of the life or death of his company that was experiencing difficult times following the war and cancellation of government aircraft contracts, he had committed one of the finest jobs of perjury he had ever heard.

The House Armed Services Committee hearings revealed that strategic planners in the United States Air Force did considerable wavering on the subject of intercontinental bombers, on one occasion even debating whether any aircraft with intercontinental capabilities was actually feasible. Gen. George Kenney, commander of the Strategic Air Command in 1949, was a most persistent opponent of the Convair B–36 during its post-war development, favoring Northrop's YB–49 or the B–50 as a standard USAF bomber, until the six-jet Boeing B–47, then in the final stages of development, could replace the older aircraft as the next generation heavy bomber. Kenney believed there were other capabilities more important than non-refueled long-range, that future strategic bombing operations would always require use of advanced bases or aerial refueling. An alternative version of the eight-jet Boeing B–52 was considered, using the Northrop-designed prop-jet *Turbodyne* engines for substantially increased range, or to keep the higher speed of the jet-powered design, suggestions were made to modify B–36s then coming off Consolidated Vultee's Fort Worth production line into aerial tankers for the B–52s. Kenney believed the effective range of the B–36 would never be greater than 6,500 miles, so why build such inadequate aircraft?

The continuing debate revealed many contradictions in the Pentagon's evaluation of the heavy bomber program, including use of an "envelope curve as a new criterion of measuring bomber performance," which placed primary emphasis on speed at various altitudes over maximum range, but since this measurement of suitability seemed to give Northrop's YB–49 the edge, especially when modified to the same extent as the B–36 was currently undergoing, this method was mostly ignored. USAF generals consistently attempted to match the performance of the original eight-jet YB–49 with the ten-engine (six piston engines plus four jet engines), modified B–36D, with seemingly no understanding that such a comparison was tantamount to comparing bananas with grapefruit. Criticism was also still being made of the Northrop YB–49 as being a poor bombing platform because its yawing characteristics made the Norden bombsight unusable, a problem then being corrected by use of automatic pilot devices; soon, this would no longer be a problem at all, with the installation of newly developed radar bombing systems.

Gen. Kenney clashed often with Gen. Curtis LeMay over tactics to be used in intercontinental bombing missions using the B–36, Kenney asserting that the B–36 was unsuited for daylight operations and could easily be shot down by Soviet MiGs. "The B–36 is a night bomber. I would not use it in the daytime. If I sent 100 B–36s on a long-range bombing mission, I would expect to get 100 back, barring mechanical troubles," Kenney said. The exception was important, for over-heating problems in B–36 engines was a matter of concern at high altitudes, when the pusher engines would routinely catch fire. The problem was so serious that the original B–36 order for 100 planes was cut back to 61, when no solution to in-flight fires was found. On the first long-range B–36A flight, two engines overheated and were shut down during most of the flight. Again, in a later B–36A endurance test, another engine was inoperative most of the flight, hardly a worthy demonstration of aircraft reliability.

"The [Pratt & Whitney *Wasp Major*] engines overheated so badly the XB–36 was lucky to get to 30,000 feet and stay there . . . It was impossible to tell how high the airplane would really go," Kenney testified. He was not satisfied with Air Material Command assurances that B–36 troubles could be cured, and he did not share their optimism over the promise of the Pratt & Whitney VDT engine in its proposed

B–36 application. The USAF later admitted the VDT engine installation was a "complete failure" when it cancelled the B–36C VDT program.

Kenney considered the Northrop YB–49 potentially the better aircraft, but he was outvoted by top level USAF staff, who agreed to provide monies for needed modification of the Convair B–36 while denying Northrop's request for funds to modify and improve YB–49 performance. Re-engineering of the YB–49 airframe to enable the flying wing to take full advantage of higher thrust jet engines then becoming available, would have pushed the YB–49 flying wing top speed close to supersonic without sacrificing long-range performance. The YB–49 airspeed indicator was already redlined at 550 mph in the original XB–35 airframe, unchanged with the installation of eight jet engines.

The House Armed Service Committee investigating USAF strategy and procurement of Convair B–36 aircraft after cancellation of $573 million in other aircraft contracts, including Northrop's flying wing, asked LeMay about the controversy, and LeMay took full responsibility for being the chief USAF advocate of the B–36, and told the committee, "The Convair bomber was a round-the-clock bomber capable of attacking in daylight or darkness. I believe we can get the B–36 over a target and not have the enemy know it is there until the bombs hit."

In his testimony, LeMay preferred not to mention the fact that ground-based long-range early-warning radar systems were already in place guarding Soviet airspace, and were being steadily improved to give increasingly accurate information on approaching aircraft to its operators. The day when radar could identify and guide defensive missiles to destroy an incoming target before seeing it, was not far off. LeMay did not comment on the argument that increasingly larger bombers were not entirely a good thing. Not only were they more expensive, with inferior performance, but they also presented larger radar images easily picked up at a greater distance from enemy targets. LeMay placed greater emphasis on tactics, speed, high altitude flying, and deception techniques, preferring to ignore the large, undisguisable radar target presented by huge bombers like the B–36, and even the much lauded Boeing B–52, both aircraft reflecting back to the enemy clearly identifiable radar signals. Neither aircraft would be able to sneak up on the enemy as LeMay envisioned in his testimony.

Kenney knew that the Northrop YB–49 radar image was exceptionally small. The YB–49 had already been tested in overflights approaching U.S. radar installations and had been found to be virtually invisible. Like the much later Lockheed SR–71, designed twenty years later, which was often visually observed on its landing approach before being detected by airport radar, Northrop's flying wing design was the plane of the future, potentially able to fly higher, faster, and more stealthily; the USAF bureaucracy in 1949, however, failed to recognize stealth as a valuable attribute in their haste to build the old-fashioned Convair B–36. Top level endorsement of LeMay's views eventually forced Kenney out of his command position, and Kenney was replaced by LeMay as head of the Strategic Air Command. There would be no further arguments pro and con over merits of the Consolidated Vultee B–36.

Aviation Week magazine reported at the time that:

Gen. Hoyt Vandenberg, USAF Chief of Staff, supported LeMay's views on strategic bombing, stating that LeMay had had more experience participating in and planning for strategic bombing than any man in the world. Vandenberg said the USAF was faced with the alternative of buying more B–36s to carry out its assigned primary mission of strategic bombing or not buying any bombers at all since no other plane would do the job.

Former Secretary of the Air Force, Stuart Symington confirmed these conclusions in a later statement, when he said the person who was most involved in choosing the B–36 over other planes was Gen. Curtis LeMay. It was Maj. Gen. Oliver Echols, head of Army Air Force Procurement, and later to become postwar Chairman of the Board at Northrop, who actually awarded the contract to Consolidated Vultee for the first 100 Convair B–36s, after Convair's president, Tom Girdler, claimed he was unable to find any subcontractors to work on an order for only two experimental aircraft. Jack Northrop never raised any such problem in accepting orders for his experimental flying wing bombers.

New York Daily News columnist Danton Walker reported that Secretary Symington, "might resign to head a big new aircraft syndicate promoted by Odlum." There was a Philadelphia newspaper story by Nicholas Gregory about proposed aircraft company mergers, and assertions on the floor of the House by Pennsylvanian Congressman

James Van Zandt, a naval reserve captain, calling for investigation of "ugly reports" that the USAF decision to only buy the Convair B–36 was influenced by Secretary of Defense Louis Johnson, a former director of Consolidated Vultee, and a major fund raiser for the Democratic party in the 1948 election. Symington denied in detail all the charges contained in Van Zandt's allegations, saying, "There was no consideration other than national security influencing the purchase of B–36 bombers and cancellation of contracts for other kinds of aircraft."

Gen. LeMay at one time did propose the substitution of five medium bomber groups for the two heavy bomber groups, suggesting use of Boeing B–50 or B–54 aircraft, plus a reconnaissance group that was to have been equipped with Northrop RB–49 flying wings, but it was later decided to spend the budgeted monies available to modify all B–36s by the addition of four jet engines. The USAF strategic reconnaissance conference then picked the extensively modified Convair B–36D with four additional jet engines in pods, as the best long-range reconnaissance plane. The Boeing B–47 and B–54 were rated as second and third choices. On July 12, 1949, the B–36D, in a test flight with four jet engines added to the six piston engines, reached an altitude of over 50,000 feet and a top speed of over 435 mph. On July 19, six days later, in another test flight, the Convair B–36D lost three engines at 40,000 feet. One burned and fell out of its wing nacelle, in the process severing electrical connections to two other engines. The plane made an emergency landing without further damage.

As far as USAF strategic planners were concerned, the deteriorating international situation in 1948 that eventually resulted in the Russian blockade of Berlin, made necessary the early acquisition of intercontinental bombers for possible immediate action as Soviet foreign policy became more aggressive. Their concern resulted in a shortsighted agreement to rely on only one bomber, the B–36, the aircraft immediately available, and not to proceed with acquisition and research of Northrop's flying wing, YB–49. Northrop, having refused Symington's demand for merger with Consolidated Vultee, was dropped from any consideration, and only Boeing's B–47 and B–52, then in advanced stages of development, were considered to be acceptable future bombers. A modified version of the YB–49, using more powerful jet engines, would have been available by 1951, and another, very long-range version, powered by prop-jet *Turbodyne* engines would be flying in 1952–53. It was Secretary Symington's decision to ignore this delivery schedule and not only cancel purchase of additional YB–49s, but to destroy those already built, effectively halting flight testing of modified aircraft and the use of advanced jet power that would prove the Northrop YB–49 flying wing to be the superior intercontinental bomber of the future. The strategic bomber monopoly desired by Floyd Odlum, president of Atlas Corporation, and Consolidated Vultee board chairman, was assured. Within months, Consolidated Vultee became one of the nation's largest military contractors, second only to Boeing. Odlum left the House hearing room, saying, "There is not one rivet of politics in the B–36; there is not one ounce of special favoritism in its more than 300,000 pounds of loaded weight."

Jack's company was never the same again. Basic changes took place in the philosophy of top management as Jack lost heart in his work. He had become emotionally involved with the development of the beautiful YB–49 flying wing. The physical destruction of the flying wing aircraft already completed was not to be forgotten. He was very uncomfortable with being forced to lie about the reasons for the flying wing cancellation, against his own personal principles of ethics and morality. The Air Force had made it clear there could be no hope for the plane's revival. Even the future of the company was on the line.

Older members of management became discouraged, and a number of them began to look for new jobs elsewhere, as they were replaced by a new team of executives. The group who had left shortly after the war ended included the veteran Gage Irving, vice president, La Motte Cohu, chairman, Graham Sterling, legal council, Moye Stephens, secretary, and myself, vice president and sales manager. The next exodus of key management included Claude Monson, vice president and general manager, who left to become general manager of Air Research, a subsidiary of Garrett Corporation, and John Myers, former test pilot and later vice president-sales, who resigned later, when he acquired the Pacific Airmotive Company of Burbank, which owned the Cessna airplane distributorship for southern California. B.G. Reed, an original Northrop employee who had become plant engineer, moved over to join Northrop's erstwhile rival, Consolidated Vultee, as general manager of their Fort Worth manufacturing department.

Of the original members of top management, only George Gore, secretary and legal council, remained. Among the first engineering and production managers, Tom Quayle, Dick Nolan, and Walt Cerney stayed on. Nolan was later to reach the position of senior vice president in the renamed Northrop Corporation. My car pool companion, Grant Macdonnell, stayed, eventually retiring as vice president and comptroller of the corporation after over thirty years at Northrop.

Dr. William Sears, chief of aerodynamics, resigned to join the Cornell University Aeronautical Laboratory. His mentor, Dr. Theodore Von Karman, after resigning from Northrop as a consultant, moved rapidly from chief scientific advisor to the Army Air Corps at the end of the war, to chief scientist of UNESCO in Europe, and finally to retirement in Pasadena where he had started the Aerojet Corporation.

Following organization of the original Northrop company, and during the years of World War II, Jack Northrop had surrounded himself with a remarkable team: people with imagination, drive, and enthusiasm. When war ended, as could be expected, many of these key individuals began to disperse, seeking new and better opportunities. After the Air Force B–49 contracts were cancelled and no airline could be found that was interested in a flying wing transport, it was evident to many there was no future with Northrop in a peacetime world. It was understood by most departing executives that Northrop would have a difficult time adjusting to lower military budgets in a peacetime economy. The Soviet Union had been an ally in the war. At the time it seemed unlikely that we would soon be required to protect the United States from Soviet aggression.

Like many others in the aircraft industry, Northrop attempted to get away from dependence on the U.S. military for the majority of their business, but as is typical of an organization dominated by engineers, Northrop was finding it difficult to break into the postwar civilian market and develop the different techniques involved in marketing civilian products. Management found it was not just a matter of "building a better mouse trap" that would get the customers flocking to the door.

One of La Motte's last assignments for me before we left the company was to accept responsibility for postwar planning, presenting me with the problem of what we were to do with 12,000 war workers soon to become laid-off employees. How could we continue to report profits to our shareholders? How could we keep Northrop alive?

Accompanied by Walt Cerny, assistant chief engineer, I made a trip throughout the Midwest and East, conferring with airline executives and anyone I could think of who might want to buy a new airplane. Northrop was prepared to design to order. Within a week we had called on Terry Drinkwater, a Denver lawyer running Continental Airlines while its founder, Bob Six, worked overseas for the Air Transport Command; Jack Frye, who headed TWA from Kansas City; Pat Patterson, president of United Airlines, and my Caltech friend Jim Moore, also of United, both in Chicago; Bill Littlewood, chief engineer for American Airlines; and Eddie Rickenbacker of Eastern Airlines in New York.

The end of the war found the aircraft industry scrambling to keep busy, to keep as many skilled personnel employed as possible while waiting for new airplane contracts. I was able to pick up orders for immediate reconditioning of wartime transports for peacetime use and Northrop took on the mundane task of changing Douglas C–47 cargo planes back into civilian DC–3s, taking out the cargo door, putting in lightweight floors, insulating interiors, and installing passenger seats to replace canvas slings. A firm in Montebello that made the original DC–3 seats before the war was put back to work making new seats. Northrop delivered twenty-eight newly refurbished DC-3s to United Air Lines and twenty-five to Eastern.

Except for Jack Frye, who suggested that Northrop design and build a modern tri-motored transport capable of operating from small and unimproved airports similar to those used by TACA, the TWA Central American subsidiary, no other airline executive gave us any encouragement. Their requirements for new domestic airliners had already been given to Boeing and Douglas. We learned that Lockheed, Martin, and Convair had new airliners already on their drawing boards. Four-engine Douglas DC–4s, developed during the war and extensively utilized as troop transports in all theaters, planes capable of flying across either the Atlantic or Pacific nonstop, had already been converted to civilian use and were flying on transcontinental routes. United's experience with the DC–4 was considerable, having flown the craft on charter for the Air Transport Command. Boeing's two-deck *Stratocruiser* was about to be presented to a flying public ready for a standup bar and inflight lounge in the postwar era of flight. Douglas, Convair, and Boeing all had four-engine jet-powered airliners in development. Convair was also developing a twin-engine airliner to replace the DC–3. Boeing was in the final stages of converting their jet-powered Air Force tanker into what was to be the very successful 707 airliner. Northrop's competition had already carved out their postwar niche in the civilian transport market.

Airline executives further advised me that any new airliner not of a conventional, proven design—such as Jack's proposed flying wing transport—would have to be built first and extensively tested by the company or the military before the airlines could consider buying the radical design, regardless of its potential efficiency or how good it looked in a movie presentation.

Development of the flying wing transport at company expense, without airline orders in advance, was beyond Northrop's financial ability. I knew the company had no new money to spend on Jack's dream. When I returned to Hawthorne, tired and discouraged by Northrop's poor prospects for building a commercial transport, the future looked grim indeed. When I was summoned to La Motte's office, I had no plans for the future.

La Motte had an idea.

I've just received a call from Jack Frye, and he is urging us to build a new tri-motor transport. He claims that it would meet the needs of all the Third World countries where airlines will be expanding their services. I have talked with Jack about it, and while he is not very enthusiastic about this design, which he considers to be obsolete, he admits that a tri-motor plane has advantages when used on short fields. I'm told there are many cheap surplus radial engines available that could be used in the plane. Jack will assign some engineers to a project if the company thinks we can sell enough airplanes. I have a friend, Paul Riddle, who is running a large aviation training school for the Brazilian government in Sao Paulo. Let's go down there and find out if Jack Frye is right. If the plane can be sold in quantity we might build a factory there where labor is cheap. This would be a simple plane to build.

Characteristically, La Motte had already made up his mind, and had confirmed airline reservations to Brazil. My question of how a new small transport could possibly compete with the hundreds of war surplus Douglas C–47s then flooding the market at cheap prices, was ignored. "How long will be we gone?" I asked La Motte. "I have just gotten home and I'm tired."

"I have wired Paul Riddle that we will be there in two weeks, so get some rest before we leave. You should take an extra shirt and your tux. They dress for dinner in Brazil. We will be gone about a month."

With nothing more than this sketchy plan of action to go on, I cleared my desk of details and prepared to fly to Rio. For years I had been given no chance to stay in one spot for long. Over half of my time had been spent away from home during the war. I had unfinished company banking business to attend to in New York, so I flew there before proceeding to Miami, where I met La Motte and Paul Riddle's wife at the airport. Paul was the veteran pilot who had taught Charles Lindbergh to fly in the early 1920s and had been asked by General "Hap" Arnold to go to Sao Paulo in 1944 to open up an aviation training school for the Brazilians, after they had joined the Allies and sent troops to join ours in Sicily.

We flew the long trip to South America on a Douglas DC–3, leaving Miami the next morning and island hopping south, stopping in Cuba, Puerto Rico, and the Dominican Republic before stopping for the night in Port of Spain, Trinidad. We were flying the same route scouted out for Pan American by Charles Lindbergh in a twin-engine flying boat fifteen years earlier. We were flying the route in a DC–3 carrying a full load of passengers, mail and baggage, cruising at 180 miles per hour, stopping every three or four hours for fuel.

The second day we flew on to Belem, at the mouth of the Amazon, stopping at British, French, and Dutch Guiana, and continuing down the lengthy coastline of Brazil, with more fuel stops at exotic Forteleza, Racife, and Salvador. Approaching the 4,000-foot runway at the Santos Dumas Airport, surrounded by downtown Rio de Janeiro, the pilot misjudged his speed and came in too fast. By the time he was ready to land, I could see the end of the runway at the water's edge. Almost touching the ground, the pilot pushed the throttles full forward and climbed into the air, to circle the airport and try again. The second approach to Rio was better. It was a nerve-shattering ending to the long three-day flight from Miami.

That evening we were guests of George Guinlee, a wealthy Brazilian, at a gala party at Copacabana. In spite of our exhaustion from the long flight, La Motte and I enjoyed ourselves. The hotel boasted a large gambling casino on the mezzanine floor, full of well-dressed Brazilian men and their formally gowned ladies. I wore my wrinkled tuxedo. We were introduced to "Baby" Pignatori, who owned an aircraft factory where Palistinia lightplanes had been built for the Brazilian civil airplane market before production was interrupted by the war-caused shortage of aircraft engines imported from the United States. Pignatori told us of the great interest in aviation in Brazil, due to the great distances between cities on the coast and the vast, rapidly developing interior of the country.

The next day, Paul Riddle introduced us to Air Minister Trompowski and his aide, Captain Alvis Lima. They were both enthusiastic when La Motte mentioned that Northrop was considering building a new transport plane in Brazil, even suggesting a name for the new plane, *Pioneer*, pointing out that cargo as well as passengers and mail could then be carried by air. I was skeptical, having noticed the many war surplus Douglas C–47s parked around every airport runway we saw. The planes were badly in need of new paint, and dents in the aluminum were numerous, but the twin-engine veteran of hard knocks appeared to be doing the job in Brazil quite well, and at a fraction of the cost of a new airplane. I felt that La Motte was doing much wishful thinking in his anxiety for garnering new postwar business for the company.

We called on representatives of several local airlines, among them Varig, Pan Air do Brazil, and Cruziero de Sol. They were pleased to see us and learn that a North American company was interested in building a new transport airplane for their market. But they seemed satisfied with the Douglas planes they were flying and the low prices of surplus military aircraft available everywhere—even spare parts were cheap. They expressed no interest in buying new airplanes.

Disregarding my contrary opinion, La Motte decided Northrop should build the *Pioneer* trimotored transport. Jack was talked into the project, despite being very lukewarm about the whole idea. I strongly disagreed with the decision; I knew there was no way Northrop could compete in the commercial market with a small transport, when hundreds, if not thousands of surplus military transports were available at cash-and-carry prices. However, when the board voted, I was in the minority. My efforts to find a satisfactory postwar commercial aircraft for Northrop had failed. The company should obviously remain in the business of designing and manufacturing aircraft, where Jack Northrop's design abilities were outstanding, but the *Pioneer* was not that kind of aircraft.

The *Pioneer* proved to be a rather costly venture for the Northrop company. No planes were sold to any airline anywhere. Later, the Air Force bailed the company out by ordering twenty-four modified versions of the *Pioneer* to be used as assault transports, renamed the C–125 *Raider*. It was in this airplane that Northrop's able test pilot, Slim Perett, was killed. If Jack Northrop had been listened to, there might have been a happier decision in the attempt to build commercial aircraft; but the company was desperate for postwar business of any kind to keep itself busy. It was a time when other aircraft companies were also making similar unprofitable mistakes. Even Convair tried to diversify into commercial products like gas and electric ranges, freezers, and buses, succeeding only in proving that war work was hardly an adequate preparation for unrelated peacetime consumer products.

The Northrop aircraft company tried almost everything, buying into companies that made products which seemed compatible with an aircraft production line. There was the attempt to manufacture and sell aluminum hand trucks and ground handling equipment, made by the Gaines foundry subsidiary, but Northrop could not compete with better-known products already in the marketplace. Northrop acquired the Salsbury motor scooter, but successful merchandising of a civilian product proved too difficult and the business closed down, with the product line sold back to the original owner. Jack Northrop's personal involvement in designing prefabricated houses, conducted for a short time as a postwar subsidiary operation, called Normak, did return a small profit, but it was hardly the image desired for an aircraft manufacturing company.

As Northrop had developed the *Pioneer* transport, Convair also designed a medium-range airliner to replace aging DC–3s, their Convair 240 series. As Northrop had learned in advance, probable airline customers were reluctant to buy new aircraft while their older planes still flew and were having difficulty financing the purchasing of new planes. Development of the Convair 240 proved much more costly than anticipated, leading a Convair loss in 1947 of $16 million. This evidently prompted the sale of Convair to Floyd Odlum's Atlas Corporation. Over 1,000 twin-engine Convair transports were eventually sold, mostly military versions, a far more successful program than Northrop's ill-fated *Pioneer* venture. Odlum, as chairman, then concentrated the company's manufacturing operations around military business. After winning the heavy bomber contract away from Northrop, he was able to report a financial turnaround, and a profit for Convair of nearly $4 million.

Northrop was awarded a development contract by the Air Force to design and build the *Snark* guided cruise missile, one of the first long range ground-to-ground missiles. This was a pilotless aircraft capable of carrying heavy explosives and hitting a predetermined target hundreds of miles distant from its launching point. To perform this mission with precision, celestial navigation was incorporated into the design, whereby the missile would automatically take sidereal readings on previously located stars. A new lightweight electronic computer was carried that made the necessary calculations and fed navigation data automatically into the autopilot as the pilotless flight progressed toward the target. When Northrop's electronic equipment, designed to input celestial navigation data into the missiles operating system, was first tested in the *Snark* over the Caribbean, it was found that existing maps of the area were totally inadequate and had to be redrawn in keeping with the more accurate celestial readings. Old-fashioned methods used for ocean and land surveying had suddenly become obsolete using an airborne computer.

At the time the *Snark* contract was awarded, there was no lightweight, digital electronic computer in existence. Most electronic computers of the late 1940s were quite bulky, occupying space about the size of a garage. To fly the *Snark*, Northrop engineers, under project manager Eldon Weaver, suddenly found themselves pioneering in the electronic computer field. They developed a very lightweight, small computer, which they named MEDIDA, for Magnetic Drum Digital Differential Analyzer. MEDIDA was light enough to be carried in the *Snark* missile, the forerunner of the modern cruise missile. The computer was accurate enough to guide the missile to a target 5,000 miles from its launching pad.

The engineers who developed one of the first microelectronic computers, MEDIDA, left Northrop when the company turned down their proposal to form a Northrop Electronic Computer Division. Jack Northrop said the company should remain primarily an airplane manufacturing business, the business he knew best, repeating the same business blunder he made when turning down a partnership with General Electric to develop the first turbine jet engine, the *Turbodyne*, to be designed by Northrop engineers.

Several of Northrop's electronic engineers formed their own small development organization, called Computer Research. It was not profitable and the principals soon went their separate ways, doing advanced research and design work for the leading business machine corporations. Twenty years later one of the former Northrop engineers, Richard E. Sprague, writing in the Association of Computing Machinery publication, claimed that, "One airplane company, Northrop Aircraft, spawned no less than 14 computer companies, and no less than 23 types of electronic computers. The list, which includes IBM and National Cash Register, reads like a 'Who's Who' of today's computer industry."

The only successful commercial acquisition during the post-war period was Radioplane, a builder of remote-controlled airplane models, purchased from Whitney Collins, who followed Oliver Echols as chairman of the board. Radioplane later became Northrop's Ventura Division, a leading manufacturer of self-propelled target drones for the military.

The Northrop company lost money in 1950, for the first and only time. The outbreak of war in Korea brought new money and life to the makers of military equipment and aircraft and the losses were soon recovered as the company entered a new era of profitability with new corporate management. Air Force orders for the Northrop F–89 all-weather fighter and the *Snark* guided missile were greatly increased. Even Radioplane contributed to the profit line; for every drone shot down, a new one was ordered.

In the late 1940s, Jack Northrop and his wife, Inez, surprised their friends and family by seeking a divorce. Jack married his loyal executive secretary, Margaret Bateman, in 1950. He had always kept his personal problems to himself, and his intimate friends suspected that differences in religious beliefs as well as his professional disappointments brought on by the cancellation of the flying wing may have caused the separation from Inez. She moved back to her old home city of Santa Barbara. Both she and Jack remained close to their children and many grandchildren.

I had helped make a valuable contribution to the war effort and to the Northrop company. While I enjoyed my association with Jack Northrop and all my other company associates, I had no desire to spend the balance of my working life making weapons systems for the government. I was looking forward to a peaceful world and to becoming my own boss. In some respects I was thinking like Jack.

The trip to Brazil played an important part in my decision to leave Northrop and organize my own export airplane sales company. Brazil seemed like a good place to start, and I had already received a wonderful introduction to this rapidly developing country. I had trained John Myers to take my place as vice president for sales. While parting with Jack and many other friends was hard, I would continue to keep closely in touch with Jack and the company that I helped create, and where I was happy helping Jack make his dream of a flying wing come true. A drastic shrinkage of Northrop employees was inevitable. I would be among those to go.

15

CREATIVE THINKING AND MISSED OPPORTUNITIES

Despite the heavy workload at Northrop during the war, the company continued to develop new military aircraft. Some of the new airplanes had the appearance of design-by-committee rather than being marked by the individual genius of Jack Northrop. Whenever a group of adventurous Air Force officers at the Pentagon conceived of a new idea for aircraft to be used in aerial combat, they first thought of Northrop as the only company capable of translating immature sketches into flight.

There was the all-wing bat bomb, JB–1, the Northrop version of a robot flying bomb, developed as a result of the experiences of Great Britain with the German V–1 bombing in World War II; the flying beer bottle, the XP–56; and the flying ram, reminiscent of Spanish galleons in hand-to-hand combat. The U.S. Army Air Corps awarded Northrop a contract to design and develop the secret flying wing bomb with a pre-programmed guidance system, powered by two small pulse jet engines, and carrying two 2,000 pound warheads. The bat bomb was first tested successfully as a glider. A second version was track launched from a Florida site and subsequently destroyed, which proved it would work. With the surrender of Germany and the shift of attention to pulse jet design, the contract was terminated.

The XP–56 resulted from a contract awarded by the Air Corps exploring new concepts and designs for a pusher aircraft with less drag, better pilot visibility, and more effective armament firing forward from the nose. The design evolved by Jack became the first all-magnesium, all-welded airframe in history. A new process for welding magnesium was developed for constructing the aircraft; the process, called Heliarc, was patented by Northrop. Test pilot John Myers made the first successful flight, but the plane was subsequently destroyed on another flight when a tire blew out on landing. A second aircraft was modified with a large vertical fin to assist in overcoming a yaw problem. Although pilot Harry Crosby reported the aircraft nose-heavy on a normal takeoff, the plane did reach a maximum speed at 467 miles per hour. Unique air-operated bellows rudders were installed at the wing tips, a radical and effective innovation in flight controls invented by Northrop, but the Air Corps decided the entire concept was not worthy of further development and offered no contract for additional aircraft.

Designated the XP–79B, the third aircraft in the series became the Flying Ram, powered with the first jet turbine engines then becoming available. The futuristic all-wing aircraft was built with a heavy magnesium structure and steel armor plate enabling the plane to dive on enemy bombers, slicing off tail assembles to down them. The armor plate consisted of ¼-inch face-hardened steel plate installed just inside the leading edge of the wing at forty-five degrees to the chord plane. The pilot lay prone in the cockpit wholly enclosed within the wing, the prone-pilot concept being used to raise the pilot maneuvering "blackout" threshold to twelve Gs instead of eight-G limit of an upright pilot. There was provision for four fixed fifty-caliber machine guns in the wing center section, two on each outboard side of the jet engines. The plane was a super-secret aircraft when built and one of the first aircraft flown with jet power in the U.S. The aircraft crashed on its first test flight, perhaps because of a trim tab failure, killing veteran test pilot, Harry Crosby. Following the accident, the program was cancelled and no additional Flying Rams were produced.

Jack submitted a proposal for a rocket powered fighter to the Air Corps in 1942, which, considering the state-of-the-art propeller fighter capabilities at the time, would have had performance nothing short of spectacular: 518 miles per hour at 40,000 feet altitude. However, flight endurance would be only 31 minutes, owing to the high fuel consumption rate characteristic of rocket motors. Development of the Aerojet engine intended for installation was beset by a seemingly endless series of problems. The plane never reached flight stage.

In April 1946, under tight security, the Air Force awarded Northrop a contract to develop two experimental swept wing aircraft without horizontal stabilizers to explore supersonic speeds, an effort sponsored jointly by the Air Force, the Navy, and the National Advisory Committee for Aeronautics (NACA). The X–4 *Skylancer* was a 7,000 pound aircraft with wing span only two feet longer than its length, 23 feet, 4 inches, powered by two Westinghouse XJ–30 turbojet 1,600 pound thrust engines. The plane was equipped with split dive brakes and hydraulic boosted elevons on the wing trailing edge. Unlike the Bell X–1, which had previously flown faster than the speed of sound but was launched from a bomber in flight, Northrop designed his aircraft to takeoff from the ground in a conventional manner. The first flight was at Muroc Dry Lake in 1948, with Charles Tucker at the controls. Chuck Yeager also flew the aircraft on later flights attempting to exceed Mach 1, but found the *Skylancer* was unable to break the sound barrier in level flight, although it was rumored unofficially that the plane did exceed Mach 1 in a dive. It was something that Yeager would have liked to do.

Jack was the perennial inventor and innovator. He inspired not only new designs but new techniques for building and operating his inventions. When his airplanes didn't fly well, he designed new controls so they would fly properly. Some of the methods were quite unorthodox. In his Flying Ram, the prone pilot controlled pitch and roll by means of a crossbar with hand grips at each end, in addition to maneuvering brakes operated by foot pedals, power boosted by air operated bellows. It was all quite ingenious—by Jack Northrop's standards, routine.

But aviation was not the only area of Jack's interest. During the war years Northrop and his top engineers developed several new products and manufacturing techniques that later became important sources of income and profit to other companies and industries. As Jack put it, his policy at the time was "to make this our contribution to the nation."

One of the leading hospitals in southern California approached Jack to assist them in a rehabilitation program for war veterans who had lost their arms. Northrop had already established a shop in the hospital where veterans able to work assembled airplane parts for a regular salary. This served the dual purpose of helping the company's production and boosting the veteran's morale while being rehabilitated. Medical supply firms had failed to improve artificial arms and hands, which were heavy, awkward to use, wood and leather contraptions. Jack explained the techniques developed for controlling airplane ailerons, wing flaps, and other remote, movable parts, and how the same controls could be applied to move artificial limbs.

These ideas were turned over to his engineers for development at no cost to the hospital or the veterans. At Jack's insistence, it was to be at company expense. New lightweight prosthesis devices, utilizing aircraft materials and airplane control principles, were designed and experimental devices built for veterans at the hospital to test in actual use. Veterans who had lost one or both arms enthusiastically volunteered to try out the new artificial limbs, finding them to be a considerable improvement over the old arms then being sold by medical supply houses. Patent rights for the new artificial arms were offered without royalty to leading prosthesis manufacturers, representing another important Northrop innovation for which hundreds of amputees were most grateful. With their new arms they could now perform tasks that were not possible before.

Jack Northrop's compassion for his fellow man was evident in all his endeavors, whether in consideration for war veterans or in relations with employees on the production line. Associates working closely with Jack learned to appreciate his views and practices in dealing with company workers, whom he thought of as fellow employees. Although he did not have the responsibility of administering company personnel and industrial relations departments, Jack, by personal example, established the relationship he wanted between employee and employer. He had more influence in making Northrop an excellent place to work than any other key member of the organization. It was an early beginning for a corporate reputation that continues today.

As early as 1940, Jack fostered a policy of management seeking out views of the average worker. It was company practice from the beginning that employees have the opportunity to know and talk with all levels of management, and be encouraged to go up the line if their suggestions or complaints were not listened to by immediate superiors. Northrop and Gage Irving, together with most of the original group who had worked for Douglas Aircraft, had the experience of going through an unsuccessful and frustrating sit-down strike at the El Segundo Division. They were convinced that better communications between management and workers at the time would have prevented the strike.

Jack encouraged everyone to call him by his first name, and he made a point of frequently circulating through the various departments, finding opportunities to get better acquainted. Jack had a good memory for names and enjoyed being with his employees. He carried his own lunch tray in the company cafeteria, and was opposed to the establishment of an executive dining room. He drove a medium-priced car, a Studebaker, and frowned on those who found it necessary to display their wealth.

An old-timer tells of the day when he was working on the installation of engine wiring and plumbing for the N–3PB, reaching up inside and behind the cowling in front of the firewall, and in the process getting their forearms oily and well scratched.

Somebody tapped me on the back and I turned around on my work stand to see Jack. I couldn't imagine the big chief coming around the shop, but he asked us how it was going, and we told him, laughing, waving our scratched arms. He didn't say anything, but two days later the foreman brought over a new pair of gloves for us with long cuffs so we wouldn't scratch our arms.

Jack had made no comment, but he could see the problem.

Jack used to get us all out in the back yard where the big dies used to form parts were piled up and we would sit on the dies, and he would stand up on the tallest one and give us a kind of state of the union report on the company, and on the planes we were making. I remember when he called us out there to tell us Germany had invaded Norway, but we would still be making the seaplane. He would come out at lunch hour and talk to the whole group, telling us the good news and the bad news. He kept us informed about the war, personally, at lunch hour so we wouldn't have to stop work. Sometimes he would bring out movie stars. He would always ask us how it was going. He was very interested in what we had to say.

Shortly after World War II had ended, Northrop was approached by an Air Force aero-medical officer, Colonel John Stapp, who volunteered to ride a test sled propelled by rockets. The aluminum sled would travel on a two-mile-long, straight railroad track built to exacting standards on the flat desert floor. Stapp would ride the rails at high speeds, strapped on the sled in an experimental harness, before being brought to an abrupt halt by a water brake at the end of the track.

Stapp was convinced that a good pilot safety harness for high speed jet-powered flight had not been adequately developed and tested, procedures that would save the lives of pilots and crew in an accident.

He had not succeeded in convincing automobile executives that their automobiles should be equipped with seat belts, already mandatory in airplanes. Automobile manufacturers believed that the public should not be reminded of the dangers in a possible collision.

A test track was built at Edwards Air Force Base on the Muroc Dry Lake; high speed tests began with Colonel Stapp riding the sled. He preferred doing the job himself rather than risk exposing others to the dangers of sled travel at hundreds of miles per hour with the tremendous forces involved in acceleration and deceleration at high speeds. Several Northrop engineers were assigned to the project, designing and building both sleds and test facilities for this challenging field of aerospace medicine.

The rocket-powered sled ran in an outdoor wind tunnel environment, testing airfoils at transonic and supersonic speeds and the effect of severe deceleration forces on the human body. Colonel Stapp became the "fastest man on earth" when he attained a speed of 632 miles per hour on the second 10,000-foot research track at Holloman Air Force Base in New Mexico. Photographs of Stapp, his facial features contorted into grotesque shapes by wind pressure, appeared in publications around the world.

After returning from Brazil, I organized the Coleman Engineering Company. With Northrop's cooperation, my firm began to specialize in rocket test track testing, building and operating the Supersonic Military Air Research Track facility for the Air Force at Hurricane Mesa, Utah, near Zion National Park. Here we tested pilot ejection systems for escape from supersonic aircraft. It was a source of great satisfaction to work with Colonel Stapp, to contribute to the saving of lives of air personnel forced to eject themselves from high-speed aircraft in an emergency. Stapp was not allowed to ride our rocket-propelled sled at Hurricane Mesa, because it was too dangerous. Our track ended at a 1,500 foot cliff, at which time the sled occupant was ejected by parachute. Only life-like dummys and a chimpanzee made the high-speed trip. The chimpanzee survived without harm.

Northrop's first production jet aircraft was the last major design effort of a Jack Northrop-led engineering team, and, fittingly, one of his most productive military designs. The twin-jet XP–89 all-weather aircraft was developed as a modern successor to the radar-equipped P–61 *Black Widow*. The most heavily armed fighter interceptor of its day, over 1,000 F–89 *Scorpions* were delivered to the military. The bulk went to the Continental Air Defense Command and the Alaskan Air Command, serving until the summer of 1969. The *Scorpion* was operational in the military service for almost 20 years. A clearly recognizable and distinctive feature of the XP–89 was the upswept tail, designed to keep tail surfaces clear of the wing downwash and engine exhaust. It was the Muroc Dry Lake ground crews who dubbed Jack's plane *Scorpion*, because the upswept tail reminded them of the angry desert insect ready for attack. Later the name was officially approved by the Air Force.

Design of the new fighter, which was to become the first airplane to fire an air-to-air nuclear weapon, began with the requirement for a fighter capable of guarding the United States against the possibility of attack from arctic regions, from "over the top of the world." The fighter would be operating in harsh northern climatic conditions, during periods of low visibility and at night, with a two-man crew consisting of pilot and radar operator. In the radar-equipped nose, ready to fire, were six twenty-mm rapid fire cannon. Each wing provision was made for four rocket launchers capable of carrying a total of sixteen rockets. In later versions, the F–89D, the cannons were removed and rockets installed in wing tip containers, with fifty-two in each pod. The pilot could fire 102 rockets in clusters, called by them, "the Sunday Punch."

The plane was equipped with many of Jack's innovative control ideas. One noteworthy feature was the split or clamshell ailerons, located just outboard of the slotted landing flaps on the wings. When they were opened both top and bottom, a drag was created to slow the airplane down, a design feature especially useful in combat situations, where the pilot wanted to close rapidly on the target and then decelerate to a slower speed while firing guns or rockets. The decelerons, as they were called, were also of critical use in braking the aircraft when it was occasionally put into a dive and achieved supersonic speed. All flight controls, including flaps, decelerons, elevators, and rudder, were operated by dual, engine-driven hydraulic systems. The rudder control operated as part of a yaw damping system with a force-producing device so the pilot received a natural "feel" in flight. As a result the aircraft earned a reputation as a high-performance machine with unusually easy-to-fly and "forgiving" characteristics.

At the beginning of flight testing all did not go well. The first XP–89 crashed during a high speed pass over Hawthorne Field, killing the flight test engineer, Arthur Turton, although the pilot,

Charles Tucker, escaped with injuries. A post-accident investigation revealed that horizontal stabilizer-elevator flutter had caused structural failure. All subsequent aircraft were modified with the addition of large mass balances to the horizontal tail surfaces. At this time a Lear F-5 autopilot and ILS zero visibility landing system were also installed.

Early "C" model aircraft in service with Air Defense squadrons were involved in a series of unexplained crashes occurring as a result of wing structural failure in flight maneuvers. All F-89s were grounded. An intensive investigation launched by the company disclosed that wing attach fittings were cracking and failing in combat flight attitudes. The wing also had a tendency to twist under certain aerodynamic loads, a new phenomenon little understood in the 1950s. Northrop engineers subsequently devised key structural changes, including strengthened wing attach fittings. As a result of the improvements, the F-89 became one of the safest airplanes in the Air Force inventory, establishing new standards for low accident rates for operational fighters, but not before traumatic changes within the Northrop company engineering staff.

Jack had already begun investigating the problem when the new Northrop chairman, Oliver Echols, insisted on bringing in an outside engineer, Edgar Schmued, to be in charge of finding the source of the structural failures, to investigate the phenomenon of aeroelasticity, and to redesign the wing. Bringing Schmued into the Engineering Department over his objections antagonized Jack, and he let his displeasure be known. The two previous general managers, La Motte Cohu and Claude Monson, had always left decisions on basic engineering procedures and personnel selection for Jack to decide himself. Engineering problems were always his problems alone. When Echols insisted on naming Schmued Assistant Chief Engineer, and likely successor to him, Jack protested, but to no avail. Northrop had been discussing the same position with Eugene Root, a talented Lockheed engineer. Jack felt that Root would make a better future chief engineer and his possible replacement.

Within days Jack Northrop submitted his resignation. The F-89 *Scorpion* was the last plane designed by Jack. His final parting with the company he had founded and so faithfully served occurred in December 1952. It must have been ironic to Jack that the final decision to leave his own company was prompted by similar conditions that prevailed when he departed Douglas in 1938 to form his own company—and from Lockheed before that. Jack felt that he no longer had authority to run his own department, and his time was again being diverted from his true love, the designing of new airplanes.

In the opinion of most executives who worked for Northrop at the time, the ascension of Ed Schmued to be chief engineer at Northrop set the company back twenty years. Schmued was not interested in anything new, even in experimental designs, especially if they had not been tried before by someone else. The spirit of the entrepreneur, Jack Northrop's style of being willing to take chances, entirely disappeared upon the arrival of Schmued. It was a radical change that seemingly occurred overnight, resulting in an increased rate of turnover in personnel as those with new ideas moved on.

Schmued had been with North American Aviation, builders of the famous P–51 *Mustang* fighter of World War II, and no small reputation preceded him. The *Mustang*, initially conceived by Dutch Kindelberger while the company was still small, made North American famous. The automotive mentality brought over to Northrop by Schmued prevailed in the company under President Lee Atwood, who replaced Kindelberger in the postwar period. General Motors, a major shareholder in the company, had applied their old-line management styles to the aviation industry, and Schmued learned the techniques of Detroit well. Schmued did not last long at Northrop, but during his tenure made decisions still felt negatively in the company today. Apparently believing that engineering drawings of the various flying wing projects, particularly those of the cancelled XB–35, YB–49, and YRB–49 aircraft, would be of no further use to the company, and definitely of no value to the Air Force, he ordered their removal from the files and had them destroyed. In the process he also removed the inventive spirit of Jack Northrop from the company. Bill Ballhaus, an able engineer and Caltech alumnus, replaced Schmued, but he was soon lured away from Northrop by Beckman Instruments.

Possibly even more than Echols or Schmued, it was Whitney Collins, who replaced Echols as chairman and CEO, who most dramatically changed the mood of the company away from the innovative, family-style management of La Motte and Jack. Collins had become director when Northrop purchased his Radioplane company, builder of "drones" for military target practice, as a post-war investment. The small radio-guided planes were expendable, and therefore profitable repeat business would be assured for the company.

Jack Northrop's name, in the word of an employee at the time, became "verboten" in the company. The new management tried their best to discourage anyone from supporting Jack, or from saying anything about his cancelled flying wings. Word came down from the executive offices to forget the flying wing, and not to speculate on the reasons for Jack's resignation—officially for reasons of failing health, but known, in conversations across Engineering Department drafting tables, to be a result of keen disappointment on the part of Jack, and a need to start all over again on the part of management. Many employees were convinced that Echols and Schmued were brought in to move Jack out. Former General Echols had been part of the Air Force heavy bomber command and boasted of a close relationship with General "Hap" Arnold and the Air Force. It was clear that Echols was cleaning house to bring Northrop Aircraft Inc. back into good graces with the Air Force. Management orchestrated a transfusion of new blood from the North American company, famed designer of the P–51 *Mustang*, to create a new team they felt would greatly benefit the new Northrop. Employees called it, "the North American invasion."

Collins' personality presented a considerable contrast to that of Jack and La Motte. He was rather pompous, and always appeared quite confident of himself, having started his own business making model airplanes for display purposes when the war ended. Soon, his business grew in size as the models became radio-controlled, powered target planes, and proven moneymakers. Radioplane turned out to be Northrop's only profitable postwar investment, and the enterprise continued as a separate business.

Collins rode to work in a chauffeur-driven limousine, insisting on the proper corporate image. He expanded office space by taking over the building formerly occupied by Northrop Aeronautical Institute, next to Plant 1 in Hawthrone. The aviation training school established by Jack was sold and moved to new quarters in Inglewood. Collins then decided that Beverly Hills would be a better corporate address and moved all the executives to leased offices away from the factory in Hawthrone, which he renamed the Aircraft Division. Soon after, corporate offices were again moved, into a company-owned skyscraper at Century City.

Collins was a tall, good-looking man, impeccable in his dress and appearance. At a dinner occasion with Northrop executives, the wife of Grant Macdonnell, a member of Collins' staff, was sitting next to Collins, carrying on a conversation with her hands flaying the air at a moment when Collins leaned over to sip his soup. Her moving hand accidentally brushed against his head, dislodging his toupee into the soup. No one had realized that Collins was getting bald. The next day Grant Mcdonnell was transferred out of the executive offices to the comptroller's office, where Collins wouldn't have to look at him.

The Collins-Echols-Schmued regime, which represented the ultimate in change, did not last long. Collins died prematurely, and Tom Jones replaced him. Jones was an able engineering planner who joined Northrop in an engineering position, but soon rose in management ranks to become chief executive officer in a newly renamed Northrop Corporation. A new era of prosperity and growth began with the development of T–38 trainers and F–5 *Freedom Fighters* that sold in volume around the world. The *Snark* cruise missile formed the basis of a new Electronics Division. One of the leading manufacturers of gyroscopes, located on the East Coast, was acquired. The Korean War, and later the war in Vietnam, coupled with increasing defense requirements of the cold war, marked the turning point of Northrop's discouraging postwar years.

Jack and Margaret Northrop moved to the Hope Ranch in Santa Barbara, where they built a lovely home. He retained an active interest in the Northrop Aeronautical Institute, successor to the Northrop Training School he founded during the war, and became an active official in the national Boy Scouts of America, reviving an old interest in scouting. Sale of his Northrop stock provided him with ample financial resources for the first time in his career, and Jack and Margaret began to relax and take life easy. He joined the Valley Club in Santa Barbara and was often seen on the golf course, a new kind of challenge for an aeronautical engineer. He didn't leave his company entirely, however, for when Collins sold the Northrop Aeronautical Institute, Jack drove back to Hawthorne to help Jim McKinley and other school administrators acquire ownership of the school and move to new quarters in Inglewood.

Jack Northrop felt the need to keep closely in touch with aviation, and the decision of the new Northrop management team to discontinue the training school at Hawthorne, which had changed its name to Northrop Aeronautical Institute, gave him this opportunity.

Jim McKinley, the able director who had pioneered the valuable training school approached Jack in 1953, and together they talked to a number of potential backers who might, together with Jack, be willing to supply the money to acquire a new facility in the nearby city of Inglewood. One of these prospects were Dr. Ulrich Bray, the former Assistant Research Manager of the Union Oil Company. Dr. Bray became a National Research Fellow at Caltech during the years when

Jack Northrop had close personal and professional ties with Dr. Von Karman. Bray had admired Jack, only a high school graduate, for his major accomplishments in aviation and his willingness to work with the leading scientists in the fields in which he was interested. Like Jack, Ulric Bray was an imaginative pioneer.

When Dr. Bray was told that the very successful Northrop Aeronautical Institute was available for private development, he felt that a practical training institution could be developed not only for potential aircraft employees, but for foreign students who would be attracted to this country for general technical training after they had first mastered the English language. He convinced Jack and Jim McKinley that all foreign students must be given intensive training in the English language and the other humanities before subjecting them to the more advanced technical subjects generally taught in engineering colleges.

After this program had been adopted, Dr. Bray helped Jack attract a number of influential trustees, and a substantial number of tuition-paying foreign students, to provide the revenue to enlarge the original Inglewood campus by adding new buildings and staff to the modest-sized Inglewood building.

This basic recognition of the importance of first teaching speaking, reading, and writing in English to bright foreign students when they enrolled at the Northrop Aeronautical Institute gave them an advantage over many of the more prestigious technical colleges in the country. Jack Northrop served as Chairman of the Board until replaced by Donald Cook, who was later replaced by Ulric Bray in 1972.

Five years after becoming independent, the staff and curriculum had been enlarged to permit the awarding of a Bachelor of Science Degree, and the two-year junior college or trade school status was changed to that of a four-year college. The name was changed to Northrop University in 1975, after full college accreditation was granted.

When the dedication ceremony for the new Aviation Technician School Campus was held on November 4, 1972, Donald Douglas Sr. and Arvin O. Basnight, Director of Western Region, FAA, were the main speakers. The list of Trustees, headed by John K. Northrop, Honorary Life Chairman of the Board, read like a "Who's Who" in southern California. The ceremony marked the completion of a twenty-year, $16 million campus development program, and was a proud day in the 77-year-old founder's life.

When I organized my own engineering company, I found that

many Northrop Institute graduates had practical advantages over the graduates of many of the other engineering colleges, including my own alma mater Caltech. They, like founder Jack Northrop, had learned how to get along with their fellow workers, and did not try to impress them with their superior knowledge and training.

In the early 1960s, while still completely separated from the aviation business, Jack organized a land syndicate that acquired a large tract of ocean view property in Santa Barbara. He had retained an active interest in prefabricated housing, and was persuaded that the site was ideal for an attractive, moderately priced residential development. After buying the undeveloped land, his development company, in which he had made a very substantial investment, was informed by the city of Santa Barbara that no building permits would be issued for the site because of an acute shortage of water. After an extended wait and increasing legal expenses, most of Jack's personal fortune was lost when the development syndicate was dissolved, with the land sold for a fraction of its original purchase price.

When Dick Millar, who had remained a director of Northrop and become a vice chairman of the Northrop board after Tom Jones was named chairman, learned of Jack's unfortunate situation, he brought Jack's plight to the board's attention. He explained Jack's need for more income to meet his modest living requirements and suggested that, in light of Northrop's considerable past service to the company, that he be made a Director Emeritus, with provision for a salary as a consultant. In this way, the company that he founded came to his rescue when he was badly in need of help. The friendly contacts were resumed, and remained until his death in 1981.

Jack Northrop had always maintained a high standard of ethics, and it was his decision to not embarrass the company by making any public statements about the cancellation of the flying wing contracts by the then-Secretary of the Air Force, Stuart Symington, and the role of the Air Force in ordering the destruction of the flying wing bombers already built. It was not until the Northrop company agreed that sufficient time had passed that he granted an interview to comment publicly upon those fateful days in 1948.

Thirty years after the YB–49 contract cancellation, Clete Roberts of Los Angeles Public Television Station KCET, talked in front of a television camera with Jack Northrop. Release of the complete interview, with added comments by other participants and dramatic color motion picture photography of the YB–49 in flight, was delayed for fourteen months while Roberts made futile attempts to obtain comments from Symington. The former Secretary refused to talk with Roberts personally, and threatened the television station with legal action if the interview was broadcast. Symington later issued a denial through his secretary that he had ordered the Northrop company to merge with Consolidated Vultee in 1948, saying he "never did that sort of thing."

Floyd Odlum and General McNarney, who had participated in the 1948 meeting in San Marino, had died in the interim. Only Dick Millar and Jack Northrop were still able to tell their story, and they did, along with test pilot Max Stanley and the only two living Air Force officers who had flown the YB–49 flying wing at Edwards Air Force Base in the California desert. Jack had the satisfaction of viewing the taped interview with Clete Roberts from a hospital bed shortly before he died.

There were many who wished Jack Northrop had said nothing, who felt that the interview only opened up old wounds from what, to some of those involved, was an emotional issue they had hoped would remain dormant. The Northrop company itself would have preferred the subject not be brought up for public discussion. In the filmed interview, photographed under a shade tree in the back yard of his son's residence, Jack was seen as an old man, frail, with watery eyes and halting voice. He was 85 years old, but his words came across clearly, and his convictions were still strong as he related to Roberts his version of the 1949 YB–49 cancellation of his lifelong dream.

Well, it's a very strange story and perhaps difficult to believe, but it certainly is seared into my memory, and I'm quite sure I can give you the absolute facts as they occurred.

The same day that General McNarney, who was the chief, the military chief, of the Air Forces, came to my office with that additional order for thirty-five airplanes, which he said was a drop in the bucket as far as the ultimate order was concerned, Mr. Millar and I were requested to visit Mr. Symington. At that meeting, he lectured us rather lengthily on the difficulties of a Secretary for Air in keeping things in hand, and told us that he did not want to sponsor any new aircraft companies entering the business and having to be supplied with business over the years, and that he wanted us without question to merge with Consolidated Vultee, which was then operating a government-owned plant in Fort Worth, building the B–36, as a competitor to the B–35 or YB–49.

After the lengthy diatribe on Mr. Symington's part, I said, "Mr. Secretary, what are the alternatives to this demand you're making of our merger with Consolidated Vultee?" He said, "Alternatives? You'll be goddamned sorry if you don't!"

General McNarney said, "Oh, Mr. Secretary, you don't mean that the way it sounds," and Mr. Symington said, "You're damned right I do!"

Well, this was a rather staggering termination of the meeting . . .

Northrop went on to tell of his receiving a telephone call shortly after the merger talks were broken off. "I got a telephone call a few days later from Mr. Symington. He said, 'I am cancelling all your flying wing aircraft.' And I said, 'Oh, Mr. Secretary, why?' And he said, 'I've had an adverse report,' and hung up. That was the last time I ever talked to him, and the last time we could ever reach him by phone or any other way."

Jack then told Roberts how the money that was to be used to buy the YB–49 went to purchase the rival B–36 instead, that contracts for the bombers were given to Consolidated Vultee for construction of the B–36 in the Fort Worth plant. As Roberts added, "So, in fact, the contract was taken from you, and given to Consolidated because you had refused to merge with Consolidated, as you were ordered to do by the government, is that accurate?" Jack Northrop nodded his head, "That is absolutely accurate."

Further on in the interview, Clete Roberts asked Jack what he had to say regarding his quite different testimony before the House Armed Services Committee in 1949, when Congress was investigating the flying wing cancellation and allegations of conflict of interest by the government. Jack answered carefully, "My reaction is that, under pressure of the life or death of Northrop Corporation, I committed one of the finest jobs of perjury that I've ever heard." Roberts asked him again, "You did not tell the truth?" And Jack replied, "I did not tell the truth."

Roberts continued, "And the reason for doing that was. . ."

"The reason for doing that was fear of the Secretary, the Air Secretary, Mr. Symington, fear of his complete obliteration of Northrop Aircraft Corporation."

Roberts inquired further, "How does it happen, Mr. Northrop, that for thirty-one years this story has not been told?"

Northrop replied, "The reason . . . is the same as the reason for my initial perjury, and it was the fear . . . that any intimation of this circumstance would result in a complete cancellation and obliteration of the company."

Dick Millar corroborated Jack's reasons in a separate interview. ". . .[T]he meeting with Mr. Symington was so, shall I say, brutal . . . barefaced . . . so obviously, if you will, a power play, that you almost had to assume that he would be prepared to take further steps if we didn't go as good boys and go along . . ."

This interview was Northrop's last public word on the subject. In a letter to a friend, Jack wrote of having "finished dictating a question and answer autobiography, and it was typed from the tape. When I got the typed document I was horrified at the lack of logical continuity in thought and expressive English. Therefore, I procrastinated for weeks on the miserable job of correcting it so that it would make some sense . . . The fact that I have never kept much in the way of photos, documents or mementos makes the job even more difficult, so let's not be concerned if the project dies on the vine . . . As I feared, it makes reading which is dry as dust, and without considerable research and gathering of interesting incidents . . . it would be hopeless as far as any public interest is concerned." It was typical of Jack Northrop's lifelong modesty to assume that his own words, no matter how awkward, about the design and development of his great achievement, the flying wing, would be of little public interest.

He preferred to consider other matters, as in the same letter, he wrote, "Mrs. Northrop and I live on a hilltop adjacent to a flyway where the gulls come back and forth to a small fresh water lake. There, flocks of various sizes glide in to wash their faces. They land on the water, to insert their bills and oscillate their heads from side to side rapidly to get rid of the salt water encrustation and other contaminants. They then take off, climb back to an altitude of two or three hundred feet and return home. When they approach the lake they set their wings in the attitude of great soaring birds, and make a long, beautiful, motionless glide to the water. It is one of the many things we enjoy here in Santa Barbara." Those who were privileged to see the flying wings in flight say that Northrop's genius, translated from his drawing board into an aircraft, flew not unlike a soaring bird.

Eleven Northrop XB–35 flying wing bombers in final assembly on the ramp at Hawthorne, 1949.

Flying wing Northrop XB–35s
on the assembly line in 1950,
before scrapping after the
production contract to build
thirty aircraft was cancelled
by the Air Force.

The last aircraft designed
by Jack Northrop, the F–89
all-weather *Scorpion* fighter,
1951.

Jack Mannion, Production Supervisor, 1943–1970; Vice President, Aircraft Division, 1970–1985. Retired after forty years with Northrop.

Oliver P. Echols, Chairman and General Manager, 1950–1954. Formerly U.S. Air Force General and Chief, Air Material Command.

Richard W. Millar, Board Chairman, 1947–1949; Vice Chairman, 1970–1982; Director 1947–1982.

Whitney Collins, Northrop Chairman and Chief Executive Officer, 1955–1959.

Squadron of Northrop T–38 supersonic jet trainers over the Rockies, 1961.

Welko Gasich, aircraft designer and Executive Vice President-Programs; F–5 Program Director.

Jack Northrop with Tom Jones, Northrop Chief Executive Officer, at F–5E *Freedom Fighter* roll-out party. Courtesy John Northrop Jr.

Rollout of the F–5E *Freedom Fighter* at Hawthorne.

Kent Kresa, President and Chief Operating Officer.

Jack and Margaret Northrop, 1970.

Jack Northrop with General Jimmy Doolittle, 1971. Courtesy John Northrop Jr.

Jack Northrop's 80th birthday celebration, at Northrop Corporation Family Day, Hawthorne, June 6, 1976.

The controversial official Air Force rendering of the Northrop ATB Stealth bomber (B–2).

Jack Northrop with Mary and John Northrop Jr.'s family, La Canada, 1979. Photo courtesy John Northrop Jr.

Northrop F–20 *Tigershark* takeoff. General Charles "Chuck" Yeager lifts F–20 off the runway at Edwards Air Force Base, marking the 35th anniversary of the first supersonic flight, also by Yeager. General Yeager reached a planned speed of Mach 1.45 in the Mach 2-class *Tigershark*, saying, "It is one of the most beautiful planes I have ever flown."

Tom Jones shows President Reagan the F–20 *Tigershark*, 1982.

The 200th F/A–18 *Hornet* shipset, an aircraft designed by Northrop. The center and aft fuselage sections being prepared for delivery to the prime contractor, McDonnell Douglas in St. Louis.

NORTHROP ATB

The Stealth Bomber

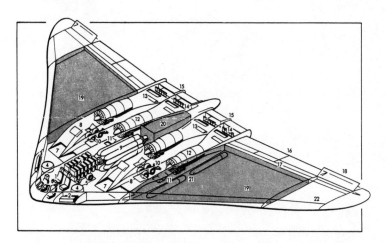

1 Four-man crew
2 Covert strike radar
2 Electronic warfare antennae
4 Retractable packs for FLIR and laser radar systems
5 Nose-wheel bay
6 Shielded avionics bay
7 Completely flush ventral vents
8 Serpentine, RAM-treated duct with internal
     streamwise baffles
9 Common Strategic Rotary Launcher (eight cruise
     missiles or B83 thermonuclear gravity weapons)
10 Main landing gear
11 Auxiliary air inlets
12 Four modified General Electric F101 engines
13 Auxiliary inlets for IR suppression
14 Absorbent baffles for IR and radar suppression
15 Two-dimensional vectoring/reversing nozzles
16 Flaperons, possibly with flexible covering
17 Roll/lift-dump spoilers
18 Split wing-tip surfaces function as elevators,
     rudders and air brakes
19 Wing fuel tanks
20 Fuselage fuel tanks
21 Possible conformal carriage of Advanced Cruise Missiles
22 External RAM

One of the many conceptions of the top secret Northrop ATB Stealth bomber, the B–2.
From the book *Stealth Aircraft* by Bill Sweetman. Reprinted by permission of Motorbooks
International.

16

NEW HORIZONS

The rapid growth enjoyed by the Northrop Corporation after 1952, when Jack Northrop resigned as president and chief engineer of his company, can be largely attributed to the rearmament program that began with the war in Korea and with the wise and farsighted leadership provided by Thomas V. Jones and his new management team. The ill-advised management decisions of several executives during the previous years were corrected and Northrop Corporation was placed on a sure course for the future, by long-range planning and inspired direction.

Tom Jones, heading the new management team, came to Northrop from the Rand Corporation, a consulting firm and "think tank" begun by Douglas Aircraft personnel, primarily concerned with long-range planning. Jones possessed an unusual aptitude for the complex planning involved in aircraft development. This was what Northrop needed as the business began to rebuild without the long-range vision of its founder. As far as Tom Jones was concerned—and in this he differed little from Jack—the aircraft manufacturing industry, and a new element in the defense lexicon—aerospace—must demonstrate consistency, persistence, and determination. An important aspect of this was serving your customers effectively, and Jones looked at all the world as a potential customer of Northrop. His intention was to stay in close touch with their problems and requirements, their worries, attitudes, and goals. It was Jones' view that customers must know everything about Northrop, and have total confidence in the Northrop Corporation. Nor would the modern aircraft and aerospace industry be able to function in a static environment. Northrop would grow in a world environment.

A bright engineering student at Stanford University, Tom graduated in 1942, working first for the Douglas Aircraft Company in Santa Monica. After the war, he moved for awhile to Rio de Janeiro, where he served as technical advisor to the Brazilian Air Ministry and taught as a university professor. Returning to California, he joined Rand, where he directed and wrote a widely used logistical study: "Capabilities and Operating Cost of Possible Future Transport Airplanes." Long before joining Northrop, Tom had become convinced that aeronautical engineers were not concerning themselves enough with the basic economic factors affecting the aircraft they were designing. Technical excellence and performance in the air were considered by the engineers to be more important than cost and delivery of airplanes on schedule. Tom's view was that if a new airplane was required to meet too high a performance target it might also be too costly or take too long to develop and maintain.

It had been different during wartime, when priorities were quite simple—build a plane fast and make it fly high and fast, no matter what the cost. The postwar decade marking the change of leadership from Jack to Tom was one in which the aircraft industry was forced to abandon the old fraternal spirit that had prevailed prior to and during the war. It was now a time when a new breed of businessman and bureaucrat took over control of the industry, which was no longer run by individualistic aviation pioneers. The romantic days were gone.

To build a larger and more profitable company, a corporate planner was needed at the top, a president with a different kind of vision of the future, one who was willing to compromise to achieve his goal. To build a better airplane was not enough. Just as Tom Jones could not have been the imaginative innovator who inspired the confidence of the original group who had staked their futures with Jack Northrop to build a new career for themselves based upon visions of flying wings, it was also true that Jack could never have built the company he founded into the large multinational corporation that Northrop became after his retirement.

Jones expressed other strong views as well, believing that government should not subsidize the aircraft industry, should not provide government-owned plants and equipment—GOCO, as it was called. The practice had been initiated during World War II, when aircraft manufacturers were small and undercapitalized, but the production assistance programs still continued. This meant that the vast proportion of the plants and equipment used by defense contractors to help to defend the free enterprise system wasn't owned by the free enterprise system at all. It was owned by the government—equipment, plants, and factories.

Most aerospace executives depended on this type of subsidy. Convair (then Consolidated Vultee, now General Dynamics) moved their airplane production from company-owned facilities in San Diego to a government-owned plant in Dallas to manufacture their B–36 bomber. This practice gave the companies with government-owned facilities an advantage that competing companies did not share: enhancement of the military services' incentive to keep government-owned facilities busy, in addition to financial advantages enjoyed by the company by not tying up limited capital in "bricks and mortar."

Except for a brief period during World War II, Northrop has always owned all its plants and equipment, and has never relied on government facilities. Capital investments of Northrop over the years have averaged nine percent of sales, while the average for the rest of the U.S. aircraft and aerospace industry averages less than five percent. Jones was always aware that this high level of capital investment reduced current earnings, but Northrop had always been looked upon as a technologically sound company, and one that had long used innovative business arrangements. Substantial capital investments provided the means for future earnings growth for a company that lost money in only one year of its history (1950).

Tom Jones disliked the commonly employed cost-plus-fixed-fee contract, a kind of contract that, he felt, killed any incentive to operate efficiently. Fixed price, or a fixed price incentive type of contracting, was strongly advocated by Tom. This became a consistent negotiating posture adopted by Northrop, representing a substantial change from previous company practices. It did not please his competitors.

Tom Jones was promoted rapidly, and the Northrop Board elected him Chairman and Chief Executive Officer in 1960. At his insistence, the name of the company was changed from Northrop Aircraft Inc. to Northrop Corporation, to reflect the changes taking place in the newly diversified firm. As CEO, Jones proved himself adept in dealing with his customers—the politicians and military bureaucrats. Intensely ambitious and hard working, he demands respect as the head corporate executive for over 28 years. During this time Northrop

Corporation has become one of the major aerospace designers and manufacturers in the world. The design and building of airplanes, a primary business conducted during Jack Northrop's era, became the Aircraft Division in Jones' reorganization. The company grew into a widely diversified corporation through the establishment of a number of new divisions and the acquisition of subsidiaries. A substantial portion of sales were soon derived from businesses other than aircraft, including electronics, navigation, communications, and aviation-related products and services.

In addition to Radioplane, which became the Ventura Division, manufacturer of target drones, the corporation located an Electro-Mechanical Division in Anaheim, specializing in the development and manufacture of electronic-passive sensor systems—systems that gather information but do not reveal where they are. This division was later combined with an enlarged Electronics Division in Hawthorne, which specialized in missile guidance and control systems. This division was later to create unexpected problems for Northrop managers responsible for permitting apparently inadequate inspection of components being assembled into guidance systems controlling the controversial MX intercontinental guided missile, causing unexpected embarrassment for the ordinarily trim corporate ship run by Jones.

A new laboratory was built in the Palos Verdes Estates to specialize in advanced technology and research. A worldwide aircraft service division was established in over thirty different countries; Wilcox Electric of Kansas City, a leading producer of airport instrument landing systems and navigational aids, was purchased; and a precision products division for manufacturing gyroscopes was opened in Norwood, Massachusetts.

One of the major manufacturing programs expanded by Jones had begun when Northrop produced engine cowlings for the World War II Boeing B–17 *Flying Fortress*. An agreement was made in 1966 to team with Boeing again, to engineer, tool, and build the main fuselage of the Boeing 747 airliner. This program was established entirely on a risk-sharing basis with Boeing. Northrop put two-thirds of its corporate net worth on the line for the 747 project, because Jones was convinced that the project made good business sense for the company, the stockholders, and one of Northrop's oldest customers. Northrop's task was to do the detail design and build the 153-foot long, 21-foot wide main passenger fuselage section. By the end of 1987, Northrop had delivered 678 complete 747 fuselage panels to Seattle, contributing nearly $3 billion to company revenues. The half sections traveled in enclosed railcars built especially for the purpose, by Southern Pacific tracks from the Hawthorne plant to Boeing's assembly line. In 1988 Northrop continued work for Boeing on the 747–400, the newest in the line of Boeing jumbo airliners. A considerably modified version of two of the new jumbo aircrafts are destined to become a flying communications center and the new Air Force One.

Northrop was associated with Boeing during the aborted development program for the proposed Boeing 2707 Supersonic Transport, the American SST. In addition to all-titanium wing test sections, the company also produced a full-scale test cabin section fabricated entirely of titanium. This forerunner of the aircraft flight control cabin, with a distinctive downward articulated nose section, would have been produced by Northrop under contract to Boeing, if the SST program had not been cancelled.

Northrop stepped on the threshold of space when the company, in competition with four other bidders, was awarded a contract to produce two "lifting reentry bodies." These were to be used as spacecraft that could reenter earth's atmosphere without burning up, and still maintain enough maneuverability to land back on earth. The lifting test bodies were intended to explore only the earth landing phase of orbital flight. They were dropped from a B–52 at an altitude of 45,000 feet, gliding back to earth for a "dead stick" landing on Rogers Dry Lake in the Mojave Desert. The program ended after forty-three flights, with a rocket-powered flight to nearly 90,000 feet and a speed of Mach 1.7. It was later concluded by NASA that a delta wing shuttle designed by Rockwell International would be more useful in the space program, but Northrop's early experimental flights in the lifting body proved that a returning space ship was a very practical idea.

After phasing out of production of the Northrop F–89 *Scorpion* all-weather fighter and the *Snark* guided missile projects, Tom Jones, then deputy chief engineer, initiated studies for a lightweight, easily maintained fighter to sell to allied nations, a design designated the N–156 *Freedom Fighter*. The design concept was influenced mostly by what Jones called "life cost," meaning the cost of the aircraft over its entire life span.

Following the Korean war "the country was on a technological binge," as Jones later explained. "But nobody mentioned that you only had so many hands and feet and could run in only so many directions." Jones sought an answer to this dilemma in a series of concentrated studies for a new type of manned weapons system. Out of his studies emerged a totally new design philosophy incorporating certain key features: a future fighter had to be small; it had to be lightweight and low in cost, with high thrust-to-weight engines; it had to be simple to maintain. Northrop technical teams had toured Europe and Asia, and found increasing concern over the rise in complexity, weight, and cost of modern military aircraft. Third World countries were looking for a high performance fighter they could afford, and that would possess a low attrition rate for both plane and pilot.

Advanced lightweight, high-thrust jet engines to power cruise missiles were then under development, and Jones was quick to recognize their potential for the new aircraft under study. The new engines were small enough so that a "safety package of two" could be installed in the aircraft, actually enhancing weight savings over use of a larger single engine. The first complete prototype N–156 was developed by an advanced design team headed by Welko Gasich. Key specialists were Robert Katkov and Art Nitikman, aerodynamics; Art Ogness, structure; Lee Begin, configuration; and George Gluyas, performance. In applying the latest state-of-the art design concepts, Gasich's team utilized area ruling and all-movable "flying" horizontal stabilizers. Popularly called the "coke bottle" design, area ruling was an application of the Whitcomb theory of area distribution for reduction of drag, a "pinching in" of the fuselage at the wing root, enabling the aircraft to accelerate more easily from transonic to supersonic speed. The main landing gear retracted into the fuselage, for the aerodynamically efficient wings were too thin to accommodate the wheels.

The plane appeared to be perfect for operation from small jeep carriers, but Washington decided to mothball the Navy's entire jeep carrier fleet. Perhaps influenced by the Northrop design for a lightweight carrier plane, the Air Force proposed a competition for a supersonic trainer to replace the rapidly aging Lockheed T–33A. Northrop quickly shifted emphasis, using the basic N–156 technology to develop the T–38 *Talon*. The trainer prototype made its first flight with test pilot Lew Nelson out of Edwards Air Force Base. On the third test flight, Nelson exceeded the speed of sound. The fighter version of the T–38 eventually became the F–5 series of aircraft.

Looking back on the first flight, Nelson said the *Talon*'s performance was "exactly what we expected. When I got back on the ground, I told the crew, there were no surprises." Nelson had flown the NACA variable-stability aircraft at Moffett Field, a plane that simulated some of the aerodynamic characteristics of the T–38. As a result of those flights, the *Talon's* vertical tail was changed to its production shape. Nelson said, "This was the only configuration change ever made on the airplane, and it was made before the first flight." The only other change in the T–38's appearance was the removal of a fuel vent from the stabilizer and the installation of a stainless steel separator between the tail pipes. Engineering excellence was evident before a single plane was built. The only criticism heard about the plane—if it can be called criticism—is that the trainer is much easier to fly than the planes the students will graduate into, but perhaps that is what a student trainer should be. Students don't have the split-second reaction time and ability to deal with emergencies that experienced pilots have. They need a safe, easy-to-fly aircraft.

The first T–38A *Talon* was delivered in 1961 to Randolph Air Force Base, Texas. At the time it was heralded as the nation's first "space age" trainer specifically designed to close the gap between subsonic trainers and increasingly sophisticated combat aircraft. The plane soon became the standard trainer in the U.S. Air Force.

Northrop *Talons* have been used to train more than 52,000 Air Force and foreign national military pilots, including the first astronauts to walk on the moon and the first USAF women pilots. Citing the *Talon's* cost effectiveness as well as its exceptional safety and maintenance records, in 1974 the U.S. Air Force Thunderbird demonstration squadron aerial acrobatic team replaced its F–4E *Phantoms* with T–38A *Talons* and traveled the country impressing a new generation with the excellence of Northrop-produced aircraft. It is the aircraft used for astronaut flight proficiency maintenance, and astronauts are seen regularly in television newcasts flying their *Talons* to keep flight time current. The aircraft continues in its role as trainer of pilots for the newest, most advanced aircraft. Northrop built a total of 1,187 T–38A *Talons*. More than 1,000 still fly today. The T–38A has the best safety record of any supersonic aircraft in the Air Force inventory—only 2.2 accidents per 100,000 flying hours—about five times less than that for the Air Force's fighter aircraft and about half the rate of all Air Force aircraft. Its service life has been doubled three times. According to General Thomas Ryan, former commander of Air Training Command, "We are going to use the T–38A for pilot training into the next century."

In the mid-1950s, European NATO countries embraced a military philosophy of massive retaliation as a defensive strategy. Under this concept it was expected that an initial attack by the Soviets using conventional forces would be repulsed by large numbers of small aircraft dispersed throughout the countryside of Europe, parked under overpasses, inside haystacks in pastures and inside barns. On signal, the swarms of small fighters would take off from autobahns, unimproved airstrips, and pastures and attack enemy airfields, various targets, and advancing forces. It was later decided this was not a good idea, and the NATO competition for purchase of these lightweight airplanes—between an Italian G–91, the British Gnat–Folland, and the U.S. Northrop N–156—was cancelled. NATO changed their strategy from massive retaliation to selective response, deciding against parking airplanes under overpasses.

It was company president Jones who initiated the well-timed gamble to build a prototype N–156F fighter as a company-sponsored project, without government funding. U.S. Defense officials had begun to recognize the logic of buying a new airplane more suited to mutual assistance programs than the expensive, highly sophisticated aircraft currently in the Air Force inventory. In 1958 Northrop was authorized to build three N–156F prototypes. Commonality with T–38 parts and shortened tooling production time made possible the first flight of the new fighter at Edwards, less than four months after the first flight of the T–38. Further work was halted, however, when no immediate purchasers for the aircraft was evident at home or abroad.

In 1961, a competition to furnish fighter needs for southeast Asia was conducted between Northrop, Lockheed, Ling-Temco-Vought, and McDonnell Douglas. Lockheed attempted unsuccessfully to introduce a less complex F–104 using a simpler radar system, but the F–104 was deemed too sophisticated for underdeveloped nations to keep flying without substantial U.S. maintenance assistance. Northrop won the competition with their basic F–5. The plane was selected as a defensive arm for favored nations under the Military Assistance Program.

This was the beginning of a famous line of aircraft called *Freedom Fighters*, eventually sold to thirty countries around the world. It was capable of a multitude of military roles: as interceptor, strike aircraft, ground support, and reconnaissance. The fighter boasted an unusually high ration of firepower payload per pound of aircraft weight. In addition to low initial cost and low maintenance requirements, it could still be flown as a trainer.

The Northrop F–5 was a low-cost, new production, multi-mission fighter that could perform both air-to-air and air-to-ground missions; it could be put into development quickly and at relatively low cost; its performance was sufficient to meet the threats of known enemy aircraft—at the time principally the MiG–15 and 17. Yet it was simple enough to be operated and maintained by air forces of developing nations.

Up to this time the bulk of grant-aid aircraft provided to both industrialized and less sophisticated nations of the free world had been surplus U.S. Air Force fighters, with some exceptions, like the F–86s, which were new production aircraft. But the expected availability of surplus airplanes did not materialize, at the same time when it was also realized that Third World educational and mechanical capabilities were limited, and their industrial base would be unable to provide even common hardware support for U.A. Air Force fighters if available.

The U.S. Air Force launched a program in 1965 to evaluate twelve F–5C aircraft in the Vietnam environment of limited war operations. Commonly identified as *Skoshi Tigers*, they flew across the Pacific after being modified with aerial refueling systems, jettisonable pylons, armor plate, and camouflage. Within three months of readiness alert, the planes were modified, Air Force crews trained, trans-Pacific flights made, and first combat sortie completed. On their Vietnam tour, the aircraft flew 2,600 sorties over a period of 150 days at an operational-ready rate of 85 percent.

Use of the Northrop F–5 in southeast Asia, also constituted the first effort on the part of the United States to "Vietnamize" the air defense of South Vietnam with a jet fighter Vietnamese military personnel could operate and maintain on their own. It was still considered possible that a much less sophisticated aircraft, made available at the earliest practicable date, would permit the United States safely to withdraw regular Air Force and Marine aircraft operating in the war zone. The F–5 was expected to improve and modernize the self-defense capabilities of South Vietnam. As it turned out, though, the aircraft didn't make a difference in Vietnam.

Bringing the F–5 into operational status overseas did bring forth disagreement in Congress. Senator J.W. Fulbright, chairman of the Foreign Relations Committee, said it was "disgraceful" that the House–Senate Conference Committee was persuaded to included "$28 million for a *Freedom Fighter* jet plane that the Pentagon had not even requested." Fulbright called the F–5 jet fighter appropriation "back-door foreign aid," saying it amounted to providing a subsidy to private companies for development of an airplane suitable only for use by foreign countries.

In 1963, the F–5 family of aircraft was selected as the *Freedom Fighter* to be provided by the U.S. to allied nations using military assistance program funds. Following the decline of grant aid assistance and the return of a reasonable level of self-sufficiency to Third World countries, the F–5s began to be used by the U.S. government as "carrots" to persuade allied countries to begin buying some on their own. Many did. Morocco was one of the first, purchasing a squadron of 12 F–5 airplanes. Some 687 F–5s were sold by Northrop as grant aid aircraft, 202 supplied with U.S. credit assistance financing. In all, 889 F–5s were built at the Hawthorne plant, not including F–5s produced under license in Canada, and 70 co-produced in Spain. More than 2600 Northrop F–5A, improved F–5E, F–5F, and RF–5E *Tigereyes* were eventually flying somewhere in the world. The plane, conceived by Northrop and produced completely with Northrop funds, proved to be tremendously successful and very profitable. They still fly.

When Northrop delivered the last *Talon* to the Air Force in 1972, the chief of staff of the Air Training Command, Brig. Gen. Michael C. McCarthy, said, "I have never heard anyone describe the T–38 as anything but a beautiful airplane. It is reliable in every parameter, a great performer, a remarkable airplane." Dubbed "The White Rocket," it was the world's first—and still the only—supersonic trainer, the airplane set four time-to-climb records and, with pilot Jacqueline Cochran at the controls, set eight women's flying records.

With Northrop aircraft flying around the world, the ground work was laid for Northrop to operate a worldwide airplane service subsidiary. Foreign sales of the popular *Freedom Fighters* enabled the company to open offices in Paris, Madrid, Rome, Teheran, Bangkok, Athens, Seoul, Bonn, Cairo, Rio de Janeiro, Saudi Arabia, Malaysia, Luzerne, Zurich, and Taiwan. The company had definitely moved from a modest beginning into the "aerospace big league."

After a quarter century of production, Chairman of the Board Tom Jones spoke of the important changes taking place in the world where Northrop conducts business, saying,

> These are times that can be challenging and productive, and perhaps more important, they represent a real opportunity for Northrop . . . We are going to have to compete strongly, and use our

resources wisely, to win new programs in this new environment. We cannot and do not intend to rest on the hard-earned position we hold today. We have many new programs in their early stages of development with an expanding future ahead of them.

Jones told of his attendance at the "Gathering of Eagles," a bringing together for a few days of many of the greatest airmen of America and the rest of the Free World. Jimmy Doolittle and his Tokyo Raiders, Curtis LeMay, Chuck Yeager, Gabby Gabreski—great names in American history—were all there. He told of stories he heard from them—sometimes unbelievable, but true legends—about them and about others that aren't with us anymore. The personal tales were marvelous. "Sometimes they moved you spiritually," he remembered.

There were other incidents that people recalled. Those weren't as dramatic—they hardly could be, compared to the human exploits. But those stories had a particular significance of their own. Jones said, "They were accounts of how people had tried new ideas—crazy ideas, they were usually called crazy ideas at the time—how they had innovated—how they had broken the 'other sound barrier.'" We all know Chuck Yeager broke one kind of sound barrier. The "other" sound barrier is the continuous sound of people saying, "that can't be done," or, if it could be done, "then you won't be able to get it done because the system won't let you."

Listening to those Eagles must have reminded everyone of what this country is really about, and about the kind of people who have devoted their lives throughout history to pursuing a better idea and a better way of doing something.

Jack Northrop would have been at home at the Gathering of Eagles.

17

CONTROVERSY, FAILURE, SUCCESS

Never to be more than a wooden mock-up, never to fly, the company-funded P–530 *Cobra* was nevertheless the prototype that ushered in a new era of air superiority fighters for Northrop. Wing leading-edge extensions along the fuselage were aerodynamically curved, giving it a hooded "cobra" look. Like the N–102 *Fang* that preceded it by 12 years, its advanced features were to be far-reaching. Its progenitors influenced not only the design of future high performance fighter aircraft, but military procurement procedures and congressional debates as well.

Weighing less than half the competitors first-line, twin-engine fighters, the *Cobra*, while still on the drawing board and in the computer, promised nearly twice the range, maneuverability, and acceleration of contemporary aircraft. The plane, like the child of the F–5 it was, possessed certain F–5 configuration characteristics: the shape of the F–5 wing, a stretched F–5 fuselage, and two jet engines side-by-side in the tail. It was the twin-canted vertical tail that visually separated it from the old F–5 family. It was a new generation of aircraft, to be sure.

Lee Begin, who had been active in the N–156 program, headed the *Cobra* project office. Walt Fellers, then manager of advanced systems, was responsible for seeing the *Cobra* through the usual series of design refinements. Jerry Huben was in charge of configuration integration—fitting all the external parts together. After a year of wind tunnel testing and analysis, Huben changed the configuration to a high wing location, for maximum ordnance flexibility and maneuvering ability and moved the cockpit forward for better pilot visibility. The basic design was patented in 1970, with Walt Fellers, Lee Begin, John Patierno, Jerry Huben, Adam Roth, Hans Grellman, and Vern White sharing the honors.

The Mach 2 class *Cobra* represented a continuation of Northrop's design and manufacturing philosophy. It combined a military arms program with international industrial and economic requirements to provide an aircraft ideal for overseas countries from several standpoints. In some respects it was an extension of the F–5 program, modernized and brought up to date—a multipurpose weapon capability, low-cost purchase price, and opportunities for large-scale industrial participation and state-of-the-art technology exchange. In addition to aluminum, steel, and titanium, graphite composites were used for light weight and strength in doors and panels, leading-edge extensions, wing trailing edge, and other control surfaces. Advanced technology features of the aircraft included new radar, enabling pilots to detect enemy aircraft at low as well as high altitudes. The Air Force, perhaps influenced by the design, requested proposals for an aircraft highly specialized in the day-fighter role, with particular emphasis on light weight and low cost. It was evident that Northrop's *Cobra* could be a winning candidate for the new Air Force fighter contract, and the design was further refined to match U.S. requirements. The Air Force evaluated specifications from four companies, choosing Northrop and their erstwhile flying wing competitor, the Convair Division of General Dynamics, to produce two flying prototypes. Northrop's design was designated YF–17; General Dynamics' aircraft, the YF–16. The stage was set for a new confrontation between old competitors.

The Air Force proposal called for an aircraft highly specialized in visual, clear weather day-fighting, to achieve air superiority over future battlefields. The new fighter must sustain high rates of turn and increased supersonic maneuvering capabilities below Mach 1.6. It had to be able to accelerate quickly yet present no compromises that might take away from its ability to maneuver inside the combat zone. The Defense Department made no promise of production contracts, but the Air Combat Fighter, as it came to be known, was expected to be a supplement to the McDonnell Douglas F–15, and to exceed performance requirements that the weighty, longer range, and more heavily armed F–15 fighter could not meet.

The first YF–17 flying prototype was completed in April 1974, and trucked to Edwards Air Force Base, to be prepared for its first flight by Northrop chief test pilot, Hank Chouteau. Landing after 61 minutes over the desert, Chouteau praised the new aircraft, "When our designers said they were going to give the airplane back to the pilot, they meant it. It's a fighter pilot's fighter." Two days later, the YF–17 flew supersonically in level flight without an afterburner—a first for any U.S. designed airplane.

Information obtained during the flight test program clearly established the superior high performance and low cost characteristics of the Northrop YF–17. However, Air Force procurement officers decided that the more expensive, heavier, more complex, more difficult to maintain, and less maneuverable General Dynamics YF–16 would be better suited for its specific operational requirements, mostly in supplementing the older air-to-air fighter aircraft already in their inventory. As they put it, "including considerations of its force structure mix and logistics commonality." Among other differences the Northrop YF–17 was equipped with a more powerful General Electric jet engine than the Pratt & Whitney jet powering Convair's YF–16. The Air Force decision was final. They had concluded it was unwise to mix up old planes with new ones, even if the new planes were better able to fight. The Convair Division of General Dynamics was awarded a succession of contracts for production quantities of the F–16, which was to become one of the two standard U.S. Air Force fighters. Several thousand F–16s have been built, and they fly in many foreign Air Force squadrons.

The U.S. Navy felt differently. The Northrop YF–17, designed for mission versatility, could just as easily fly from a carrier as a paved airfield. The YF–17 went on to win the Navy air combat fighter competition where multi-mission suitability was a greater consideration. The YF–17 design was redesignated the F–18. The Navy wanted the aircraft for carrier operations, with modifications for longer range, strengthened fuselage, and landing gear. The new F–18 would replace aging F–4 *Phantoms* and A–7 *Corsairs* with one airplane that could be used for both defense and attack missions. It would be the Navy version of commonality. Navy procurement officers were impressed by the performance and the price of the Northrop F–18. They wanted to buy it but their regulations required competitive bids from more than one contractor.

Northrop had not built a shipboard fighter incorporating the special needs of Navy carrier operations before. They joined with

McDonnell Douglas, who had more experience with carrier aircraft, in making a proposal to the Navy. The agreement between the two aerospace firms, stated that ". . .they will jointly develop and propose an air combat fighter for the U.S. Navy which is based on the YF–17 design. . .Under the teaming agreement, McDonnell Douglas will have prime contract responsibility for a carrier-suitable version of the YF–17 to meet the requirements of the proposed NACF (Navy air combat fighter). Northrop will have prime contract and design responsibilities for YF–17 land-based variants for use by NATO nations and other allies."

As was to be expected, General Dynamics' Convair also sent in bids for a version of their F–16, but the combined McDonnell Douglas-Northrop proposal was not to be beaten. They won the large Navy contract for a new shipboard fighter-attack aircraft with the Northrop designed F–18, now to be called the McDonnell Douglas F/A–18 *Hornet*. By previous agreement, Northrop became the major sub-contractor on the project manufacturing 40 percent of the aircraft in Hawthorne—the center and aft fuselage sections, twin vertical stabilizers and associated subsystems. The St. Louis plant of McDonnell Douglas would build the remainder of the airframe, wings, and be responsible for final assembly. Design rights were turned over to McDonnell Douglas, to be modified for carrier operation. Sales and manufacturing rights for the original land-based model of the F/A–18, the already built and tested YF–17, would be retained by Northrop, for they expected an active demand for the new plane, originally designed with allied overseas requirements in mind.

Because of strengthened airframe structures necessary to withstand the shock of arrested carrier landings and catapult launching, the plane was slightly larger and about 10,000 pounds heavier than the YF–17. It now featured folding outer wing panels for carrier storage, greater internal fuel capacity, and a nose section enlarged to accommodate the Navy's 28-inch search radar antenna. In the spring of 1976, plans were formalized with the Defense Department for a land-based version of the multi-role F–18 *Hornet* strike fighter, to satisfy worldwide requirements for an advanced aircraft able to operate from conventional runways. It must be economic to maintain, yet still reflect a balance between the latest advances in technology, mission requirements, and cost-weight considerations—all part of the Tom Jones credo for Northrop aircraft. The Northrop sales department went looking for customers.

After a substantial number of F/A–18 *Hornets* had been delivered to the U.S. Navy, and they became operational, their reputation spread. Both Canada and Australia approached McDonnell Douglas to buy a land-based version. McDonnell Douglas accepted their order for *Hornets* and agreed to modify a number for early delivery to their respective governments. This action, in the view of Tom Jones, was obviously contrary to the intent of the original contract between the two companies, when Northrop turned over the design rights. After conversation failed to resolve the issue, Jones authorized a suit for damages against McDonnell Douglas. Rather than have the suit go to trial, McDonnell Douglas settled the disagreement out of court by paying Northrop $60 million. Northrop agreed that future orders for modified land based F/A–18 *Hornets* may be accepted by McDonnell Douglas.

As principal subcontractor to McDonnell Douglas for the Northrop-designed *Hornet*, Northrop has rolled out of the Hawthorne plant more than 1,000 shipsets—a shipset being the back 26 feet of the aircraft. There appears to be no absence of constructive collaboration between the two companies, Northrop–McAir, as the team is sometimes called. It had been suggested that the lawsuit between the two might preclude cooperation, but that has not been the case. Northrop and McDonnell Douglas have brought their individual strengths and the undeniable asset of successful team experience to work for them in soliciting and winning future contracts. As the president of Northrop, Kent Kresa, said in commenting on the legal differences, "Lawsuits tend to be between the lawyers rather than the builders. As they say, the airplane and the factories never knew the trouble that was brewing in the law departments." The lawsuit was undoubtedly an embarrassment to both parties. The F/A–18 *Hornet* turned out to be an excellent airplane in all respects, is still being ordered, shipsets are still leaving the Hawthorne factory for the St. Louis assembly line, and the business is profitable for both companies.

Specially modified Northrop-McDonnell Douglas F/A–18 *Hornets* are the official airplane of the U.S. Navy Blue Angels acrobatic flight demonstration squadron. Eleven of the aircraft replaced the team's A–4 *Skyhawks* at the end of the 1986 season. At sea, both pilots and operational commanders concur on the *Hornets* capability. Its reliability is twice the fleet average, and pilot comfort levels are higher than any other aircraft on the carrier deck. The engines wear out before the airplanes do.

The catapult shot of the *Hornet* is an eye-opener for most of the old "tailhookers," as carrier pilots are called. It is a hands off shot into the air, with flight control computers automatically rotating the aircraft to the proper attitude for lift-off, based on preselected trim settings. This is done without using the control stick. The only problem, it is said, is a pilot-caused oscillation for those who don't believe the computer can fly and grab the stick prematurely. Pilots say this only happens once, however, "usually with the older nonbelievers."

Navy Commodore Leon Edney, writing about the *Hornet*, said that the days are gone when a pilot must compensate for aircraft weaknesses with gutsy flying and complicated stick techniques. He quotes an ex-fighter pilot:

> In most aircraft, if you put on a hard maneuver, you bleed away a lot of your air speed. You have to be very careful in those aircraft. If you screw it up—you're dead. You could put your best move on a guy, and if it didn't work—you're out of air speed, out of ideas, and you are a grape. With this aircraft, you can put your best move on a guy, and if it does not work you can unload and you get your speed back quicker than the other guy.

It is the best of testimonials.

Considering the success of the *Freedom Fighter* and the *Hornet*, it was not surprising that Tom Jones had been thinking of another fighter for Northrop to develop with company funds, using the same speculative philosophy as before. President Jimmy Carter's administration felt that a new fighter plane was needed that was designed specifically for foreign customers. Carter assured aircraft contractors that his State Department would help create a Third World market for low cost fighters by refusing to license Air Force frontline airplanes for export. A definite market seemed possible, and Jones decided it was time for Northrop, following up on the F–5 success, to build still another lightweight fighter and offer it for sale to the world at a fixed price. He sent his designers a single-page memo outlining expected cost and performance goals to be met. Robert Sandusky, Manager of Advanced Design, responded with a concept for a new fighter that was just what Jones was looking for. He named this new plane the *Tigershark*. It was developed from scratch by Northrop into a complete fighter program without any assistance, financial or otherwise, from the government. The company spent more than $1 billion on the program. It was typical of what Jack Northrop would have done if he were still in charge.

Jones advised his staff to design the plane in the most practical manner, to meet his requirements as they saw best, without preconceived ideas of construction or materials. He wanted money saved in manufacture, in operation when the plane was flying, and in easily accomplished maintenance to keep the plane flying. Designing was to be accomplished without Pentagon restrictions. There would be no need to pass memos back and forth. When there was a problem to solve or when revised design made a change in production procedures necessary, it was only necessary for the individual making the change to consult with Sandusky and then walk down the hall to speak with production personnel. Jones formatted a plane and a factory to build it in at the same time, a production matter easy for Northrop to decide on since, unlike most government contractors, they owned all their own production facilities and buildings. The General Dynamics F–16 is built in a government-owned plant, where there is little incentive to modernize production lines and assembly techniques or to manufacture airplanes with less expensive methods.

Rather than invent new manufacturing equipment that would increase costs and take time to develop, Northrop searched out existing processes that could be converted to use by F–20 production engineers. Graphite-composite stocks that must be kept cold before processing were stored in a deep freezer adapted from one used by the kitchens of the Sara Lee Baking Company. Workers cut graphite into sections, using Gerber cloth-cutting machines found in the garment industry. When designers agreed on using injected-molded fiber glass for small parts, they drove down the freeway south of Hawthorne to the largest toy manufacturer in the west, Mattel Inc.—where Jack Northrop's son worked as a designer of toys—and adapted their molding technics to building airplanes.

When the F–20, as it was designated by the Air Force, was completed and tested, company and military test pilots were pleased to find the new plane superior in many ways to the contemporary McDonnell Douglas F–15 and the General Dynamics F–16 fighters that had been developed earlier under cost-plus-fixed-fee contracts, designed to meet certain specifications presented by the Air Force. The principal differences were in the shorter time required to prepare the F–20 for takeoff, or scramble in the event of emergency, and the much lower cost of maintaining the Northrop airplane—keeping it in the air—due to the use of fewer and simpler parts and less complicated weapon and navigational systems. Some Air Force pilots who flew the F–20 said that, in combat with frontline U.S. Air Force planes, the *Tigershark* would win. The Pentagon successfully avoided any such encounter, however, in its efforts to ignore the F–20. There was never any intention to consider adding the F–20 to active American inventories. Nothing at all was done to interest foreign customers in buying the plane, although Tom Jones did push the Reagan Administration to pressure the State Department and Air Force to try harder to sell the F–20 overseas. The way to go, however, was to convince the Air Force to buy the plane for its own use, but it would have none of it.

As journalist Gregg Easterbrook put it:

> There is one way to overcome the Air Force's institutional prejudice against an airplane that was developed somewhere else and doesn't cost enough: through the leadership of the President and the Secretary of Defense. So far neither has shown any willingness to challenge the way the Pentagon does business. Michael Burch, Secretary Weinberger's press officer, said that Weinberger has not considered talking to the Air Force about the F–20 and does not intend to consider it.

Easterbrook went on to say, "Northrop has never dared to publicly suggest that the Air Force should buy the F–20, and company officials dismiss the idea even in private, saying that nothing can possibly come of it, for bureaucratic reasons." The Air Force, with its officer corps of in-house experts, is incapable of accepting under any circumstances a fighter plane they didn't design, that wasn't built according to specifications they prepared, and more, that didn't cost enough. Apparently it would be considered by the Pentagon to be sinful to buy for less what is more.

There may be other reasons, for General Dynamics appears to have a more direct and influential connection to the Pentagon. Northrop dares not push too hard for fear of losing lucrative contracts for the Stealth ATB (Advance Technology Bomber), which will pay Northrop far more billions of dollars than any Air Force contract for the F–20 could. Jones surely remembered the Pentagon's reaction when Boeing expressed public outrage in newspaper ads over the Air Force's purchase of the expensive Lockheed C–5 *Galaxy*, with its terrible performance record and structural defects, when Boeing was offering a cargo version of the 747 at half the price. A few months after the newspaper ads appeared, the Air Force cancelled, without warning, Boeing's contract for an air-launched cruise missile. It was a lesson to be remembered.

The F–20 *Tigershark* lacked the long range of the F–15 and the more complex radar and guided missiles of the F–16. The big difference was in the price. General Dynamics F–16 fighters were costing the government over $16 million each, while the Northrop F–20 *Tigershark* was offered for a fixed price of about two-thirds that amount, or about $11.6 million. Spare parts were also offered at fixed prices over the life of the aircraft, a practice previously unheard of in military procurement programs. The F–20 *Tigershark* was a superior aircraft, available at less first cost, and with lower maintenance costs throughout its life. The government's silence at receiving this outstanding proposal was impressive—they were not interested. Three *Tigersharks* were built at Northrop's expense. None were sold. In six years of selling and promotion, with General Chuck Yeager as demonstrator, Northrop did not find a single buyer.

Northrop tried almost everything in the attempt to loosen the strong grip held by General Dynamics' F–16 on the U.S. Air Force and foreign markets. Their public affairs department worked overtime, sprinkling newspapers and magazines with F–20 advertisements and dramatic photographs of the airplane, and any celebrity that would stand next to the airplane. They co-starred the F–20 in television commercials, once with the upscale BMW, boasting of the BMW as "the ultimate driving machine" and the F–20 as "America's newest tactical fighter." The plane appeared in the background as Chuck Yeager sold Delco batteries on television. Yeager flew the plane to the Air Force Association's Gathering of Eagles in Las Vegas and showed off the *Tigershark* to everyone who cared to look. The F–20 appeared in ads with a can of Coke, which caused a touchy reaction from Northrop regarding their method of selling a multi-million dollar military airplane, but the Northrop promotion people said, "It didn't get to be popular because of the Coke ad. It got in the Coke ad because it was popular."

Northrop neither accepted nor paid any fees for the F–20 to appear on television. It may have been the only fighter free to endorse products, for the Air Force does not allow its planes to be used for testimonials. The campaign was not only created to convince the Pentagon and Congressional politicians that the *Tigershark* would be a worthy purchase, but to show the American public that there is an alternative to General Dynamics, in order to take advantage of the public's traditional support for the underdog—Northrop in this case— as compared to the big, bad, monopolistic General Dynamics and their well established F–16 *Falcon*. Les Daly, Northrop's chief corporate spokesman, said, "They [the American people] recognize this as an effort at a time when they are looking for a new effort from the defense industry. The fact we haven't sold an airplane abroad only seems to cement the feeling that something is wrong in the system."

The F–20 didn't cost the government anything to develop. The F–20 was at least equal—according to some experts, superior—to F–16s then being considered for addition to Air Force inventories. The F–20 was less expensive than the F–16, yet for reasons that the procurement bureaucracy could not adequately explain, it was the F–16 that was favorably considered for purchase, rather than the F–20. The F–16 was built to Air Force specifications; the F–20 was not, yet it exceeded Air Force requirements. It was as if some governmental network had decreed that General Dynamics' Convair Division should always be awarded a contract over Northrop; as if a replay of the Northrop YB–49 flying wing versus the Convair B–36 controversy was being constantly repeated, with Northrop's YF–17 losing out to General Dynamics' Convair YF–16, and now with a brand new F–20 aircraft, superior and less costly, Northrop would still be denied a place on the Air Force flightline. It was as if Northrop should always be second to General Dynamics, something preordained by tradition, unless Northrop designed their airplanes to be sold under another name, like the McDonnell Douglas F/A–18.

Northrop was forbidden to solicit overseas sales by the same government agencies which, in previous administrations, had encouraged them to develop the low cost F–5 for overseas markets. For some reason the rules were changed while the F–20 *Tigershark* was on the drawing boards. Now, Air Force assistance was required for a contractor to obtain foreign orders for military planes. As most of these governments were dependent on the United States for the money to pay for new aircraft, it was easy for the Air Force to convince Third World generals which plane they should buy. Indeed, it was no surprise that they preferred the same plane the U.S. Air Force was flying—there was much more prestige in that arrangement—even if the aircraft did cost more. It was well known they would not be able to maintain the complex F–16 with any degree of proficiency.

For some time, Taiwan had been trying to persuade the Pentagon to sell it a squadron of F–20 *Tigersharks* to begin replacing the 200 aging F–5 *Freedom Fighters* on the island, but the request was rejected on grounds that Taiwan does not need the planes for defensive purposes, apparently wanting to avoid upsetting China. Taiwan was not permitted to buy the planes directly from Northrop. Then, in an apparent convenient overlooking of the rules, when the government of Greece wanted to buy 40 F–16s direct from General Dynamics, and not through an agreement with the Pentagon, there was no problem with a direct purchase. Greece got their F–16s. Since introducing the made-for-export fighter in 1980, Northrop had often come close to a sale, only to have a Pentagon official or member of Congress block the deal.

The Defense Department and Air Force reserved to themselves arrangements for negotiations with allied countries. As far as anyone knows, they have never presented the F–20 on an equal basis with the F–16, always offering the U.S. Air Force fighter for sale first. This implies that Northrop's F–20 is inferior, or else, why wouldn't the U.S. Air Force also buy the airplane Northrop was trying to sell? Before Northrop's F–20 appeared, the Air Force never allowed its first line fighter planes to be sold overseas, except to very favored nations. Now, following revised directives, the newest Air Force fighter, the F–16, was made available to any Free World country able to read a price tag and borrow the money. As far as Tom Jones was concerned, the free enterprise system he championed so energetically was not working very well for Northrop. Forty-seven years after cancellation of Northrop's YB–49 contract and the destruction of the flying wing bombers on the Hawthorne ramp by order of the Air Force, the Northrop company appeared to be once more the victim of government politics, with General Dynamics–Convair the winner.

General Dynamics is the nation's largest defense contractor. Its Convair aircraft manufacturing division is based in Texas, where close friends in Congress protect the jobs of Texans and the profits of Texas corporations; Texas is the home of John Tower, who was chairman of the Senate Armed Services Committee, and F–16 production and assembly is done in a government-owned factory in Fort Worth, in the district of Jim Wright, the Speaker of the House.

Going back nearly 25 years, numerous criminal investigations have centered on General Dynamics for alleged fraud, kickbacks, and overcharges on military contracts. The indictments have grown in number in recent years, beginning with an antitrust suit filed by

Attorney General Robert Kennedy for antitrust violations when General Dynamics required firms that sell to it to buy from it. The court ordered the company to divest itself of the offending division. Seven people were indicted in 1970 in an alleged scheme to sell defective parts for use in the F–111 fighter plane, with four former officials of the company charged in the $300,000 deal. In 1983, two General Dynamics executives were paid $2.7 million in kickbacks by the former chairman of the Frigitemp Corp. In the same year a 79-count federal indictment charged a former General Dynamics purchasing agent with fraud when fictitious companies were allegedly set up to buy parts for use in General Dynamics–Convair contracts with the Air Force and NASA. The next year the Justice Department sued three businessmen and a former executive vice president of General Dynamics, alleging an elaborate bribery and fraud scheme to rig awards for subcontracts on Trident ballistic missile submarines and nuclear attack submarines built for the Navy. The former vice president fled to Greece. At the time General Dynamics was billing the Navy for $650 million in submarine excess cost overruns, Admiral Hyman Rickover admitted accepting "thousands of dollars" in gifts and jewelry given to him by General Dynamics while he headed the Navy's nuclear shipbuilding program. Rickover said, "I'm not aware that there are any excess overruns," and denied the gifts discouraged him from criticizing General Dynamics or his calling for a congressional probe of the company. A former vice president of General Dynamics, Takis Veliotis, says the company knew when preparing the contract that the submarines could not be built for the agreed price, intending to apply later for "cost overruns." The Justice Department later dropped their probe, saying there was "no reasonable prospect of a successful prosecution." Senator William Proxmire said the decision "shows the Justice Department is not serious about defense fraud," calling the Department's reasoning "baffling and disappointing."

The most recent indictment involves General Dynamics' work on a prototype weapon that became the very symbol of waste and mismanagement at the Pentagon—the DIVAD radar-controlled, four-barrel anti-aircraft gun—which, after the spending of $1.8 million, and repeated testing, couldn't hit the target aircraft. Weinberger halted work on the project and General Dynamics decided to charge the $3.2 million in production losses, which were their responsibility, to the government. Former NASA Chief Administrator James Beggs, who was a General Dynamics executive at the time, was indicted for fraud in the billing, but the charges were later dismissed. General Dynamics argued the indictment involved, "highly sophisticated regulatory and accounting matters with different interpretations." Brushing aside any corporate sins of the past, General Dynamics' new chairman, Stanley C. Pace said, "My concentration of time and effort is on the present and future," adding that all company employees would adhere to strict ethical practices or face tough disciplinary measures. Pace said he is confident that the company "can perform in the future in a way that will be acceptable to the public and Congress, as well as to the Department of Defense."

The Pentagon, increasing its public efforts to crack down on illegal behavior by its major suppliers, from time to time, suspended General Dynamics from bidding. The procedure, a temporary debarment and slap on the wrist, can be described as nothing more than window dressing. As one Air Force officer said, speaking on condition that he not be identified, when Rockwell International was suspended from bidding in the midst of a multi-million-dollar contract to build the B–1B bomber, not much didn't happen: "With a company that size, you can't stop doing business with them." On another occasion, when General Electric's bidding rights were taken away for three weeks, a spokesman for the firm said, "We know we lost some business." Among other prohibitions, General Electric was not allowed to sell electric light bulbs in the Army PX.

Northrop, with a history of government procurement machinations involving General Dynamics' predecessor, Consolidated Vultee, found itself in a difficult situation. Perhaps it was more a matter of hurt pride and prestige than anything else. Profits were still posted in the annual report. Dividends were paid as usual. Northrop was losing hundreds of millions in the ill-fated F–20 program, but found it awkward to complain, for the company was at the same time receiving contracts from the Air Force for classified advanced aircraft programs worth billions, profits that more than made up for the *Tigershark* losses.

Tragedy, too, struck the F–20 program. The company suffered the loss, in flight, of the first two F–20 *Tigersharks*. The aircraft had already been flight tested by Air Force pilots as well as company pilots, and had performed well, accomplishing all flight maneuvers without incident. Extensive investigation of the two accidents cleared the aircraft of any basic faults. As both company pilots were killed, there could not be any definitive causes determined. There were no mechanical or structural failures, but the attention the media paid to the crashes dampened enthusiasm for the F–20. The first crash occurred during a demonstration in South Korea; the second during acrobatics, when the pilot was practicing for a demonstration at the Paris Air Show. The high performance *Tigershark* apparently got away from him.

Congress entered the F–20 versus F–16 controversy in 1986, mandating by legislation a competition to select aircraft for the next Air Force purchase of 270 frontline fighters. As a result of intensive lobbying efforts by Northrop, the bill was worded in such a manner that General Dynamics could not submit a bid lower than its actual costs, language directed precisely at the F–16. Executives of both firms said they were anxious for the contest to begin, a western-style "shoot-out" between Texas and California manufacturers, to resolve the long-running debate over who designed the hotter and more cost-effective warplane.

Chief of General Dynamics Convair Division, Herbert Rogers, said, "I am delighted to have a head-to-head competition with the F–20, because we are going to win and put this whole thing to rest." Northrop Chairman Tom Jones, said he expected to win. "We are the more modern airplane. We believe we have them beat on [overall] cost. When we win, we can see the doors opening wide to many other customers. People say we have lost to the F–16, but we haven't lost any competitions, because there haven't been any. We have been in the on-deck circle, but this is the first time we have been in the batter's box."

Former General Dynamics Chairman David Lewis was quoted in the *Los Angeles Times* as once saying that he would do everything possible to ensure that the F–20 never entered production. Indeed, General Dynamics has proven to be a tough opponent. "This is not just a competition between airplanes," said Northrop spokesman Les Daly. "It is a competition between ways of life. It is competition versus monopoly." Vice President for General Dynamics, Herbert Rogers, commenting on the F–20, said, "I think Tom Jones has a fine little aircraft, but so what? His 1,500 hours of test flight is almost laughable if he thinks that he has accomplished anything. All it has accomplished is losing two out of three airplanes."

Northrop's proposal—all 18,900 pages—in containers totaling five feet-by-five feet-by-sixteen feet in size were ferried to Washington in two airplane loads. According to the Northrop vice president for

technology and planning, the bid proposal represented "an unequivocal commitment by Northrop to stand behind the F–20, both plane
and program, for as long as the *Tigershark* serves our Air Force
customers. If there was ever a program that demonstrated Northrop's
willingness to innovate—from concept to engineering, from development to production tooling, and from business guarantees and war-
ranties to pricing—that program is the F–20 *Tigershark*." There was
also something else worth noting. The F–20 introduced competition
into the U.S. fighter business, where a virtual monopoly prevails. The
benefits of the competition, regardless of the outcome, will not go
without notice by the Air Force and Congress. Suddenly, after years
of steady price increases, new ways of lowering the cost of other
fighters seem to have been discovered.

Tough lobbying and acrimonious debate set the stage for the
climax of a five-year sales battle between two of America's largest
aerospace companies. The several tons of documents submitted by the
two bidders were studied by Pentagon experts to determine the
winner of a contract that could be worth more than $4 billion. But it
was not to be a Northrop victory.

Air Force General McMullen, under whose direction the competitors proposals would be evaluated, said, "I encourage your innovation." He got it from General Dynamics, who took advantage of their
long experience with the F–16 *Falcon*, by presenting to the Air Force
a package they could accept without much criticism. In a cleverly
conceived exchange proposal that won the contest and effectively
eliminated Northrop from serious consideration, General Dynamics
would sell the Air Force kits to upgrade existing F–16s already
purchased. Those planes would in turn be replaced by new F–16C
models. The old upgraded planes would then be transferred to Air
National Guard squadrons. Which fighter was the better was never
resolved by the Pentagon; it was simply a matter of how best the Air
Force could squirm out of the controversy and still fly their favorite
airplane, the F–16. Because of Northrop's competitive pressures, the
new F–16Cs would be sold to the Air Force at considerably less first
cost. The Air Force also said the F–16 had better "intercept capability."

Like another Air Force program thirty-six years before, when
Northrop's YB–49 flying wing bomber was scrapped in favor of the
Convair B–36, the Northrop F–20 program would now be cancelled in
place of a Convair-built F–16. The new Secretary of the Air Force used

the same excuse the old one had offered; only the words had changed. Secretary Edward Aldridge said the F–20/F–16 weapons program was hurt by Gramm-Rudman-Hollings budget restrictions in a "reduced funding environment" that was a factor in his decision.

In a bittersweet conclusion to the competition, the Air Force announced that Northrop would be the prime contractor, teaming with McDonnell Douglas to develop and build a prototype of the next generation of combat aircraft, called the Advanced Tactical Fighter (ATF). Northrop will have responsibility for total systems integration of the ATF and will share $691 million over four years. After flying the prototypes, the Air Force will select one as its premier fighter, to enter service in the 1990s. Also a winner of an ATB development contract, was Lockheed, which will team with General Dynamics and Boeing.

In November 1986, two weeks after the Pentagon decision, Northrop halted all work on F–20 *Tigersharks*. After investing $1 billion of its own money and relentlessly battling government bureaucracy, Northrop closed the books on a unique and risky initiative that it had hoped would demonstrate the feasibility of a commercial approach to government contracting, as well as an ability to design on their own an airplane second to none. The last word may have been spoken by aerospace analyst Paul Nisbet of Prudential-Bache Securities, "The F–20 is an edifice to private enterprise in the defense business. The lesson is, don't go spending your own money on weapons that politics can influence."

Without Tom Jones at the head, Northrop would surely have thrown in the towel much sooner. It is also true that Northrop would not be where it is today without Tom Jones. It has been his executive skills that have transformed Northrop from the twenty-sixth largest defense contractor several years ago into what may emerge as the leading defense contractor of the 1990s. As if to underline the measure of a successful future, the 545th shipset of F/A–18 *Hornets* was delivered to Northrop–McAir, and *Hornets* began to interest overseas buyers. If the F–20 wasn't to be available, perhaps other Northrop-designed aircraft would be. Singapore requested pricing information and the French Navy expressed an interest in obtaining F/A–18s. Japan, Korea, the United Arab Emirates, Kuwait, and Switzerland want *Hornets* for their air defense systems. If Northrop can't sell one plane, they'll sell another.

At Northrop aircraft, history has repeated itself with considerable regularity, as the company competed with the best of their contemporaries and pushed their products and advanced ideas into the marketplace, even when the products were a little out of their regular line of work. As often as not, Northrop paid for developing new programs themselves, to get recognition by the bureaucracy, and even challenged government procurement procedures when it seemed the way to go. In 1988, Tom Jones and his top executives faced problems of corporate survival similar to those which many years before confronted Jack Northrop, following government demands to merge with Consolidated Vultee—which would have made Northrop part of the future General Dynamics. There was cancellation of the flying wing bomber contracts, cutbacks in government spending, rapid expansion that at times was beyond the capacity of the company, sometimes calling into question the ability of the company to continue as an independent firm, making its own decisions. Northrop, and now Jones, were kept busy solving the same engineering, corporate, and political problems.

The modern Northrop Corporation suffered severe growing pains after rapidly expanding the Electronics Division from a modest beginning, with about 600 technically minded employees, to a manufacturing unit with ten times that number. A major contract was awarded to Northrop—in competition with Rockwell International, a firm well established in the field of developing and manufacturing long range guidance systems—to build the key guidance element for the controversial MX missile.

The MX guidance device, an inertial measurement unit, or IMU, is perhaps the most complex device ever designed and constructed for the military, containing 19,401 parts manufactured to better than fine watch precision, all contained within an IMU container the size of a basketball. The guidance device functions like a compass and speedometer, telling the onboard computer, also inside the ball, how to steer the missile to its target. Rockwell's International Autonetics unit had already built 2,258 inertial guidance computers used in the ICBM Minuteman missile programs, and had considerable experience in the work, but when the newer MX went into production the Air Force was convinced it would be better to split the system contracts, giving the integration work and assembly of the complete missile to Rockwell and the IMU to Northrop.

Northrop's Electronics Division did well until IMU production was increased; unfortunately, at the same time, Northrop's electronics specialist, David Ferguson, fresh from MIT where research began on the guidance system, was promoted to Senior Vice President of Northrop and moved away from day-to-day production problems. With Ferguson's expertise sitting at a desk in another building, quality control suffered. Production also fell behind schedule, and to catch up, short cuts were made in quality testing. In essence, they kept testing faulty components until they found a good one, instead of determining what was going wrong in their fabrication. Delivery of completed IMU's were delayed and some delivered IMU's failed in Air Force tests after assembly into the MX missile.

The problem became public knowledge when Congressional hearings disclosed serious problems with the MX guidance system. Northrop management was criticized on television in testimony by Les Aspen, Chairman of the House Armed Services Committee, who, in the presence of CEO Tom Jones on *60 Minutes*, made the startling assertion, "So far as we know, the MX missile could land on Chicago." Within the week Jones moved Ferguson back to a hands-on position personally overseeing IMU production and quality control; however, this move came too late to avoid continuing unfavorable publicity, and when the Air Force withheld contract payments totalling $130 million because of problems in late deliveries of the IMU, questions were raised regarding Northrop's financial position. There had already been concern over the company's finances after payments on the ATF Stealth bomber were suspended when Northrop failed an Air Force review of its purchasing system at the Pico Rivera Advanced Systems Division, where ATB components were produced. Following these disclosures, and after the severe drop in the stock market in late 1987, Northrop stock plummeted from its previous high of $50 to a low of close to $25 a share.

While the company was not facing serious financial difficulties, the write-off of losses from the MX and ATB programs, plus the prior $700 million loss written off earlier when the F–20 *Tigershark* program was dropped, greatly depressed earnings. The losses caused securities analysts to raise questions as to whether Northrop management could maintain control over the corporation and continue receiving support from the hundreds of Northrop common stock shareholders. One analyst commented on the ominous possibilities when he said, "It is a dangerous position for the company if it wants to remain autonomous."

Hostile takeovers had become common during the stock market boom period of the mid-1980s, and with Northrop stock selling at a fraction of its true book value, the fortuitous opening for an opportunistic investor syndicate, or even a contemporary Floyd Odlum, might be too great to ignore. It had already been the experience of others in the aircraft industry, as Carl Icahn, with no previous interest or experience in aviation, took over TWA. The Northrop Corporation, with its many profitable divisions, would be a worthy purchase to an investor primarily interested in making a quick profit by splitting up the company and selling off its assets.

The unfavorable financial publicity caused Les Daly, Northrop's Senior Vice President for Public Affairs, to announce, "The company has had a standard defense against hostile takeover for several years." Nevertheless, Joseph Campbell of Paine Weber observed, "Loss of control has a basis of disappointed shareholders and a low stock price. I am reviewing carefully the Northrop bylaws and certificate of incorporation to determine how vulnerable they could be to a hostile takeover."

As one of the founding directors, I participated in organizing the original Northrop Aircraft Company as a standard California corporation in 1939, when we had no fear of a takeover; even then, Jack Northrop made his feelings quite clear, that he wanted the company incorporated in such a way that no single outside entity could control it. According to the original papers of incorporation, whoever controls a majority of the voting common stock can elect the board of directors, who in turn appoint company officers and run the business. A common means of protecting current management from hostile takeover is for the company to buy its own shares and retire them. This is in itself a risky endeavor, because large amounts of money must be borrowed, often resulting in severe financial problems and preventing the use of company funds in long-range development programs. Northrop management made it known that it is ready to do whatever is necessary, for not only would control of the corporation be at stake, but public criticism of Northrop's performance on Air Force contracts, resulting in Congressional criticism and political demands to divide up ATB Stealth bomber production, would mean much to the future of Northrop as a major aerospace corporation.

Ironically, Tom Jones faces the same serious problems which confronted Jack Northrop over forty years ago. In 1988, it is Rockwell International, not Consolidated Vultee, who would benefit from changes made in procurement of both the MX guidance system and the ATB B–2 Stealth bomber, which was designed as the next generation bomber to replace Rockwell's already obsolete B–1B bomber, designed before stealth was considered a primary requirement. In early 1987, as the B–1B neared the end of its original production contract, political pressures were mounted by Rockwell to keep their Palmdale final assembly line alive, delivering more B–1Bs. Should Rockwell have succeeded, fewer Northrop ATB B–2 Stealth bombers would have been ordered, or none at all, setting the stage for a repeat of the unfortunate cancellation of the Northrop YB–49 flying wing bomber over 40 years ago. Another Northrop flying wing would become a political victim of government procurement practices that do not always deliver the best military aircraft for the nation's security.

Another worry to Northrop hovers on the horizon. Just as President Truman's budger reductions forty years ago forced cancellation of the YB–49, it may be determined within the year that after new strategic arms control treaties have been negotiated with the Soviet Union, fewer long-range strategic weapons will be needed, causing cancellation not only of the stealth bomber, but the entire MX missile program as well.

Tom Jones and his able management team, face many of the same problems Jack Northrop did in dealing with Northrop's single most important customer, the Federal Government and its military agencies. Only the airplanes are different, half a century later. It has always been a struggle for corporate survival in a dangerous world, a struggle made perhaps more difficult as Northrop enters the future in a possibly peaceful world.

18

STEALTH AND THE FLYING WING

What some observers have described as a "Luke Skywalker-type jet," the ATF (Advanced Tactical Fighter) radar evading, Stealth fighter plane, has won a contract for Northrop as one of two prime contractors—along with Lockheed—for the Air Force. The fine print in the contract may have intrigued Tom Jones more than anyone else. In a statement about the contract, Colonel Albert C. Piccirillo, ATF system program director, indicated that he must have been reading Northrop's proposal for the F–20 *Tigershark* and the credo Jones had previously outlined to his staff in a memo years before. The colonel wanted Northrop and other contractors to stay within the fixed price quoted in the contract. Piccirillo also explained that the flexibility in contract provisions would enable Northrop to design and build aircraft unfettered by the Pentagon bureaucracy that in the past had often enforced accepted theories and regimented aerospace research. Northrop and their partner would have the opportunity to break out into areas of technology and production techniques that Northrop had long considered the only way of producing aircraft. With this new Pentagon credo, building the ATF would be easy with Tom Jones in charge. He had already begun.

Another aspect of this new opportunity to compete with General Dynamics-Convair was knowing that the Air Force wanted the new ATF to ultimately replace the F–16 for striking ground targets, as well as replacing other older aircraft in Navy and Marine Corps inventories. Perhaps Northrop aircraft could again be part of the Air Force frontline inventory. Herbert Rogers of General Dynamics–Convair said of the ATF, "[It] is the only new fighter program that we can see all the way into the distant future." The program is assuredly one of the most important Pentagon contracts ever awarded. If Northrop successfully develops the winning plane, thousands of jobs for southern California are assured for more than a decade. This will propel Northrop into the preeminent ranks of aerospace giants. The Air Force wants to buy 750 ATF Stealth fighters at $35 million each, in a program worth a total of more than $36 billion.

The primary function of the ATF will be to knock out enemy fighters and airborne warning and control systems, protecting ground forces and clearing the skies for other aircraft. The ATF mission also includes air superiority. It is going to fly supersonic: very high, very fast, and very far. The Air Force wants a fighter that cannot be seen, that has twice the combat range of current aircraft, that can turn in half the space, take off in less than 2,000 feet, and incorporate advanced trouble check systems which will determine maintenance problems by plugging into a computer. The plane will require only a minimum of personnel on the ground to repair it and keep it flying. It will use new technology that Northrop has in development to pioneer tactics in air combat. While the airplane will be almost invisible on radar, it will fly like a fighter, and if seen, fight accordingly. The new offensive fighter will be needed to counter two Soviet supersonic, all-weather fighters, the MiG–29 *Fulcrum* and the SU–27 *Flanker.*

Describing the demonstration/validation phase of the ATF program, Colonel Piccirillo said, "The Air Force will consider renegotiating any single ATF requirement that is found to be a design-to-cost driver. The service is serious about its $35 million unit flyaway cost goal." Until now the ATF teams were only defining roles, keeping proprietary secrets from each other, but now that contracts were issued they could get down to work. Northrop and McDonnell Douglas were soon conferring, assessing specific areas in which the two risk-sharing partners could share advanced technology to further the program.

Piccirillo himself speculated that the ATF program would benefit from both companies' collaboration on the Navy's F/A–18 *Hornet* strike fighter, the Northrop YF–17 derivative that both have been producing for years. Although security controls on ATF shared information will be considerably more strict, the companies' well-established management and electronic data exchange systems can be easily adapted to operate accordingly, yet without bureaucratic restrictions. This is an ability that Northrop prizes, since swift internal communications and shared data between engineering specialists is a Northrop trademark in designing more for less.

In announcing the 50-month, $691 million ATF contract, Air Force Secretary Edward C. Aldridge Jr., said Northrop will be allowed to decide "the best way to introduce the engine into the aircraft," indicating some of the open, flexible features of the contract. Northrop will decide whether to design its aircraft with a common engine bay perhaps accepting a degree of performance loss or with differences in inlets and other features to optimize each engine installation. The engines will be required to power the ATF at sustained speeds of twice the speed of sound at 50,000 feet altitude and higher. The ATF will be made largely of non-metal composite, radar-absorbing materials, with an array of new technology, including radar-evading devices. The radar's field of view, to be much wider than current aircraft, will also be treated flexibly, with consideration of alternatives where it might make sense to relax contract requirements. Other design features would be balanced against their cost and weight, with consideration of adverse aircraft performance that might occur. It is expected that forty to forty-five percent of the cost of the ATF program will involve electronics rather than airframe.

It was evident right from the beginning that this was not the kind of Air Force contract that had resulted in so many flying compromises in past years. In their contract proposal, Northrop had already defined fallback positions to be initiated if technologically risky elements of the ATF designs didn't work out. Northrop also had a great advantage in five years of design and development work on the Advanced Technology Bomber (ATB), the Stealth bomber now being assembled in the Mojave Desert at Northrop's Edwards Air Force Base facility, a lonely building on the edge of the desert runway. Problems encountered on the Stealth bomber would be of considerable help in resolving technological problems in the Stealth fighter. In the light of recent past experience, it was obvious that Northrop would emphasize risk reduction during the next four years of the ATF contract for an aircraft that would probably be the last Air Force weapon to be a subsonic as well as supersonic fighter.

Northrop would also be keeping an eye and ear on what Rockwell International was doing with their X–31 fighter contract, a concept by the Pentagon to make close-in air combat viable. In some ways this would be a return to the dog fight days of 1918. In recent years greater emphasis has been placed on fighting at long range with missiles, beyond visual contact (BVC), calling on the aircraft's ability to detect an enemy with powerful radar. No guns in the conventional sense would be needed, but an internal weapon is expected to be installed on the Northrop ATF.

Rockwell may have lost the ATF competition to Northrop and Lockheed by placing their emphasis on what they called the next generation fighter, beyond even the ATF, where maneuverability would be an asset. Northrop may have won with an emphasis on stealth characteristics and powerful radar, yet there is considerable evidence that BVC combat may be something that actually does not exist, that all aerial flights, if they continue at all, will quickly degenerate into an old-fashioned dogfight. Critics of BVC combat also speak of the basic problem of communications, of whether the target is actually the enemy. Some systems, used to identify friend or foe are notoriously unreliable and vulnerable to jamming or deception.

Unfortunate experiences from Vietnam, during which a number of U.S. planes were shot down by friendly fire, caused the Pentagon to impose a rule—followed ever since—that aircraft be clearly identified visually before any missiles are launched. Success rates of long-range missiles have also left much to be desired. According to a Congressional Budget Office analysis, the long-range *Sparrow* missile scored only seven successful kills in the 1973 Arab-Israeli War. The short-range *Sidewinder* missile scored 200 kills. The concern will not be academic in future conflicts, as high-performance aircraft begin to look more and more alike. The most recent Soviet and U.S. fighters, the Sukhoi SU–27 and the F–15 *Eagle*, look like copies of each other. From a few miles away they are indistinguishable.

This is where close-in combat and high maneuverability will resume the important role played in past conflicts. One critic has said, "If you really believe in BVC, then you don't need any maneuverability at all—all you need to do is get a C–5 cargo plane and load it full of missiles." It will be up to Northrop and their partner, McDonnell Douglas, to come up with an invisible BVC ATF that will have the maneuverability of an F–20 *Tigershark* or F–16 *Falcon* with onboard computerized combat ability to create 1918–style fighter aces in the 1990s.

The challenge is awesome. The winner will receive more than a contract. The Northrop ATF, designated by the Air Force as YF–23A, will be expected to fill close-in air support and battlefield interdiction

roles, fight deep within enemy territory, intercept high-flying bombers with long-range missiles, and be able to operate from battle-
damaged runways no longer than two or three thousand feet. It is a
challenge that Tom Jones will accept with full understanding of his
responsibility, for the winner of the next conventional war may well be
determined in Hawthorne.

Northrop has another aircraft, already designed and off the drawing boards, assembled, ready for test flying by the Air Force. It is a
bomber that cannot be seen. In the name of national security, billions
of dollars have been spent on the Northrop B–2 Stealth aircraft, the
Advanced Technology Bomber (ATB) that hopefully will be invisible to
a future enemy. As the *Washington Post* put it, "What you don't see is
what you get." The Pentagon has also tried to keep the ATB invisible
from the public. Already concealed from most political accounting are
at least fifty Lockheed XST strike fighters that probably cost about
$40 to $50 million each (known as Project Harvey, after the invisible
six-foot rabbit that haunted James Stewart in the movie of the same
name); a new General Dynamics cruise missile program that is expected to cost about $7 billion (a Stealth missile for use by Rockwell's
B–1B bomber); and the most expensive warplane ever built, Northrop's secret ATB Stealth bomber, with projected program costs between $35 billion and—according to hostile competitors—$80 billion.
Over the past six years U.S. Air Force total ATB expenditures have
been about $12.5 billion. The only specific cost data the Defense
Department has ever released publicly about the Stealth bomber
reveals that they plan to buy 132 aircraft for deployment in the 1990s
at a cost of $36.6 billion dollars—$278 million each, but most analysts
say that would only be the beginning if all the B–52s and B–1Bs are
going to be replaced.

According to the *Wall Street Journal*, Northrop received a Pentagon contract in early 1988, estimated at $2 billion, to begin produc-
tion of Stealth B–2 bombers. The awarding of the contract would seem
to indicate that delays and cost overruns might not be as bad as
rumored, and that assembly of the first nuclear bomb-carrying Stealth
has never been far behind schedule. There had been speculation about
whether the Air Force would award the production contract exclusively to Northrop, or split it between Northrop and another company. With Northrop having received production monies, it would
seem that the Pentagon is sufficiently satisfied with progress on fixing

bugs in the plane to move on to production, with Northrop as the prime contractor.

There was a time, a few years back, when all was in doubt, when partisan demagoguery by Air Force generals and Rockwell International lobbyists attempted to scuttle Northrop's advanced B–2 flying wing penetration bomber in favor of the already outdated Rockwell B–1. Cancellation of the B–1 bomber by President Carter precipitated an aggressive scramble by the Air Force and Rockwell to keep the B–1 program alive, in one form or another, by any means possible, including cancellation of Northrop's Stealth bomber. There was the possibility of a replay of the expensive 1948 cancellation of Northrop's first flying wing bomber, the YB–49.

Fortunately, from Northrop's point of view, the Pentagon had classified the Stealth bomber a top secret "black" program with appropriated monies hidden within various parts of the budget. Opponents trying to kill the Stealth B–2 and replace it with the B–1 operated at a serious disadvantage—neither the Air Force nor Northrop would admit that a Stealth program even existed, much less as an airplane under construction. Comparing the B–1 with the B–2 was not possible, because, as an exasperated Rockwell executive said, "I can't make a comparison with the Stealth because I'm not allowed to know anything about it." Even the thousands of peace activists picketing in every major city at the time did not know of the Stealth bomber—only the B–1 received their noisy opposition. The preferred way of keeping the millions of Stealth development dollars away from political scrutiny and public criticism was to keep the Stealth secret. It was not a matter of *national* security, but of *congressional* security.

While newly-elected President Reagan had promised in his campaign to authorize construction of the B–1B (a modified B–1), during the early months of his first term there was considerable debate in the new administration as to whether to skip consideration of the B–1B in favor of Northrop's B–2 Stealth. Pentagon brass would have none of this, but soon found themselves lobbying for both bombers so they could keep at least one. The Rockwell B–1B was backed by Republicans and the House. The Northrop Stealth B–2 was pushed by Democrats and the Senate. Air Force generals found themselves lobbying with rival political factions and voters living near bomber bases for two different bombers, arguing that the B–1B was "a bird in the hand," and would be available first, with the more advanced B–2 becoming operational at a later date. Active duty officers in uniform appeared in Senate and House hallways, lobbying Congress in direct violation of Title 18 of the U.S. Code, which forbids members of the executive branch from arm-twisting Congress and trading bomber bases for votes for their preferred bomber. The military-industrial complex, described by President Eisenhower many years ago, demonstrated its capability within the American system of organized irresponsibility.

Defense Secretary Weinberger was at first opposed to the B–1B, claiming that not building a hundred B–1Bs would save over $20 billion with little strategic loss, since Northrop had promised delivery of the Stealth B–2 by 1987. The industrial and political competition was not ended by Reagan's eventual decision to build 100 B–1Bs. Rockwell wanted to build 100 more and sign a new contract before their Palmdale assembly line shut down. Northrop rushed to deliver the first B–2 Stealth at an earlier date, and thereby block additional funding of B–1Bs. Rockwell hired one of Reagan's close associates, Michael Deaver, for $100,000, to persuade the administration to buy the second hundred aircraft, and Deaver was indicted and convicted for his unsuccessful efforts. Tom Jones, CEO of Northrop and an old personal friend of Reagan, had only to reach for the telephone to offer arguments for his Stealth B–2s. It was a strange way to contract for aircraft to defend the country. Whether either plane was worth their tremendous cost, as part of a strategic deterrent triad, was never debated.

Over half of Northrop's current business is classified, as a consequence of a political philosophy of hiding defense allocations that might be criticized by Congress and slashed from the budget. A better understanding of the Stealth bomber's role in national security could well have been public knowledge if those in Washington who fully supported Stealth bomber expenditures in place of the exorbitant costs of the Rockwell B–1B bomber had only explained the need for stealth while the aircraft was being designed and monies were first appropriated. The last of the already obsolete B–1Bs manufactured by Rockwell International rolled off the final assembly line in Palmdale in January 1988. The first of Northrop's B–2 Stealth bombers flew in the same year.

Under the circumstances, perhaps if the Stealth secret is kept with the Air Force until Northrop's ATB becomes operational, the program will continue to be adequately funded before interceptors, in the form of Congressional defense critics, will be able to shoot it down.

While Northrop may be able to design an aircraft that Soviet air defenses cannot see, it remains to be seen if the bomber is too big to hide from inquiring Senate committees looking for a way to reduce the national deficit.

The Stealth bomber seems to have broad bipartisan support in Congress, so there is little reason to keep the fact of a flying wing Stealth bomber secret, except for traditional military attitudes—if it's new it's secret. While Lockheed's ATF Stealth fighter only flies at night so Soviet spy satellites cannot photograph the new airplane—although scale plastic models of the ATF and ATB can be purchased at your local hobby shop—the first flight of the large Northrop Stealth bomber will be seen immediately by Soviet satellites photographing Edwards Air Force Base on a daily basis. It is Air Force policy to test-fly heavy aircraft only during daylight hours, so the Stealth bomber will be seen as soon as it flies, even if radar doesn't see it.

Air Force Secretary Russell Rourke has said the ATB "is on a smooth glide path" and is "going very, very nicely, and the technology is extraordinarily satisfying." The same year, Secretary of Defense Weinberger said, "The ATB program is on schedule, the technology is well understood and working, and we expect the system to be operational in the early 1990s." The decision for Northrop to produce an operational ATB appears to have been made. "In terms of mission capability," added Weinberger, "the ATB's unique low observable characteristics make it far more survivable than the B–1B."

Northrop has been operating in somewhat of a frenzy in recent years as they've tried to keep the ATB on schedule and away from politicians supporting the B–1B or nothing at all. Full page newspaper advertisements alerted needed engineers working at competitors of superior benefits at Northrop. Hefty inducements were offered to experienced engineers with special skills. On one occasion the personnel department enticed an engineer away from McDonnell Douglas with a $10,000 bonus and twelve percent pay increase. He later returned to his former employer because of the long hours required at the Northrop shop. Overtime work at the stealth Pico Rivera facility, Northrop's Advanced Systems Division, is routine as the company rushes to meet contract schedules.

In July 1986, an Air Force Lockheed C–5A *Galaxy* delivered "a set of wings" (in the case of a flying wing that's almost all of it) to Northrop's new Palmdale facility, site 4. Major parts of the ATB aircraft have been transferred from key subcontractors and Northrop's Pico Rivera, California, plant as assembly of the ATB proceeds apace. The first flying prototype will be tested at Edwards Air Force Base, where a large hanger for "testing of advanced aircraft" has already been completed on the flight line.

Information on the Stealth bomber is not easy to come by. The windowless exterior of the Pico Rivera facility, once a Ford automobile factory, discloses nothing about Northrop's top-secret activities. A story is told of the employee who has become a folklore hero at the plant, according to the *Los Angeles Times*. Several years ago he climbed upon the roof of the plant and painted a vulgar insult in Russian cyrillic lettering, large enough to be visible to the orbiting Soviet satellite on its daily passes over the factory looking for any shred of information about the ATB program. Soviet intelligence agents puzzling over their collected photographs of U.S. defense plants received an unexpected greeting from the employees of Northrop. The Pico Rivera site is the largest secret industrial plant in the United States, with 12,000 employees developing and building the revolutionary stealth aircraft.

The configuration of the ATB is no longer a secret. The Northrop ATB Stealth bomber is a flying wing, albeit shaped rather more like an arrowhead than the sweptwing boomerang of Jack Northrop's early designs. Senator Barry Goldwater said so. The aviation trade magazine, *Aviation Week*, confirms the fact. Several Northrop employees interviewed by the *Los Angeles Times* described the bomber's design as awesome. "It looks like a living creature," one said. "I can see why the Air Force is willing to give Northrop all this money. They'll do anything to have it."

Jack anticipated the contemporary delta-shaped flying wing for supersonic flight in a lecture to the Royal Aeronautical Society in London, some forty years ago, in which he described the development of all-wing aircraft, "From the aerodynamic point of view it appears that with the delta wing it is possible to eliminate a substantial portion of the [sound barrier] wave resistance and thus realize fairly favorable life-drag rations at supersonic speeds."

High performance characteristics of a Stealth bomber are not necessarily measured in terms of speed—it need not fly fast. It's primary function, other than to carry bombs, is to remain invisible. The aircraft is not intended to "surprise" the enemy, it is intended to do its job without being detected—without the enemy knowing what hit it—then it is to turn around and get out. The plane must have a long range, but except for turning around fast, it need not be as maneuverable as a fighter. Its defensive armament need be little more than short-range missiles like the *Sidewinder*, since if successful as a Stealth design, far distant fighters would not be able to find the bomber with their airborne radar. Only those close-up would have a shot. A new sophisticated radar, called Over-The-Horizon-Backscatter, that bounces its radar signals off the ionosphere, would be able to detect Stealth bombers, but only in mid-journey, not near the target. High flying aircraft with look-down radar might see the ATB, but onboard electronic counter-measures would be sending out false radar echoes and confusing infrared light to make the ATBs large triangular silhouette fuzzy when viewed from above. As if to anticipate problems posed by enemy radar, Northrop is also involved in developing a tactical cruise missile, called *Tacit Rainbow*, to search out and destroy radar transmitters that might be searching for their stealth aircraft.

Stealth is not a simple magic trick, but a means of designing an airplane so that its radar signature is reduced to a minimum. It can have no large flat surfaces, such as fuselage sides and vertical fins, wings and tail surfaces that meet at right angles, or large engine intakes and exhausts. All of these trap and then reflect radar waves. Bombs and fuel tanks hanging from the wings also create highly visible reflectors for radar emissions prowling the skies. Open skin joints and vents, gaps, sharp corners, and sudden changes in reflectivity of the airplane's surface produce radar echoes. Stealth airplanes must have a smooth and seamless finish, like a fine sculpture of polished marble. "We've never contended that stealthy means invisible," said Air Force General Lawrence Skantze. "It means difficult to detect—and more difficult to track."

To have a long range, the Stealth bomber must be a highly efficient aircraft, with low drag and large fuel capacity. Requirements for a Stealth bomber, as detailed by the Air Force, sounded familiar, and they were. Northrop had designed and built an aircraft meeting the same specifications over four decades ago. It was Jack Northrop's concept for a flying wing bomber, designated by the Air Force YB–49, that first flew forty years ago, on October 1, 1947. In fact, the bomber had already been purchased by the Air Force, and tested for its invisibility to radar, and radar at the time couldn't see it. Northrop's solution for the new ATB was quite simple—design and build a more efficient flying wing, constructed of modern composite materials, powered with the latest jet engine, and incorporating new electronic gear, airborne radar, inflight sensors and high-speed automatic flight control systems.

Composite materials are high-tech fibers of carbon or boron embedded into lightweight plastic, producing fabricating materials stronger than steel, yet lighter than aluminum. These graphite composites are similar to materials used in fishing poles, sailboats, and secondary structures in airliners—anywhere that weight-saving is more important than cost, which is their drawback, for composites often cost ten times more than aluminum, mostly because of the elaborate production techniques required.

It is the advanced design, combined with composite materials, and carrying "star wars" electronics, that make the ATB a plane of the future. As Jack would have described the ATB, it is the ultimate airplane—the most efficient possible—the last great airplane to fly in the earth's atmosphere, before rocket powered ships take off for space. When Jimmy Carter's Defense Secretary, Harold Brown, first announced the ATB program, he described the plane as "a major technological advance." It will be the Northrop Corporation's crowning achievement and the ultimate accolade to Jack's design genius.

In 1976, a letter to Jack Northrop from the National Aeronautics and Space Administration (NASA) confirmed a study by aeronautical engineers and their own staff that the flying wing concept had decided advantages over conventional designs in load-carrying ability and fuel economy at high subsonic speeds. The NASA study also pointed out advantages of span loading—spreading out payloads throughout the wing span—inherent in a flying wing, but not possible in the fuselage of a large cargo or passenger plane of conventional design.

The letter from Robert Frosch, NASA Administrator, commented on Jack's recent meeting with members of the NASA aeronautical research staff, saying how in a field as dynamic as aviation, "we sometimes lose track of important historical lessons.

As you know, our studies of technology needs for potential future large cargo/logistics aircraft have led us to investigations of span-loaded configurations during which we have, in effect, rediscovered the flying wing. Obviously, we recognized the pioneering Northrop work in that area as an essential source of information, and in the course of our investigations we reexamined considerable NACA B–35/YB–49 wind tunnel data. Our analyses confirmed your much earlier conviction as to the load-carrying and efficiency advantages of this design approach, and studies performed for us by the major manufacturers of large airplanes have further corroborated these findings.

We do not yet know when the commercial market or military requirements will create demands for new long-range cargo carriers. We are continuing our related research and technology efforts, and have as yet found no reason to disagree with you as to the potential benefits of the tailless span-loader approach for such applications.

The letter was an exciting affirmation of Jack's vision. Within the year a number of the principal commercial cargo and passenger aircraft manufacturers, including Boeing, Lockheed, and McDonnell Douglas, were investigating the feasibility of flying wings for future commercial applications in the twenty-first century. A typical flying wing concept was a Boeing "span-loader," essentially a flying wing that would carry a half-million pounds of cargo inside a thick wing with a 250-foot span some 5,000 miles at subsonic speeds. Some variations of the concept envisioned wingspans of 500 feet, and a takeoff weight nearing 5 million pounds, powered by as many as twelve turbofan jet engines of 52,000-pounds thrust.

Scientific papers and technical memoranda on the design of flying wing cargo aircraft began to multiply. The preliminary design department of the Boeing Commercial Airplane Company prepared a report on technical and economic aspects of "sweptwing span-distributed load concepts" for civil and military air cargo transports. R. V. Turriziani of Kentron International investigated YB–49 baseline studies for use in advanced technology applications. McDonnell Douglas evaluated the technical and economic aspects of "span-loaded cargo aircraft" concepts. NASA prepared design criteria for a "flying wing cargo airplane."

Flying wings have not been forgotten by aviation enthusiasts wanting to build and fly their own planes. There must be tens of thousands of ultralight flying wing hang gliders in the world, some powered, most not, many carrying such nicknames as Minibat and SuperWing. In 1987, as the big flying wing began to take shape again in Palmdale, Gilbert Davis of Boise, Idaho, decided to build his own, with the help of a talented old Northrop protege by the name of Joe Rosales. The Daviswing is an up-to-date version of Northrop's prototype N–1M, retractable geared, with a single pusher mounted engine, constructed of composite materials. In flight, the Davis flying wing is said to be responsive, fairly stable, and exhilarating, with little that is tricky or objectionable in its handling. Its yaw instability is no more than that exhibited by the V-tail general aviation Beechcraft. Davis wants everybody to fly one, and intends on manufacturing kits for building your own flying wing at home.

Meanwhile, a group of volunteers out in Chino, California, home of Ed Maloney's Planes of Fame Museum, are resurrecting a rare relic of Northrop's pioneering days, a 1942 Northrop N–9M prototype flying wing, one of only two survivors, the other being a non-flying restoration in the Smithsonian Air & Space Museum of the original N–1M flying wing. Ed Maloney intends to fly his. He found it in the Edwards Air Force Base boneyard in very bad condition, the wood parts rotten, not much more than junk. Panel by rib by aileron by longeron, the wood and aluminum boomerang from the past is being returned to flight. Say the workers restoring Northrop's experimental dream, "Our concern is to rebuild this airplane and get it back up in the air as a flying memorial to Jack Northrop."

A dinner honoring Jack Northrop and Donald Douglas Sr., sponsored by the Boy Scouts of America, was held in Los Angeles in 1978. Both of these aviation pioneers had made substantial contributions to the scout movement, and a boy scout camp in the San Gabriel mountains is named for Northrop. Up to this time, in the years of his retirement, Jack had shunned the limelight, and avoided discussing his personal role in the development of aviation, telling interviewers he was "just lucky." He called himself a "technically advanced high school graduate," and no one questioned him.

When Donald Douglas was asked to comment about his friendly rival, Jack Northrop, he said, "Don't let the old buzzard kid you. When a guy like this starts getting modest, it's time to look out. Any formal education he lacked he didn't need. Jack Northrop was a man with a million ideas—all of them good. He was an innovator and a dreamer whose innovations succeeded and whose dreams became real. There is a little of him in every airplane that flies."

When Jack rose to speak he was embarrassed by the flattery. After complimenting Douglas on his own major accomplishments in aviation, Northrop said, "They called it the golden age of aviation, that period between World War I and World War II, when California was the developing ground for almost every advancement in the field. Let me add amen to the thought. It was before the computer age;

before the growth of giant corporations where every decision is made by a committee. We were never told, 'You can't do this or don't experiment with that.' No one was big enough to say such things and make them stick. So we did as we pleased—and what we pleased was to make better airplanes."

Not long after the Boy Scout dinner, Jack began to lose his health. Up until then he had been able to get around by himself, in spite of the sad loss of his wife, Margaret, in 1977, which came as a great blow. They had sold their home at Hope Ranch and moved into an apartment near the Santa Barbara Biltmore Hotel. After Margaret's death Jack lived with his son, John, and his wife Mary.

He missed playing golf at the Valley Club in Santa Barbara, where I occasionally played with him, enjoying his company. He rode a cart around the course, but was still competitive, even as the years began to catch up with him. On these occasions Jack was reticent about talking about why the YB–49 flying wing bomber had been so suddenly cancelled by the Air Force, but his continued disappointment was evident, and he felt that his career had been prematurely terminated by this unfortunate incident. However, after the PBS television interview in which the facts came out for the first time, and the public finally learned of the sad events, Jack seemed to become more cheerful.

Six months before he was hospitalized in October 1980, an old friend and executive of Northrop Corporation drove to Jack Northrop's home and picked him up for a visit to his old company, now spread out in numerous divisions and plants in the Los Angeles basin. They drove to the Advance Systems Division in the Palos Verde Hills, where research and engineering work was in progress on new products and aircraft for Northrop. He wanted Jack to know about the important advanced thinking he had inspired so many years before.

They looked at drawings together, as Jack's frail, thin features contemplated the amazing sight before his eyes. It was almost as if the engineering drawings spread before him were restorative in some magical way. Sitting quietly in the wheelchair, he seemed to become more erect and alert as a smile crossed his face. Months before, Jack had lost his ability to speak, but it was clear to those at his side that his mind was as bright as ever. He was very pleased. He was looking at drawings of a new flying wing. A long-range, high speed, flying wing aircraft was on the drawing boards. He saw that his flying wing would fly again, and as a Northrop aircraft. It was the Stealth B–2.

With these thoughts assuredly uppermost in his still-agile mind during a six-week stay in the Verdugo Hills Hospital, near his son's home in La Canada, California, Jack Northrop died, at ease and pleased, a smile on his face, on February 18, 1981. He was eighty-six years old.

While Jack spent much of his life designing warplanes, he was a peaceful man. In some ways he was disappointed that the art of flying, often in airplanes incorporating his inventions, was in part made possible by monies from a government that must defend itself in a war-infested world. That he was dependent on the success of his warplanes was a contradiction to Jack. He did think of a world in the future that was more stable, where military defense work no longer received top priority. As he sketched drawings for flying wing civilian airliners, he thought of the time when his Northrop company would no longer be dependent on defense contracts for survival. It would be in the future that the hopes and aspirations of Jack Northrop might finally be achieved. Since Northrop opened its doors in an abandoned hotel building in Hawthorne in 1939, the millennium had not been reached.

At an earlier time, Jack Northrop had said, "I'll be satisfied when somebody does something with the flying wing to prove how good it is. I think this is the only reason I am still here in life, because I still believe that this will happen."

The Reagan Administration has approached the North Atlantic allies with an offer to develop and produce jointly a jet fighter for the 21st century. The project, known as Hornet 2000, as outlined by high-level Pentagon and U.S. aviation industry executives to West Germany, Britain, Italy, Spain, and France, proposes that they join with the United States in developing an advanced version of the Northrop designed F/A–18 *Hornet* fighter-attack aircraft, and end their own fighter development programs. The plan is both audacious and unusual. For the first time the United States has expressed a willingness to develop and manufacture a new military fighter in collaboration with foreign companies. The Pentagon said that an upgraded *Hornet* can be built at a cost of roughly $25 million per plane, compared to $55 to $60 million for one European-designed and produced figher aircraft. Tom Jones could have told them so years ago. Perhaps Northrop is already pulling their F–20 *Tigershark* out of mothballs.

APPENDIX

35th WILBUR WRIGHT MEMORIAL LECTURE
THE DEVELOPMENT OF ALL-WING AIRCRAFT

John K. Northrop

The thirty-fifth Wilbur Wright Memorial Lecture was delivered before the Society by Mr. John K. Northrop on Thursday, May 29, 1947 at 6 p.m. in the Lecture Hall of the Institution of Civil Engineers, Great George Street, London. The chair was taken by Sir Frederick Handley Page, C.B.E., President of the Society.

The President: They had now reached the highlight of the 1946–47 session, the Wilbur Wright Memorial Lecture. It seemed incredible to think that these memorial lectures had been going on for 35 years, no sooner was one over than another one came round. The Lecture was usually given in alternate years by an Englishman and an American, and this year they were fortunate in having as their lecturer that distinguished American, Mr. John K. Northrop.

Before introducing Mr. Northrop he had another duty to perform. As was customary on the occasion of the Wilbur Wright Memorial Lecture, as President, he had cabled Orville Wright as follows:—

"On May 29th 1947 your distinguished countryman John K. Northrop will read the 35th Wilbur Wright Memorial Lecture on The Development of All-Wing Aircraft. The reading of this annual lecture is a constant reminder of those early years of this century when you and your brother laid down so clearly, yet so simply, the firm foundations of the art of flying upon which must ultimately be built that structure for world peace which can never be destroyed."

He had received the following reply:—

Heartiest greetings to the Society and to all assembled to hear my esteemed fellow countryman Northrop deliver the 35th Wilbur Wright Lecture. I believe Mr. Northrop will bring to you a good message on matters useful in peace.

ORVILLE WRIGHT.

243

He had also sent the following cablegram to the Institute of the Aeronautical Sciences:

On behalf of the Council and Members of the Royal Aeronautical Society I send you our greetings on the occasion of the reading of the 35th Wilbur Wright Memorial Lecture by your distinguished member John K. Northrop on The Development of All-Wing Aircraft.

They had cabled in reply:—

On the occasion of the reading of the Wilbur Wright Memorial Lecture by our distinguished American contemporary John Northrop the Officers and Council of the Institute of the Aeronautical Sciences extend heartiest greetings to the Royal Aeronautical Society. We are all looking forward to a period of greater collaboration between the Societies on either side of the Atlantic.

P. R. Bassett, President

He now had great pleasure in introducing Mr. John K. Northrop. Mr. Northrop was well-known on both sides of the Atlantic for his work on all-wing aircraft. Indeed, he was one of the great pioneers in that field and probably knew more about this particular type of airplane than anyone. He was chief designer, President and everything else—in fact, he was the Northrop Aviation Company. He had been designing and developing the all-wing type since about 1923. This evening they were to have the pleasure and privilege of hearing from Mr. Northrop something of the difficulties and successes connected with that development.

He had pleasure in calling on Mr. Northrop to deliver his lecture.

One cannot undertake the presentation of one of the long series of Wilbur Wright Memorial Lectures without a deep sense of appreciation of the tremendous contributions made by the illustrious group of scientists and engineers who have given such great distinction to this event. The happy precedent of inviting individuals from without the United Kingdom to make this presentation in alternate years has gone far in the past toward improving the understanding, cooperative effort and fellowship of the English-speaking peoples, and I am deeply honored to have been among those chosen to further this very worthy cause.

INTRODUCTION

In choosing the title, "The Development of All-Wing Aircraft," as the subject of my lecture I run some risk of being accused of writing a company history rather than a paper of the broad scope ordinarily presented before this time-honored institution. This is far from my intent, but being sincerely convinced that the all-wing airplane is a valuable step in the development of aeronautics, and desiring to contribute a maximum amount to the available data in the limited time at my disposal, my paper must be confined largely to experience gained by our company in its work on this subject.

Outside the efforts of the Horten Brothers in Germany there has, until a comparatively recent time, been little physical accomplishment in the development of the all-wing airplane except by our company. The contemporary Horten development has been fully described in technical reports emanating from Germany since the close of the European war. In many instances the Horten conclusions were surprisingly similar to our own. Their work was not carried so far, however, and I doubt that they had the sympathetic and responsible governmental backing and the resultant opportunities for development accorded us.

In considering the development of all-wing aircraft I would like first to distinguish between all-wing and tailless airplanes. Most tailless airplanes are not all-wing by our definition. There is a tremendous background of development in tailless types, which has been fully reported by Mr. A. R. Weyl in *Aircraft Engineering*. These articles outlined a surprising number of reasons for building tailless aircraft which have motivated the various designers and constructors over the years. Only one of the many advantages to be gained through such development has inspired our work, namely improved efficiency of the airplane.

More recently, through the rapid development of turbo-jet power plants, a second advantage has arisen, which is the elimination of design difficulties attendant upon the impinging of high speed high-temperature jets on tail surfaces. Still more recently a third possible advantage has appeared, this being the (as yet unproved) probability that problems of stability in the transonic and supersonic ranges may be somewhat more simple of solution in the tailless type than in the older and more conventional arrangements.

Only the first of these basic advantages, namely that of improved efficiency, has been readily apparent over a number of years and, as a result, virtually all our efforts have been directed toward the reduction of parasite drag and the improvement of the ratio of the maximum trimmed lift coefficient (C_{Lmax}) to the minimum drag coefficient (C_{Dmin}). It is natural, then that we were not interested particularly in tailless airplanes as such; if we could not eliminate vertical tail surfaces, fuselages, and a substantial portion of interference drag, the gains to be made seemed not worth the effort necessary for their accomplishment.

Our work, therefore, through the years has been directed solely to all-wing aircraft, by which I mean a type of airplane in which all of the functions of a satisfactory flying machine are disposed and accommodated within the outline of the aerofoil itself. Of course, we have not as yet built any pure all-wing aircraft. All have had some excrescences, such as propellers, propeller drive shaft housings, jet nozzles, gun turrets and the like. We have, however, built a number of airplanes in which the minimum parasite drag coefficient has been reduced to approximately half that ordinarily attained in the best conventional aircraft of like size and purpose, and in some of the designs completed and tested the excrescences and variations from the aerofoil contour have been responsible for less than 20 percent of the minimum airplane drag.

BASIC ASSUMPTIONS

A surprisingly large number of people, both within and without the aircraft industry, still appear to question the economic reasons for going to all the trouble to build an all-wing airplane. "Sure," they say, "after a lot of practice people can learn to walk on their hands, but it's most uncomfortable and unnatural, so why do it when nothing is gained thereby?" Actually, there are startling gains to be made in the aerodynamic and structural efficiency of an all-wing type, provided that certain basic requirements can be fulfilled by the type under question. These requirements can be simply stated as follows:

First, the airplane must be large enough so that the all-wing principle can be fully utilized. This is a matter closely related to the density of the elements comprising the weight empty and the useful load to be carried within the wing.

The dimensions of the average human body may also at times be the limiting factor but, ordinarily, in the larger types of transport or bombardment aircraft in which we are most interested, it will be found that excessive sizes are not necessary in order to secure, within a wing of reasonable thickness ratio, adequate volume for a commercial cargo or bomb load plus the necessary fuel.

The extremes explored and satisfactorily flown to date in our experience range from a "buzz" bomb having a span of 29 feet, in which the warhead was cast as a portion of the aerofoil to the 172-foot XB–35 long-range bomber airplane. The buzz bomb was practical because of the comparatively high specific gravity of the warhead, plus the fact that the configuration permitted almost all of the wing to be used as a fuel tank. The XB–35, on the other hand, is considerably larger than would be necessary to provide ample space for passenger and crew comfort and ample volume for payload, be it cargo or bombs. It was designed larger than necessary because we desired to keep the wing loading comparatively low in this first large experimental venture. It has a normal gross weight of 165,000 lb., an overload gross weight of 221,300 lb., and sufficient volume within the wing envelope so that the maximum gross weight at take-off might well be increased to over 300,000 lb., somewhat over half of which could be devoted to bombs, fuel and miscellaneous payload. It may be seen, therefore, that there is a practical range of size within which the all-wing airplane can be used. If the requirements of space and volume do not permit the full use of the all-wing principle, a rudimentary nacelle may be added without losing its economic advantages.

The second basic requirement is that the all-wing airplane be designed to have sufficient stability and controllability for practical operation as a military or commercial airplane. We believe this requirement has been fully met by hundreds of flights completed with this type, and we are fully convinced of its practicability after having built a dozen different airplanes embodying scores of different configurations incorporating the all-wing principle.

In comparing all-wing and conventional types, we may fairly assume that spans of comparative aircraft having the same gross weight are equal, and as a further simplification we may for the moment neglect compressibility effects in our comparison to the advantages of all-wing and conventional types of large bombardment or transport aircraft having maximum velocities up to approximately 500 m.p.h.

COMPARISON OF MINIMUM DRAG AND MAXIMUM TRIMMED LIFT

Based on these assumptions and on the following proved data on the all-wing type, a comparatively simple analysis of advantages may be made.

The ratio of the minimum parasite drag coefficient (C_{Dmin}) for all-wing airplanes to that for conventional types is approximately 1:2. Minimum drag coefficients for a number of large bomber and transport aircraft such as the B–29, B–24, C–54 and others average approximately .023. The minimum drag coefficients for several all-wing types have been measured both in model and full-scale configurations and vary from less than .010 to about .0113, which is the figure for the XB–35 including armament protuberances, drive shaft housings, rudimentary nacelle for gun emplacements, and so on.

The ratio of maximum trimmed lift coefficient (C_{Lmax}) for all-wing to conventional types is approximately 1.5:2.3. The latter figure is typical for a number of the large airplanes of conventional arrangement previously mentioned. The former is readily attainable in a configuration such as that of the XB–35 and may be subject to considerable improvement through the use of several types of high-lift devices yet to be proved.

For comparative airplanes of the same span and gross weight the selection of the required wing area will depend either on flight conditions, including take-off without flaps, or landing conditions. If the flight conditions govern, the ratio of required wing areas of all-wing to conventional aircraft will be 1:1 because the two wings are equally effective except under conditions of maximum lift. If landing conditions govern, the ratio will be $\frac{2.3}{1.5}$:1, assuming the same landing speed in each case. If take-off with partial flap deflection governs, the ratio will be somewhere between the above two figures.

1. $\dfrac{(D_p)_a}{(D_p)_c} = .50 \times \dfrac{S_a}{S_c}$

$= .50 \times 1.0 = .50$ (flight condition)

$= .50 \times \dfrac{2.3}{1.5} = .77$ (landing condition)

2. $\dfrac{P_a}{P_c} = \dfrac{D_a}{D_c} \times \dfrac{V_a}{V_c} \times \dfrac{D_a}{D_c}$ (at equal speeds)

$D_a = (D_i)_c + (.50 \text{ to } .77) \times (D_p)_c$

$= (1.5 \text{ to } 1.77) \times (D_i)_c$

$D_c = 2(D_i)_c$

Therefore $\dfrac{P_a}{P_c} = \dfrac{1.5}{2}$ to $\dfrac{1.77}{2} = 75\%$ to 88.5%

3. $\dfrac{R_a}{R_c} = \dfrac{P_c}{P_a} = \dfrac{1}{.75}$ to $\dfrac{1}{.885} = 133\%$ to 113%

FIGURE 1

In large all-wing bombers and transports, and to a growing extent in conventional long-range transports as well, the ratio of gross weight at take-off to landing weight will approach 2:1. Therefore flight conditions are likely to govern the selection of wing area more than landing conditions. In the following calculations both extremes are used as indicative of the range of advantage to be gained by the use of the all-wing configuration. Referring to Fig. 1, it may be seen from equation (1) that the total minimum parasite drag of the all-wing airplane in terms of the conventional airplane will vary from 50 percent if flight conditions govern, to 77 percent if landing conditions govern. In this equation $(D_p)_a$ and $(D_p)_c$ represent the parasite drags of all-wing and conventional airplanes while S_a and S_c represent the respective wing areas.

It is a well-known fact, based on the Breguet range formula, that with conventional reciprocating engines and propellers the speed for maximum range is approximately that at which parasite drag and induced drag are equal. Therefore, at the same cruising speed as the conventional airplane the all-wing type will require from 25 percent to 11½ percent less power, as shown in equation (2), and with the same amount of fuel will fly from 33 percent to 13 percent farther, as indicated by equation (3). In these equations P represents power required, and D total drag. V is airplane velocity and R range, with the suffices a and c again denoting the all-wing and conventional configurations. If the all-wing airplane is operated at *its* most economical speed, instead of the most economical speed of the conventional airplane, it will fly 19 percent to 7 percent faster and the range will be from 41 percent to 14 percent greater with the same amount of fuel as indicated in equation (4) of Figure 2.

4. $\dfrac{R_a}{R_c} = \sqrt{\dfrac{(C_{Dp}S_c)}{(C_{Dp}S)_a}} = \sqrt{\dfrac{1.0}{.5}}$ to $\sqrt{\dfrac{1.0}{.77}} = 1.41$ to 1.14

and

$\dfrac{V_a}{V_c} = \sqrt[4]{\dfrac{(C_{Dp}S_c)}{(C_{Dp}S)_a}} = \sqrt[4]{\dfrac{1.0}{.5}}$ to $\sqrt[4]{\dfrac{1.0}{.77}} = 1.19$ to 1.07

5. $\dfrac{P_a}{P_c} = \dfrac{D_a}{D_c}$ (at equal speeds)

$D_a = (D_i)_c + (.50 \text{ to } .77) \times (D_p)_c$

$\quad = (D_i)_c + (.50 \text{ to } .77) \times (D_i)_c \times 4$

and $D_c = (D_i)_c + (D_i)_c \times 4$

Therefore $\dfrac{P_a}{P_c} = \dfrac{1 + (2 \text{ to } 3.08)}{1 + 4} = 60\%$ to $81\frac{1}{2}\%$

6. $\dfrac{R_a}{R_c} = \dfrac{P_c}{P_a} = \dfrac{1.0}{.60}$ to $\dfrac{1.0}{.815} = 166\%$ to 122%

FIGURE 2

ADVANTAGES OF LOW PARASITE DRAG

Under high-speed conditions with any type of power plant the parasite drag becomes a much larger percentage of the total drag than for cruising conditions with reciprocating engines. At high speed the parasite drag may account for 80 percent or more of the total, while the induced drag drops to 20 percent or less. Using an assumed figure of 80 percent parasite drag, which is probably correct to ±10 percent for most aircraft, the power required to drive the all-wing airplane at the same speed as the conventional airplane will be from 40 percent to 18½ percent less, as shown in equation (5), and the range, at the high speed of the conventional airplane, will be from 66 percent to 22 percent greater, as indicated in equation (6). As turbo-jet and turbo-prop power plants both operate at relatively high speed for best fuel economy, the advantages of the all-wing configuration, when used in combination with these power plants, will closely approach the above figures for maximum range as well as high speed.

These advantages are all based on the simple aerodynamic values obtained with all-wing airplanes; namely, that; C_{Dmin} equals 50 percent of conventional C_{Lmax} equals 65 percent of conventional. The probabilities are that the minimum parasite drag can, within a comparatively short time, be reduced, at least for commercial types, to about 40 percent of the conventional figure and that the maximum trimmed lift coefficient (C_{Lmax}) may, within a similar short time, be increased to at least 75 percent of conventional values.

METHODS FOR INCREASING MAXIMUM TRIMMED LIFT

One of the most interesting devices for increasing maximum lift is, of course, the judicious use of boundary layer control in conjunction with turbo-jets or gas turbines. Another involves the development of a better combination of low pitching moment flaps and trimming devices which will permit of "lifting ourselves by our boot straps" in a more successful manner than we have achieved to date. Model configurations tested up to this time, employing such methods, have shown improvements of .1 or .2 C_L over the figure now used of 1.5.

A third possibility of rather unconventional nature remains to be proved in the all-wing airplane. This consists of placing the C.G. behind the aerodynamic center of the wing, eliminating inherent longitudinal stability by so doing and replacing this characteristic, which heretofore we have always considered as an essential to satisfactory aircraft design by highly reliable (and perhaps duplicate) automatic pilots which take over the function of stability from the airframe and may perhaps do a better job of maintaining the proper attitude than the present classical method. While unconventional and possibly a bit horrifying to those unaccustomed to the idea, it may have practical application to very large aircraft where the pilot's skill and strength are largely supplanted by mechanical means of one sort or another, and wherein the pilot controls the mechanism which in turn places the airplane at the desired attitude. If the C.G. is located aft of the aerodynamic centre the airplane will trim at a high angle of attack with the flaps or elevator surfaces deflected downward rather than upward from their normal position, thereby increasing the camber and rendering the whole aerofoil surface a high-lift device. It is possible that trimmed lift coefficients in the order of 2.0 may be achieved by this method, and experiments completed to date with such a device on conventional aircraft show that the C.G. may be displaced at least 10 percent of the mean aerodynamic chord aft of a normal position without any uncomfortable results in the flying characteristics of the airplane.

When these improvements in C_{Lmax} and C_{Dmin} can be realized, further startling gains in performance will accrue, as will be outlined later. It would seem, however, that the present accomplishments offer sufficient incentive to warrant all they have cost in time, effort and money, and that the question, "Why bother with an all-wing airplane?" is already well-answered.

OTHER MAJOR ADVANTAGES

There are other major advantages of the all-wing type which cannot be so definitely evaluated but which can and do contribute appreciably to improvement in efficiency and range. Two of these, namely the elimination of jet-tail surface interference, and the possible elimination of wing-tail surface shock wave interference, have already been mentioned. The third, and the most immediately applicable to designs of the near future, is the improved adaptability of all-wing types to the distribution of major items of weight empty and useful load over the span of the wing. While such distribution can be made to a limited extent in conventional airplanes, it can be much more fully accomplished in the all-wing type. Such weight distribution results in substantial savings in structural weight which have important effects on the ratio of gross weight at take-off to landing weight. An analysis of the range formula indicates that this ratio is one of the most important range parameters. Competent authority has shown that distribution of fuel in the wings instead of the fuselage of a large conventional modern transport would allow an increase in gross weight of 16 percent without increase to weight empty, with a corresponding increase in range up to 30 percent

It is fairly obvious that the all-wing airplane provides comparative structural simplicity, plus the possibility of structural material distribution in a most effective way at maximum distances from the neutral axis, plus an opportunity to stow power plant, fuel and payload at desirable intervals along the span of the wing, which cannot be equalled in conventional types. These matters are rather intangible and difficult to illustrate by numerical relationships. They depend to a large extent on the type and size of the airplane, what it is designed to carry, and what the desired high speed may be.

PROBLEMS INVOLVED IN ALL-WING DESIGN

Having demonstrated, perhaps, that the advantages of the all-wing type are fully worth striving for, let us consider the problems involved and their solution. Based on our present experience these difficulties do not appear now of surpassing magnitude, but in 1939 several of them seemed so serious as to discourage the most hardy optimist.

To one testing a swept-back aerofoil having a desirable root thickness, taper ratio and symmetrical section, together with reasonable washout at the tips such as might be designed from the then available data, the first results were a bit terrifying. The elevator effect was erratic, changed in sign with varying deflections, and was entirely unsuitable for the control of an airplane. It was also seen that the degree of static longitudinal stability indicated by the average slope of the pitching moment curves was less than that considered desirable in a conventional airplane. Experiments involving visual observation of tufts on the model indicated a separation along the training edge of the aerofoil which was apparently due to the planform configuration, and which was responsible for the erratic curves. In early experiments a simple addition of 10 percent to the chord length with a straight line contour from approximately the 70 percent chord point to the new 110 percent chord point, almost completely eliminated the difficulty.

N–1M, FIRST FULL-SCALE AIRPLANE

It was soon determined that date applicable to conventional wings with little or no sweep were completely unreliable for the degree of sweepback required in practical all-wing designs, and that a whole new technique had to be developed to determine the limits within which taper ratio, sweepback and thickness ratio could be combined for satisfactory results. All these variables were explored in a series of wind tunnel models, and when a reasonably satisfactory group of configurations had been determined it was decided to build our first piloted flying wing, the N–1M (Northrop Model 1 Mockup).

Because of the many erratic answers and unpredictable flow patterns which seemed to be associated with the use of sweepback, it was decided to try to explore most of these variables full scale, and the N–1M provided for changes in planform, sweepback, dihedral, tip configuration, C.G. location, and control-surface arrangement. Most of these adjustments were made on the ground between flights; some, such as C.G. location, were undertaken by the shift of ballast during flight. The variations to which this first airplane was subjected involved two extremes of arrangement in which the airplane was found to be quite satisfactory in flight.

It is an interesting commentary on the comparative ease with which the basic problems of controlled flight were solved to note that no serious difficulties were experienced in any flight attempt, or with any of the various configurations used. Some "felt" better to the pilot than others, but at no time was the airplane uncontrollable or unduly difficult to fly. The principal early troubles were related to the cooling of the small "pancake"-type air-cooled engines which were buried completely within the wing, and because of the pusher arrangement did not have the benefit of slipstream cooling in taxiing, take-off and climb. Engine-cooling problems seriously handicapped the early flights but later, somewhat larger engines were installed and the design of the cooling baffles was sufficiently improved so that repetitive sustained flights were accomplished easily.

The first flight was more or less an accident in that, while taxiing at comparatively high speed over the normally smooth surface of the dry desert lake bed used as a testing field, the pilot struck an uneven spot. He was bounced into the air and made a good controlled flight of several hundred yards before returning to earth. Altogether, this first airplane was used in over 200 flights of substantial duration, during which numerous configurations were tested and a great deal of work was done in the determination of the best types of control surface and surface control mechanism.

ELEVONS AND RUDDERS

From the inception of the work, longitudinal and lateral controls were combined in the "elevon," which word was coined to designate the trailing edge control surface members which operate together for pitch control and differentially for roll control. At no time during early tests did control about the pitch or roll axes give any appreciable difficulty. The control which was least expected to cause difficulty gave the most, namely the rudder.

Early in the test program it was found that the airplane had quite satisfactory two-control characteristics that is, a normal turn resulted from a normal bank without the use of rudder controls and as a result, throughout the program we have often considered the elimination of rudder controls entirely. It was indeed fortunate that the first airplane developed such docile characteristics, for many of the rudder configurations tried proved to be ineffective—or worse, affected the flight characteristics of the airplane adversely.

From the start it was determined to eliminate, to the greatest extent possible, vertical fin and rudder surfaces; first, because they violated the all-wing principle and added drag to the basic airfoil; second, because with the moderate sweepback employed in our early designs the moment arm of a conventional rudder about the C.G. was small, and an excessively large vertical surface would have resulted had we tried to achieve conventional yaw control moments. The rudder development was therefore concentrated on finding a type of drag-producing device at the wing tips which would give adequate yawing forces without affecting pitch or roll. To this end we tried 25 or 30 different configurations in flight which were first tested in the wind tunnel. As a result of this experience it was concluded that dynamic reactions were likely to be very different from static reactions; some of the configurations which looked best in the wind tunnel proved to be quite unsatisfactory in flight.

The best and most practical rudder found was one of the simplest in concept and one of the first to be flown, namely a plain split flap at the wing tip which could be opened to produce the desired drag. This flap was later combined with the trimming surface needed to counteract the diving moment of the landing flaps, forming the movable control surfaces at the wing tip of the XB–35.

Among the many flights accomplished with the first experimental airplane were several in tow of other aircraft where the distance to be covered, or the altitude to be gained, made it impractical to depend solely on the airplane's own engines. After a few minutes of acquaintanceship with the slight differences brought about by the presence of the tow cable, the airplane behaved well in tow and several comparatively high altitude flights were made to investigate the spin characteristics. These appeared to be quite normal, based on preliminary tests of this airplane. Later experience, however, indicated that the spin characteristics of tailless types vary from one design to another, in the same fashion as may be expected in conventional types, and that no broad generalization as to spin behavior can be made with safety.

N–9M FLYING MOCKUP FOR BOMBER

The N–1M was first flown in July 1940 and for about a year was consumed in a combination of aerodynamic tests and attempts to solve engine cooling problems. As soon as good sustained flight demonstrations could be made on schedule the Army Air Forces took active interest in the program and top-flight officers, including General H. H. Arnold and Major General Oliver P. Echols, encouraged us to investigate the application of the all-wing principle to large bomber aircraft. To this end it was decided to construct four scale models of a larger airplane. These were designated N–9M (Northrop Model 9 Mockup) and they duplicated, except for the power plant and propeller arrangement, the aerodynamic configuration of the proposed XB–35 airplane.

The first of these aircraft was completed and test flown on December 27, 1942, and had completed about 30 hours of test flying with pilot (and sometimes an observer) when it crashed, killing the pilot. The machine had been on a routine test flight across the desert away from its base, and was out of sight of technically qualified observers at the time of the accident. However, all evidence pointed to a spin, and the attitude of the airplane on the ground indisputably indicated autorotation at the time of impact.

This loss was a serious setback and work was started immediately to recheck the spin characteristics of the airplane in a spin tunnel. It was later determined, both in the tunnel and in flight, that recovery was good, although a bit unconventional (requiring aileron rather than elevator action), but that the spin parachutes which had been attached to the airplane for the low-speed stalling and stability tests then in progress were ineffective as to size and improperly located.

SPINNING AND TUMBLING CHARACTERISTICS

Subsequent models, over hundreds of flights, gave no trouble. The low-speed stall and spin tests with rear C.G. positions were accomplished without further difficulty and the N–9M proved an invaluable test bed in which various control configurations could be proved in detail. A large number of additional rudder configurations were developed and tested on the N–9Ms; likewise different types of mechanical and aerodynamic boost for the control surfaces were investigated, as well as the general behavior of the airplane in all types of air, and with different C.G. positions.

In connection with the model spin tests of this airplane, an investigation of the tumbling characteristics of the type was made in the spin tunnel. These tests showed that if the model was catapulted into the airstream with an imposed high velocity about the pitch axis in either direction, it would continue to tumble or come out of the maneuver, depending on comparatively minor differences in elevon and C.G. position. In other words, under circumstances of induced rotation about the pitch axis the recovery was marginal. However, it would never tumble from any normal flight condition, such as a stall, spin, or any other to-be-expected maneuver. In some configurations, if dropped vertically trailing edge down into the wind stream, a tumbling action would be induced which might or might not damp out. This was not judged a serious matter in view of the fact that a vertical tail slide is hardly a maneuver to be courted, even by a fighter airplane, let alone a 100-ton bomber.

The three remaining N–9Ms have been flown almost continuously since their completion dates to the present. Only recently have all desirable test programs been completed and the airplanes relegated to a semi-retired status from which they are withdrawn only for the benefit of curious pilots.

XP–79, ROCKET-POWERED AIRPLANE

In September 1942 we conceived the idea of combining the newly developed liquid-rocker motors with a flying wing in a high speed and highly maneuverable fighter. The physical dimensions of the human frame immediately became a limiting size factor and for this reason, as well as because much higher accelerations can be withstood for longer periods in the prone position, it was decided to place the pilot prone in this design. Three experimental, full-size glider versions of this little airplane were rapidly completed and a long series of glider tests undertaken. In order to achieve the utmost in low drag and light weight, the original airplanes were mounted on skids and the first glider tests were attempted with an automobile tow. Because of the rugged construction of the gliders they had a fairly heavy wing loading and the equipment provided for towing proved to be incapable of achieving enough speed for take-off.

As a second expedient, detachable dollies were built from which the airplane was expected to take off at flight speeds. Minor crack-ups occurred with this configuration and it was finally decided to compromise the aerodynamic cleanness of these first test airplanes in order to provide a rugged permanent and dependable landing gear for experimental purposes. The unusually large fin used here was required to stabilize the fixed landing gear, a substantial portion of which extended ahead of the C.G. After this gear was installed, and with another airplane as the towing medium, the take-off difficulties were eliminated and a number of successful glider flights were made.

These airplanes were flown both with and without wing-tip slots and slats which were tested for the purpose of eliminating tip-stall difficulties, as will be described later. They were also flown with a wide variation in vertical fin area, to determine the amount necessary or desirable for various flight conditions.

In one memorable test during which the airplane was equipped with a fixed slat, a rather peculiar accident occurred. The pilot, as mentioned before, lay prone within the wing contour. Two escape hatches were located approximately opposite the center of his body, one on the upper surface, the other on the lower surface. The handle which released the escape hatches was located close to the handle which released the towing cable from the tug airplane. At the start of this particular flight, after a successful climb to 10,000 ft., the pilot inadvertently released the escape hatches at the time of his release from tow, and as a result partially fell out of the airplane. The instinctive grasp on the control mechanism resulted in an indescribable wing-over maneuver. When things calmed down the pilot found himself in a steady, uniform glide with the airplane upside down. Minor movement of the controls seemed to produce little effect and the much-shaken individual crawled out of the airplane, sat on the leading edge of the center section while he checked his parachute harness, and then slid off to make a perfectly normal parachute descent. The airplane, undisturbed by the change in C.G., continued a long circling flight of the test area and finally landed in a normal continuation of its upside down glide, a short distance from the take-off point. It was rather seriously damaged but not so much so as to prevent repair. A later check in the wind tunnel indicated that there was a very stable region in inverted flight with this particular slat combination. Later the slats were abandoned as unnecessary and perhaps undesirable.

The airframe was considered suitable for the purpose intended long before the rocket motors had been developed to a degree of reliability considered safe for use, but finally a small motor having about five minutes' duration, was installed and a number of rocket-powered flights were accomplished. The first powered flight occurred in July 1944.

Although the first concept of the XP–79, as this fighter was designated, was as a rocket-powered vehicle (similar in basic idea to the Messerschmitt ME–163), it soon became apparent that the completion of the rocket motors would be far behind schedule and that serious difficulties were attendant to this development. One of the basic concepts for the full-size motor was that the fuel pumps would be driven by rotation of the combustion chambers, which were set at a slight angle to the thrust axis in order to develop torque. It was not foreseen that the rotation of the combustion chambers would have a serious effect on the combustion therein, and this difficulty, never completely solved, caused the abandonment of the particular engine which was being developed for the project.

XP–79B TURBO-JET AIRPLANE

As no alternative rocket engine was available, it became necessary to modify the design to incorporate turbo-jet power plants, and the second of the XP–79 series, called the XP–79B, was completed with two Westinghouse B–19 turbo-jets and first airborne on September 12, 1945. The take-off for this flight was normal, and for 15 minutes the airplane was flown in a beautiful demonstration. The pilot indicated mounting confidence by executing more and more maneuvers of a type that would not be expected unless he were thoroughly satisfied with the behavior of the airplane.

After about 15 minutes of flying, the airplane entered what appeared to be a normal slow roll, from which it did not recover. As the rotation about the longitudinal axis continued the nose gradually dropped, and at the time of impact the airplane appeared to be in a steep vertical spin. The pilot endeavored to leave the aircraft but the speed was so high that he was unable to clear it successfully. Unfortunately, there was insufficient evidence to fully determine the cause of the disaster. However, in view of his prone position, a powerful, electrically controlled trim tab had been installed in the lateral controls to relieve the pilot of excessive loads. It is believed that a deliberate slow roll may have been attempted (as the pilot had previously slow rolled and looped other flying-wing aircraft developed by the company) and that during this maneuver something failed in the lateral controls in such a way that the pilot was overpowered by the electrical trim mechanism.

ALL-WING BUZZ BOMBS

Several other all-wing aircraft and variations of them were built and tested during the same period. Shortly after the advent of the V–1 an all-wing "buzz" bomb was designed and built. This airplane housed the German V–1 resonator in a duct in the center of the wing and carried twice the German warhead in cast wing sections on each side of the power plant with fuel in the outer wings. Several were built and flown successfully.

The first of these buzz bombs was tested as a pilot-controlled glider with good success. It was very small and incorporated a number of extra bumps which were originally conceived to be the best way to carry standard 2,000 lb. demolition bombs. In spite of its peculiar configuration, which departed appreciably from the all-wing ideal, it had quite good flight characteristics, was flown on a number of occasions (the airplane was successfully slow-rolled) and demonstrated the suitability of the type for the purpose intended.

The one difficulty experienced in this series of tests is worthy of note. The piloted version of the buzz bomb naturally required some type of landing gear for take-off and landing, and in this case we employed tiny, low-pressure air wheels, rigidly mounted in the airframe structure and extending only a few inches below the contour of the aerofoil or, more specifically, the bomb-shaped bumps thereon. Landing on this gear involved bringing the airplane in at an altitude of approximately 15 percent to 20 percent of the mean aerodynamic chord just prior to contact, and no amount of practice on the part of the pilot produced a technique satisfactory for this purpose. In every case a change in airflow appeared to develop as the airplane approached within a quarter-chord length of the ground. The drag was apparently reduced, the lift increased and the airplane rose, in spite of anything the pilot could do, to a height of 8 or 10 ft. above the ground, at which point it stalled and flopped down out of control. This maneuver resulted in a number of rough landings but no damage to either the pilot or the airplane. It was later found that the only way to make any sort of smooth landing was to bring the airplane in at comparatively high speed and actually fly it onto the ground. This difficulty was not experienced in airplanes having normal landing height above the ground, such as the N–9M and XB–35.

XB–35, LONG-RANGE BOMBER

During all this development and testing of other types and scale versions of the XB–35, the design and construction of the big ship had been under way. N–9M airplanes had proved the practicability of the design. They closely approached the XB–35 configuration with the exception that they mounted only two pusher engines, located at positions corresponding to points midway between engines 1 and 2, and engines 3 and 4.

The problem of control-surface actuation on the big bomber involved the development and testing of a complete hydraulic control system, as none of the aerodynamic boosts or balances developed and tested in the N–9M models had proved satisfactory. The system used in the XB–35 employs small valves which are sensitive to comparatively minute movements of the control cable and which, when displaced, permit large quantities of oil to flow into the actuating cylinders. This arrangement eliminates any pilot "feel" of the load on the control surfaces unless a deliberate arrangement for force feedback is made. Rather than undertake this later step, a comparatively simple force mechanism, which is sensitive to accelerations and airspeed, was developed. This device gives the pilot a synthetic feel of the airplane which can be adjusted in intensity to anything he likes, and which has proved satisfactory in flight. For reasons to be outlined shortly, a synthetic feel was much more satisfactory than the feedback of actual control-surface loads, particularly at high angles of attack.

The XB–35 was first flown from Northrop Field to the Muroc Army Test Base in June 1946. The first several flights indicated no difficulties whatsoever with the airframe configuration. Indications of trouble with propeller governing mechanisms were discerned at an early date and it was shortly discovered that flights of any substantial duration could not be accomplished because of oil leakage in the hydraulic propeller governing system. On the last flight difficulty with both propellers on one side caused a landing with asymmetrical power, which was accomplished without trouble.

The next six months, from August to March, were spent in a vain attempt to eliminate these difficulties, plus those caused by a series of engine reduction gear failures. To date the XB–35 has not had sufficient time in the air to fully demonstrate its ability to meet its design performance guarantees. However, large-scale model tests in numerous tunnels have indicated the low-drag figures presented earlier in this paper, and preliminary speed versus power tests completed early this month have given gratifying confirmation of our original expectations. Flights accomplished to date have included all maneuvers necessary for large bombardment airplanes. So far, however, violent maneuvers have not been attempted and no exact evaluation of stability and control parameters has been possible.

Two turbo-jet powered all-wing airplanes, having the same basic shape and size as the XB–35 are virtually complete at this time and will be flying late this summer. They are powered by eight jets having a sea level static thrust of 4,000 lb. apiece. They incorporate small vertical fins to provide the same aerodynamic effect as the propeller shaft housings and propellers of the XB–35.

Let us now turn to considerations of stability and control of the all-wing airplane. They are quite different from those of conventional types and, unless reasonably well understood, may lead to discouragement at an early date concerning projects well worth further evaluation.

STATIC LONGITUDINAL STABILITY

In any airplane the primary parameter determining the static longitudinal stability is the position of the center of gravity with respect to the center of lift or the neutral point. Obviously, the neutral point may be shifted aft by adding a tail or by sweeping the wing, or the C.G. may be shifted forward by proper weight distribution, so that from the standpoint of static stability no particular configuration has any special advantage except as it affects the possibilities of proper balance. In an all-wing airplane the elimination of the tail makes the problem of balance somewhat more critical but not excessively so. Unfortunately, for any given airplane the neutral point does not ordinarily remain fixed with variations of power, flap-setting or even lift coefficient, so that the aft C.G. limit for stability is often prescribed by some single flight condition has always occurred for power-off flight at angles of attack approaching the stall.

CHARACTERISTICS AT HIGH LIFT

The pitching instability of a swept wing at high lift coefficients is by now a somewhat familiar phenomenon. The complete mechanisms involved, however, are still somewhat obscure. There are apparently two opposing effects which are of prime importance. They are the tendency for sweepback to increase the relative tip loading and also (by creating a span-wise pressure gradient) to promote boundary layer flow toward the tip. On a plain swept-back wing the latter effect apparently nullifies the former, so that there occurs in the tip portion of the wing a gradual decrease in effective section lift-curve slope with a resulting progressive decrease in stability. The tip, under these circumstances, never completely stalls, as evidenced by the stable pitching moments occurring at the maximum lift coefficient. On the other hand the addition of end plates will prevent to a large extent the effects of span-wise flow, thereby straightening the pitching moment curve but producing the normally expected tip stall, as evidenced by the strongly unstable moments in the vicinity of the maximum lift coefficient. Thus, any modification to the basic wing which affects the span-wise flow will have a noticeable effect on the pitching behavior at high lift coefficients.

In the case of the XB–35 the propeller shaft housings act to inhibit span-wise flow and straighten out the moment curve below the stall as in the case of the end plate; but in order to obtain stability at the stall, a tip-slot is provided to increase the stalling angle of the tip sections. By raising the trim flap in the outer 25 percent span and lowering the main flap in the inner 35 percent span, the stability characteristics are noticeably affected, presumably because of a decrease in span-wise pressure gradient and therefore in boundary layer flow.

Recent investigations have indicated that the problem of static longitudinal instability near the stall for plain swept-back wings depends not only on sweep but also on aspect ratio and it now appears that for a given sweepback the magnitude of the unstable break in the moment curve decreases with decreasing aspect ratio, eventually vanishing.

The possibility of controlling the stalled portions of the wing, as outlined, means that trailing edge flap controls can be laid out to maintain their effectiveness at very high angles of attack. Since a certain portion of this flap must be used to provide high lift and roll control, the amount available for longitudinal trim is limited, so that for the XB–35, for example, the total available nose-up pitching moment coefficient is .15 as compared to .30 for a conventional airplane. This limited control plus the fact that the main wing flaps apparently cannot be made self-trimming and impose a diving moment in the landing condition reduces the available C.G. range in percent of the m.a.c. as compared with conventional airplanes. The XB–35 has a C.G. range of only 5 percent or 6 percent as compared with conventional values in the order of 10 percent or 12 percent. This comparison is somewhat misleading, however, because the all-wing airplane may have a greater comparative m.a.c. in view of its somewhat lighter wing loading. It is also much easier to arrange weight empty and useful load items span-wise within close m.a.c. limits than in conventional types.

Where manual control of the elevator is employed the stick-free stability and control of all-wing aircraft are impaired by separation of the flow from the upper surface of the wing near the trailing edge, causing up-floating tendencies at higher lift coefficients. If not corrected these up-floating tendencies lead to stick-free instability and, in some cases, to serious control-force reversal at high lift coefficient. Aerodynamic design refinements devised and tested by us to date have not provided a satisfactory solution to the up-floating tendency. For small airplanes these undesirable forces can sometimes be tolerated, but for large aircraft the only solution found so far has been the employment of irreversible full power-driven control surfaces.

LATERAL STABILITY DERIVATIVES

It is when considering the lateral stability and control factors that the difference between the all-wing and conventional airplanes becomes most apparent. It is reassuring to state that despite the large differences apparent between the XB–35 and conventional aircraft, the dynamic lateral behavior of the XB–35 type is quite satisfactory, as will be discussed later.

Definite requirements for the weathercock stability $C_{\eta\beta}$, depend to a large extent on the airplane's purpose, but positive weathercock stability is always required. The swept-back wing has inherent directional stability which increases with increasing lift coefficient; but this is not considered sufficient for satisfactory flight characteristics under all circumstances and must be supplemented by some additional device. The wing-tip fin has been favored by some since it gives the largest yawing lever arm and provides a suitable rudder location. However, as previously pointed out, wing-tip fins may be unsatisfactory at the stall. For the XB–35 configuration, effective fin area is provided in large measure by the side force derivative of the pusher propellers.

RUDDER DEVELOPMENT

Rudders for all-wing aircraft are perhaps the chief control difficulty. Unless large fins are used a conventional rudder cannot be employed. If large fins and rudders are used, an objectionable adverse side force due to rudder is inherent, since the rudder moment arm is small and the side force comparatively great.

The use of pure drag rudders is feasible on the all-wing type because it is not necessary from a performance standpoint to fly at zero yaw. Thus in the case of an engine failure equilibrium conditions involving a yaw angle and the resultant corrective yawing moment do not involve appreciable side forces and associated bank angles, nor noticeable drag increases. Thus, the rudder is used only rarely for trim and its drag is therefore unimportant.

Of the many types of drag rudder investigated, a simple double-split trailing-edge flap at the wing tip has been found to have the most satisfactory all-round characteristics. This arrangement permits the simplest construction and allows combination of trim flap and rudder in the same portion of the trailing edge. One disadvantage of this type is its comparatively low effectiveness at low angles of rudder deflection, which may be remedied by the employment of a non-linear pedal-to-rudder linkage in the case of power-operated rudders.

EFFECTIVE DIHEDRAL

Considering now the effective dihedral $C_1\beta$, it is apparent that sweepback is the essential difference between the all-wing and conventional airplanes— a difference that will disappear as flight speeds increase and it becomes necessary to employ the desirable high-speed characteristics of swept wings in conventional tailed configurations. For swept-back wings $C_l\beta$ increases quite rapidly with lift coefficient which gives difficulty only when its value becomes too large. It is unimportant for either flight ease or for dynamic stability and control characteristics when it is near zero. Flight ease may indicate that a slightly positive effective dihedral is desirable while dynamic considerations point toward a slightly negative dihedral. Our practice has been to retain positive effective dihedral over the complete flight range.

ROLL CONTROL

The rolling control for all-wing airplanes is essentially normal. When elevons are used rather than separated aileron and elevator control, certain variations from conventional craft appear, in that, with the upward elevator deflection required for longitudinal trim, the adverse yaw ordinarily due to aileron deflection disappears. On the other hand, if large up-deflections are required for longitudinal trim, the up-going elevon used as aileron loses effectiveness rapidly, thus reducing the available roll control at high lift coefficients. This is particularly undesirable when considering the increased dihedral effects of swept wings at high lift coefficient.

SIDE FORCE EFFECTS

All-wing airplanes, particularly those without fins, have a very low cross-wind derivative; thus a low side force results from side-slipping motion. Some cross-wind force is probably important for precision flight, such as tight formation flying, bombing runs, gun training maneuvers, or pursuit. This importance arises because with low side force it becomes difficult to judge when sideslip is taking place, as the angle of bank necessary to sustain a steady side-slipping motion is small. This lack of side forces has been one of the first objections of pilots and others when viewing the XB–35. After flying in the N–9M or XB–35 the objection is removed, except for some of the specific cases mentioned above. For the correction of the lack of sideslip sense, a sideslip meter may be provided for the pilot or automatic pilot, and for very long-range aircraft there is a valuable compensating advantage in being able to fly under conditions of asymmetrical power without appreciable increase in drag.

DYNAMIC LONGITUDINAL STABILITY

The free longitudinal motions of any airplane fall into two modes. The first of these is a short-period oscillation. It is highly damped for conventional airplanes and also for all-wing airplanes in spite of the relatively low pitch-damping, C_{mq}. This somewhat surprising result is due to a coupled motion such that the vertical damping, Z_w, comes into play absorbing the energy from the oscillation. Also, low moment of inertia in pitch makes the small existing C_{mq} more effective than a similar value would be in conventional types. In tests on the N–9M airplane this short-period oscillation was too rapidly damped to obtain a quantitative check. The combination of low static stability in pitch, as previously described, and low moment of inertia in pitch results in periods of oscillation for all-wing airplanes that are comparable to those of conventional types.

The second mode of longitudinal motion is a long-period oscillation commonly called the phugoid. This is a lightly damped motion even for conventional airplanes, and seems slightly less damped for all-wing airplanes, because of the fact that they have relatively low drag, and drag is the chief means of energy absorption in this mode. N–9M tests indicate that calculation is slightly optimistic in this matter, but still this phugoid motion is sufficiently damped so as to give no serious difficulties. Being a slow motion, it is easily controlled.

To date the criteria for the description of airplane dynamic stabilities are vague. In the past it has been thought that consideration of damping rates and periods of oscillatory motion were adequate, but it has become evident that some further criteria are necessary. Consideration of the angular response of airplanes to various unit disturbances may supply this need.

DYNAMIC LONGITUDINAL RESPONSE

The criterion of response is probably the only category in which the flying wing is importantly different from the conventional airplane for longitudinal motion. The action of the two types in an abrupt vertical gust is especially interesting, two factors combining to reduce the accelerations experienced by all-wing airplanes. These factors are the relatively larger wing chord and shorter effective tail length of the all-wing type. The first characteristic increases the time for the transient lift to build up and is the more important in reducing accelerations. The second decreases the time interval between the disturbing impulse at the lift surface and the correcting impulse at the effective tail, so that the airplane tends to pitch into the gust. This latter characteristic is a matter of concern to pilots, since a disturbance in the air is likely to leave them farther from trim attitude, consequently requiring more active pilot control in rough air. It is believed, however, that automatic control will effectively eliminate this difficulty.

The response of the all-wing airplane to elevator deflection seems entirely adequate. It errs, if at all, on the side of over-sensitivity because of low C_{mq} and low moment of inertia in pitch. An abrupt control movement giving the same final change in trim speed for a conventional and a comparable all-wing airplane results in a larger initial swing in pitch for the all-wing.

DYNAMIC LATERAL STABILITY

As with longitudinal motion, there are two characteristic modes that are of interest laterally. the first of these is the spiral motion which is usually divergent on modern airplanes, thus uncontrolled flight results in a tightening spiral. This slight instability seems favored by pilots. All-wing airplanes have readily acceptable characteristics in this mode requiring from 15 to 20 seconds to double amplitude. In general, any time greater than five seconds to double amplitude is considered acceptable.

The second mode, the "Dutch Roll" oscillation, is more critical for all-wing airplanes, particularly at low speed, high weight and high altitude. All-wing airplanes seem comparatively bad in this respect because of the combination of relatively large effective dihedral and low weathercock stability and, for the conditions noted above as critical, are likely to approach neutral damping in the Dutch Roll mode. However, analytical determinations of this motion, using calculated damping derivatives, indicated less satisfactory characteristics than were obtained in actual flight tests. Because of a relatively low weathercock stability, the Dutch Roll is of a rather long period, in the order of ten seconds for the XB–35. It is usually assumed that for periods of such length, it is not important to have a high rate of damping since control would seem easily "inside" the motion. However, there may be particular instances where this is not true. For instance, in an all-wing airplane in which the rudder is particularly weak, the time of response to rudder control may be of the same order as the period of Dutch Roll motion. This would make directional control extremely difficult in a condition, such as landing, where the roll controls are not usable for changing heading. It is notable that for the very low weathercock stability commonly encountered in all-wing airplanes, the conventional solution of increasing weathercock stability to offset increased dihedral does not hold. Increasing C_{nr} leaves the damping essentially untouched, but reduces the period and increases the number of cycles required to damp.

Another factor contributing to the relative lack of damping of all-wing airplanes in Dutch Roll motion is the low value of the damping coefficient in yaw, C_{nr}. This appears to be inherent in all-wing designs, particularly if the use of fins is abandoned. For special occasions, when particular airplane steadiness is required (such as a bombing run), it is probable that the equivalence of such damping in yaw may be supplied by an automatic pilot, or by temporarily increasing the drag at the wing tips. This latter effect can be accomplished on the XB–35 by simultaneously opening both rudders and gives deadbeat damping in yaw.

DYNAMIC LATERAL REPONSE

As in the longitudinal motions, the amplitudes of response of an airplane in lateral motion are probably as important as the damping rates in determining free-flight characteristics. All-wing airplanes seem slightly rougher in turbulent air than conventional aircraft of similar weight. This is due chiefly to the reduced wing loading, but high effective dihedral and low weathercock stability may have an added effect. This is a matter of interest in fixing upon analytical criteria for the description of free-flight qualities. As mentioned above, increasing the weathercock stability for all-wing airplanes has a slight effect on the damping rates; however, it affects the amplitudes of response to gusts materially.

Some data from the free-flight tunnel of the National Advisory Committee for Aeronautics indicate that increasing weathercock stability, even for all-wing airplanes, materially helps the "flyability" of the airplane. Another bit of evidence that is of interest in this connection has to do with the magnitude of the side force derivative, $C_y\beta$. Increase of this parameter improves Dutch Roll damping very materially but has virtually no effect on amplitude of response to gusts, according to calculations. Free-flight wind tunnel data again give tentative support to the investigations of response as a criterion by showing little improvement of flight qualities of models with increase of $C_y\beta$.

Flight tests of the all-wing glider in which the vertical fin, located aft on the ship's center line, was varied in size from approximately 2 to 7 percent of the wing area, left the pilot somewhat undecided as to fin requirements except that the larger fin seemed somewhat easier to fly. Presumably, this was, in the light of the foregoing discussion, primarily because of the increased $C_n\beta$, the coincidental increase in $C_y\beta$ not being effective.

AUTOMATIC PILOT CONTROL

The application of automatic pilot control to an all-wing airplane has certain difficulties which are associated primarily with the low value of $C_y\beta$. In conventional applications the fact that the airplane is side slipping is detected by either a lateral acceleration or an angle of bank. In an all-wing airplane neither of these indications exists except in an almost undetectable amount. Accordingly, it is necessary, in order to fly the airplane at zero sideslip, and therefore in the direction of its center line, to provide a yaw-vane signal to which the pilot or automatic pilot will respond. This introduces some difficulty in automatic pilot design because for small disturbances the sideslip angle with respect to the wind, and the yaw angle with respect to a set of fixed axes, are nearly equal and opposite for a flying wing. The customary automatic pilot control on azimuth angle therefore tends to oppose the necessary control on sideslip. To avoid this difficulty it is necessary only to reduce the rate of control on sideslip to approximately one-third that on azimuth. This modification to a conventional automatic pilot was flown on the N–9M with complete success.

PROBLEMS OF CONFIGURATION—SWEPT *vs.* NON-SWEPT WINGS

Let us now turn to a consideration of the practical limitations in arrangement of the tailless airplane. They may be summarized briefly as sweepforward, sweepback, and a non-swept wing configuration. The sweepforward arrangement requires the use of a large fixed load forward of the leading edge at the center section for proper balancing of the airplane. Therefore, a fuselage with some substantial part of the weight empty of the airplane disposed therein is required. The swept-forward wing itself is unstable directionally and requires some type of fin for weathercock stability. To this must be added more fin area to stabilize the fuselage. In addition, it may be noted that the moment arm of the fin about the C.G. of the airplane is necessarily comparatively small, still further increasing the size of the required fin. If we add to the aerofoil a protruding fuselage and an unusually large vertical tail surface, we have departed from our basic all-wing concept. We have incorporated virtually all the elements of drag found in the conventional aircraft and have not accomplished our intent of improving efficiency. For the above reasons, which could be argued pro and con for hours, our company has done no active design and development work on airplanes with swept-forward wings.

An all-wing configuration embodying a straight, or non-swept wing, has been proposed and flown successfully in model sizes. It offers the serious disadvantage that suitable distribution of weight empty and useful load items is difficult and, if proper balance is to be accomplished, most of the structural weight and useful load must be included in the forward 30 percent or 40 percent of the wing, leaving a large volume of space within the wing unusable. Such a configuration results in an unnecessarily large airplane to accomplish a given job and for this reason has not been considered seriously.

The swept-back arrangement exemplified by the various airplanes previously illustrated and described seems to offer the best configuration for a materialization of our all-wing ideal. It can be balanced satisfactorily within quite wide ranges of sweepback, utilizing almost all available volume within the wing for storage of useful load items. It seems to fly satisfactorily in many different configurations and the arrangement is such that large payloads can be carried virtually over the C.G., with the weight empty items so distributed as to cause little variation in C.G. position between the fully loaded and empty conditions.

WEIGHT DISTRIBUTION

As has been pointed out previously, the permissible range of C.G. location is not overly critical in this type of airplane. It is, nevertheless, of great advantage to be able to load the airplane almost at will, without concern as to how the useful load is disposed and the swept-back configuration lends itself most suitably to such loading.

In the case of the XB–35, the useful load, consisting largely of bombs and fuel, can be readily disposed in suitable position about the C.G. While some fuel is located well forward and other fuel well aft of the desired C.G. location, under normal operating conditions the proper balance is readily maintained. In case of failure of one or more engines, it is necessary to pump the fuel from unused tanks to those supplying the remaining engines, but a simple manifolding system provides this facility.

Based on a great many studies of various types and applications of the all-wing principle, some practical limitations may be approximately defined. Where very dense (high specific gravity) payloads are contemplated, such as warheads or similar munitions, quite small units are practical, as demonstrated by the all-wing buzz bombs to which reference has been made. Medium-sized units having a span of perhaps 100 ft. and a gross weight of 50,000 to 60,000 lb., appear entirely practical for medium bombers and freighters. Here again the density of the useful load, both in payload and fuel, is comparatively high.

Airplanes designed to carry people need the largest volume of all. Even individual reclining chair accommodations require a minimum space of perhaps 40 cubic ft. per passenger, which is a density of only about 5 lb. per cubic ft. This is one-half to one-quarter the density of typical air cargo, and only 4 percent or 5 percent of the density of a warhead.

IMMEDIATE APPLICATIONS—ALL-WING AIRCRAFT

It may be concluded, then, that the all-wing design is immediately applicable and practical for a number of military and cargo-carrying versions, and that the passenger-carrying aircraft are likely to be of rather large size and, in the immediate future at least, will provide only comfortable seating instead of the more luxurious appurtenances associated with long-range ocean travel.

An airplane of the XB–35 configuration and size can carry 50 passengers in comfort in the existing aerofoil envelope with adequate headroom for all, and with vision forward through the floor, and upward if desired. Passenger vision in a flying wing may be more satisfactory than in conventional types if we get used to the idea of forward vision rather than that provided by side windows. The really interesting views are likely to be forward and downward rather than to the side. An airplane like the XB–35 will have cargo space for 40,000 to 50,000 lb. of air freight at a density of 10 to 15 lb. per cubic ft., in addition to the necessary crew and space for 50 passengers.

FUTURE POSSIBILITIES

Turning now to future possibilities, it seems that considerable further aerodynamic refinement can be made over that already accomplished in all-wing types. Particularly if turbo-jets are used as the motive power, the minimum parasite drag may be reduced to .008 or less. This value is obtained by subtracting the drag of propeller shaft housings, gun turrets and other military protuberances from the XB–35 configuration and assuming an improved degree of aerodynamic smoothness of the aerofoil section. Boundary layer removal and the use of somewhat thinner wing sections may further appreciably reduce this figure.

A maximum trimmed lift coefficient of 1.9 for the all-wing configuration seems attainable by methods already suggested and possibly may be further increased by judicious use of boundary layer control in combination with turbo-jet power plants. It is our opinion that the ratio of $C_{l_{max}}$ to $C_{d\ min}$ may be increased to a value of 235 within the not-too-distant future from our present actual achievement of about 130. In contrast, the years of intensive development of the conventional types already passed promise an improvement of less magnitude within a comparable time. In our judgment a trimmed maximum lift of 2.8 vs. a minimum drag of .020 seems reasonable to expect for large, long-range transport and bombardment aircraft of conventional type.

These estimates are, of course, completely arbitrary and controversial. However, if one cares to assume their validity, the following conclusions may be reached, based on methods and calculations used in the early part of this paper. The total minimum profile drag of the all-wing airplane in terms of the conventional will be from 40 percent to 59 percent. The power required by the all-wing to maintain the same cruising speed as the conventional will be from 70 percent to 80 percent and, conversely, the maximum range of the all-wing, at the cruising speed of the conventional airplane, will be 143 percent to 125 percent. The maximum range of the all-wing airplane at its best cruising speed will be 158 percent to 130 percent of the conventional, and the most economic speed will be from 125 percent to 115 percent faster.

Under high speed conditions corresponding to full power of reciprocating, turbo-prop or turbo-jet engines, where the induced drag is assumed to be 20 percent and the parasite drag 80 percent of the total, the power required to drive the all-wing airplane at the speed of the conventional airplane will be 52 percent to 67 percent and, conversely, the range will be 192 percent to 149 percent of the conventional airplane. The maximum speed of the all-wing airplane at comparable powers will be 124 percent to 114 percent of its conventional counterpart.

Different assumptions of comparative maximum lift and minimum drag values can be made to suit individual opinion, but it is believed that any reasonable assumptions will always result in an advantage to the all-wing configuration of such magnitude as to fully warrant whatever trials and tribulations may be associated with its development.

POSSIBLE SUPERSONIC APPLICATIONS

So far in this discussion we have purposely avoided transonic and supersonic considerations. The neglect is possibly a reasonable one when discussing commercial ventures, in view of the cost of higher and higher speeds. A reasonable degree of sweepback, such as is required in the type of aircraft under consideration, will permit speeds up to about 500 m.p.h. without involving great compressibility drag increases. For military aircraft, however, we cannot ignore the sonic "barrier" and its implications, and it is a reasonable assumption that sooner or later improved fuels will permit higher and higher operational speeds, even in commercial aircraft.

Based on present knowledge of supersonic flight, it will always be more difficult to carry a given payload for a given range at supersonic speed because of the additional wave drag encountered at these speeds. At transonic or comparatively low supersonic speeds, a plain swept-back wing appears to be one of the best possible configurations, provided that sufficient volume is available within the wing. Since the flow normal to the leading edge is subsonic over almost the entire wing surface, subsonic aerofoils with reasonably good subsonic flight characteristics can be used at these speeds. The all-wing design eliminates wing-fuselage interference as well as adverse interference between the tail surfaces and wing or body.

At higher supersonic speeds the problem or providing adequate volume is more difficult because of the fact that more and more fuel is required for a given range and the percentage of thickness of aerofoils suitable for such use is much less than that satisfactory for subsonic flight. Save for one compensating factor, this problem of volume and size might well rule out the all-wing airplane for supersonic use, and certainly does limit its usefulness for low altitude flight. However, an attractive field of operation exists at very high altitude where air densities are low and therefore wing areas must be comparably great if suitable lift coefficients are to be maintained. If we design a frankly supersonic airplane to fly at, say, a Mach number of 1.6, with supersonic diamond-section aerofoils, the maximum cruising lift coefficient will probably be no greater than .15, and the corresponding loading must be held to 40 lb. per sq. ft.

The above figures are based on assumed operation at 60,000 ft. and an air density ratio of .094. Such an airplane might likewise be suitable for landing and take-off at low altitude, in view of its comparatively light wing loading, which would eliminate the necessity of high-life devices. The practicability of the design depends on the relative density of the air at the altitude selected for cruising operation. If a sufficiently high altitude is chosen it seems quite possible that adequate volume can be secured in the wing, in spite of its small thickness ratio, by using low aspect ratio planforms approaching the triangular. We can compare data on two wings having the same physical depth at the root, and identical wing areas. The conventional wing is of a type already proved practical for all-wing airplanes. The delta wing has thickness ratios suitable for supersonic flight, identical thickness and only slightly reduced volume. It should be quite suitable for all-wing aircraft of reasonable size. From the aerodynamic point of view it appears that with the delta wing it is possible to eliminate a substantial portion of the wave resistance and thus realize fairly favorable lift-drag ratios at supersonic speeds.

It is gratifying to those of us who have been working on all-wing projects for years to recognize the increased interest in the type evidenced in Germany toward the end of the war, and more particularly in England and Canada in recent years. For many years we received scant encouragement and often seriously questioned our own judgment, as well as our ability to achieve a successful solution to the many problems involved in the development of this type. The goals and rewards have always seemed well worth attainment, however, and I believe accomplishments to date have justified the effort required.

I hope this discussion may provide encouragement and incentive to those in Great Britain who have pioneered all-wing airplanes and that these projects, both here and in the United States, may profit by each other's mistakes and successes, thus bringing the two countries to the forefront in this important phase in the development of air transport.

The President, Sir Frederick Handley Page: After the Wibur Wright Lecture they did not have a discussion, although Mr. Northrop had given them all a great deal about which to think. He would ask Dr. Roxbee Cox to propose, and Mr. Rowe to second, a vote of thanks. He had great pleasure in calling upon

Dr. Roxbee Cox to do this, as he had been Vice-President during the past year in charge of the technical activities of the Society, and at the Council Meeting that day he had been elected President for the ensuing year.

Dr. Roxbee Cox (President-elect of the Society, Fellow): There was nothing more inspiring than a record of high endeavor; nothing more impressive than the logical development of a great thought from a picture in the mind to an achievement in the solid. That was what they had heard in the 35th of the Wilbur Wright Memorial Lectures, and that was why this lecture must rank with the finest in that remarkable series.

Mr. Northrop was not the first to have the vision of the all-wing airplane, Mr. Stephenson was not the first to have the vision of the steam locomotive. But they both had a gift more precious than priority in vision, the gift of being the right men at the right time to turn the vision into successful reality.

Mr. Northrop's timing was, in fact, almost uncanny. Not only did he produce swept-back wings at a time when scientists agreed that swept-back wings were the things to produce; he also brought his child to maturity at a time when the only power plant which could give it aesthetic perfection—and indeed minimum drag—reached maturity as well. All that remained now was to get rid of the wheels.

There were some who believed that an airplane should have the maximum of body with the minimum of wing—a mere projectile. There were others who believed it should have the maximum of wing with the minimum of body. To concentrate on the body was gross. But to aim for wings was to be on the side of the angels.

He proposed that they accord to Mr. Northrop a most sincere and hearty vote of thanks, with admiration in their hearts for his great ideas and magnificent accomplishments.

Mr. N. E. Rowe (Vice-President of the Society, Fellow) seconded the vote of thanks. He had had the pleasure of meeting Mr. Northrop in America on two occasions. On both those occasions he had been particularly impressed both by the energy and knowledge of Mr. Northrop and by his personality. He was never too busy to talk to anybody who was interested in all-wing aircraft. He was a man of great personal kindness and modesty and was always most generous with information which would be of any assistance to others.

He had given them that night a magnificent statement of the aeronautical difficulties which had been encountered and how they had been overcome. No doubt at some later stage he would describe the great engineering, difficulties which had been encountered and overcome. Mr. Northrop had the vision of a true pioneer, but he had both feet on the ground.

He had much pleasure in seconding this vote of thanks to his friend Jack Northrop.

The vote of thanks was carried with acclamation.

Following the lecture the Annual Council Dinner was held at which the following were present:

Professor L. Aitchison, D.Met., B.Sc., F.R.I.C., M.I.Mech.E., F.R.Ae.S., Member of Council; Mr. E. J. N. Archbold, B.Sc., Grad.R.Ae.S., Member of Council.

Major General Clayton L. Bissell, G.S.C., Military and Air Attaché, U.S. Embassy; Lord Brabazon of Tara, M.C., F.R.Ae.S., Past President of the Society; Mr. Griffith Brewer, Hon.F.R.Ae.S., Past President of the Society; Sir John S. Buchanan, C.B.E., A.M.I.Mech.E., F.R.Ae.S., Member of Council; Major G. P. Bulman, C.B.E., B.Sc., F.R.Ae.S., Member of Council.

Mr. S. Camm, C.B.E., F.R.Ae.S., Member of Council; Air Marshal The Hon. Sir Ralph Cochrane, K.B.E., C.B., Officer Commanding, Transport Command; Air Marshal Sir Alex W. Coryton. K.B.E., C.B., M.V.O., D.F.C., Controller of Supplies (Air), Ministry of Supply; Dr. H. Roxbee Cox., Ph.D., D.I.C., B.Sc., F.R.Ae.S., President-elect.

Commander W. L. Dawson, Liaison Officer, U.S. Naval Attaché's Office, London; Air Marshal Sir William Dickson, K.B.E., C.B., D.S.O., A.F.C., Vice-Chief of the Air Staff; Dr. G. P. Douglas, O.B.E., M.C., D.Sc., F.R.Ae.S., Member of Council.

Mr. A. G. Elliott, C.B.E., M.I.Mech.E., M.S.A.E., F.R.Ae.S., Member of Council.

Sir Richard Fairey, M.B.E., F.R.Ae.S., Past President; Mr. W. S. Farren, C.B., M.B.E., M.A., M.I.Mech.E., F.R.S., F.R.Ae.S., Member of Council; Sir A. H. Roy Fedden, M.B.E., D.Sc., M.I.Mech.E., M.S.A.E., F.R.Ae.S., Past President.

Mr. H. J. Goett, National Advisory Committee for Aeronautics.

Professor A. A. Hall, M.A., F.R.Ae.S., Member of Council; Mr. S. Scott Hall, A.C.G.I., M.Sc., D.I.C., F.R.Ae.S., Member of Council; Sir Harold Howitt, G.B.E., D.S.O., M.C., Deputy Chairman, British Overseas Airways Corporation.

Mr. E. T. Jones, O.B.E., M.Eng., F.R.Ae.S., Member of Council.

Sir Ben Lockspeiser, M.A., F.C.S., F.R.Ae.S., Member of Council.

The Rt. Hon. Lord Nathan, P.C., T.D., J.P., Minister of Civil Aviation; Mr. John K. Northrop, President, Northrop Aviation Inc.

Rear Admiral G. N. Oliver, C.B., D.S.O., Assistant Chief of Naval Staff (Air).

Sir Frederick Handley Page, C.B.E., F.R.Ae.S., President of the Royal Aeronautical Society; Capt. John B. Pearson, Jnr., U.S.N., Naval Attaché for Air, U.S. Embassy; Mr. W. G. A. Perring, F.R.Ae.S., Member of Council; Captain J. Laurence Pritchard, F.I.Ae.S., Hon.F.R.Ae.S., Secretary of the Society.

Air, Marshal Sir James Robb, K.B.E., C.B., D.S.O., D.F.C., A.F.C., Officer Commanding, Fighter

Command, R.A.F.; Mr. N.E. Rowe, C.B.E., B.Sc., D.I.C., F.R.Ae.S., Vice-President of the Society; Sir Archibald Rowlands, K.C.B., M.B.E., Permanent Secretary, Ministry of Supply.

Mr. Livingston Satterthwaite, Civil Air Attaché, U.S. Embassy; Air Marshal Sir Hugh Saunders, K.C.B., C.B., M.C., D.F.C., M.M., Officer Commanding, Bomber Command; Lord Sempill, A.F.C., F.R.Ae.S., Past President; Sir Oliver Simmonds, M.A., F.R.Ae.S., Vice-President; Rear Admiral M. S. Slaterry, C.B., F.R.Ae.S., Chief Naval Representative, Ministry of Supply; Mr. W. R. Verdon Smith, President, Society of British Aircraft Constructors; Air Marshal Sir Ralph Sorley, K.C.B., O.B.E., D.S.C., D.F.C., Officer Commanding, Technical Training Command, R.A.F.; Mr. H. A. Soule, National Advisory Committee for Aeronautics; Professor R. V. Southwell, M.A., F.R.S., F.R.AeS., Rector, Imperial College of Science.

Captain C. F. Uwins, A.F.C., O.B.E., F.R.Ae.S., Honorary Treasurer of the Society.

Dr. H. C. Watts, M.B.E., D.Sc., M.Inst.C.E., F.R.Ae.S., Member of Council; Mr. H. E. Wimperis, C.B., C.B.E., M.A., F.R.Ae.S., Past President; Mr. L. A. Wingfield, M.C., D.F.C., A.R.Ae.S,, Solicitor to the Society.

BIBLIOGRAPHY

"Air Force Faces $800 Million Budget Cut." *Aviation Week,* July 4, 1949.
"AF Wastes $71 Millions Through Plane Cancellations." *American Aviation,* June 1, 1949.
Allison, Pratt & Whitney Team for Propfan Market. *Aviation Week and Space Technology,* March 2, 1987.
Amrein, John. Asst. Dir. Photography Laboratory, Aircraft Div., Northrop Corporation. Interview by author, 1987.
Anderson, Fred. *Northrop. An Aeronautical History.* Century City, CA: Northrop Corporation, 1976.
——. Former Northrop historian. Interviews with author, 1978–1980.
Ashkenas, Irving. Former Northrop engineer. Interview with author, 1987.
Aspin, Les. Chairman, House Armed Services Committee. Correspondence with author, 1987.
"ATF Contractors Ponder Roles, Trades." *Aerospace Daily,* November 5, 1986.
Baker, Francis J. *The Death of the Flying Wing.* Thesis submitted to the faculty of Claremont Graduate School, Claremont, CA, 1984.
Bean, David J. *The N–3PB.* Restoration of the Northrop N–3PB. Unpublished report. Hawthorne, CA: Northrop Corporation, 1980.
Biddle, Wayne. "The Invisible Airplane." *Discover,* February 1986.
——. "Pushing for Weapons That Work." *The New York Times,* July 8, 1984.
Blay, Roy, ed. *Lockheed Horizons: A History of Lockheed.* Burbank, CA: Lockheed Corporation. Special Issue Twelve, 1983.
Boyne, Walter J. "Attack! The Story of the XB–51, Martin's Phantom Strike Ship!" *Airpower,* July 1978.
——. *The Smithsonian Book of Flight.* Washington, DC: Smithsonian Books, Orion Books, 1987.
Bray, Mrs. Ulric B. Wife of former Chairman, Board of Trustees, Northrop University. Interview with author, 1988.
Braybrook, Roy. "Northrop's Lightweight Fighters." *Air Combat,* July 1983.
Brum, Christian F. Head of Special Collections, University of California Library. Taped interview with Jack Northrop, 1972.

Bryan, C.D.B. *The National Air & Space Museum.* New York: Harry N. Abrams, 1979.

Campbell, Jim. "The Wing's The Thing." *Sport Pilot,* April 1987.

Cantafio, Tony. Vice President Northrop Public Affairs. Interview with author, 1988.

Christen, Harvey. Former Lockheed employee. Interview with author, 1987.

Cardenas, Gen. Robert, Ret. Former Air Force test pilot. Interview with author, 1987.

———. Comments at Supersonic Symposium, Flight Test Historical Foundation. Edwards Air Force Base, Edwards, CA, November 7, 1987.

Chart, Dr. Ira. Northrop historian. Interviews with author 1982–1987.

———. *The F–5 Story, F–5E.* Unpublished manuscripts, n.d.

Corn, Dr. Robert. Director Photography Laboratory, Aircraft Div., Northrop Corp. Interview with author, 1987.

Cox, Dr. Roxbee. Remarks at the 35th Wilbur Wright Memorial Lecture. The Royal Aeronautical Society, London, May 29, 1947.

Daly, Les. Northrop Vice President, Public Relations. Interview by author, 1987.

Davis, Gary. Pilot and builder of the Davis Wing. Interview with author, 1987.

Davis, Dr. Lance. Professor and historian, Caltech. Interviews with author, 1982–1983.

DeCenzo, Herb. Northrop engineer and aerodynamicist, 1939–1940. Tape recorded comments, 1986.

Doolittle, Gen. James H. Ret., Correspondence with author, 1987.

Easterbrook, Gregg. "The Airplane That Doesn't Cost Enough." *The Atlantic Monthly,* August 1984.

Edwards, Capt. Glen W. "Pilot's Observations on the N–9MB Flying Wing." Memorandum Report. Air Technical Command, Army Air Forces. Bomber Operations Section, Muroc, CA, May 3, 1946.

Edmonds, Ivy G. Editor, *Northrop News.* Interview with author, 1986.

Edney, Commodore L.A., U.S.N. Commander, Carrier Group One. "F/A–18: Adding Versatility and Punch to Battle Group Options." *Wings of Gold,* The Association of Naval Aviation, Winter 1984.

Evans, Stanley H. "Cronic Sonics." *Flight,* April 20, 1950.

Everett, P.J. Former executive secretary to Tom Jones. Interview with author, 1978.

"F–18 Hornet." *Aviation & Marine International,* May/June 1979.

"Fighters, The." *Journal of Defense & Diplomacy,* May 1983.

Flight Test Report. Flight Test Division, Phase II Tests of the YB–49 Airplane, USAF No. 42–102368. Memorandum Report. Declassified from Confidential. Air Material Command, Wright-Patterson Air Force Base, Dayton OH, September 1, 1948.

"Gag Issue Raised on Eve of B–36 Probe." *Aviation Week,* July 18, 1949.

Gasich, Welko. Northrop Executive Vice President. Interviews with author, 1983–1987.

Gore, George. Former Northrop Secretary and Legal Counsel. Interview with author, 1986.

Greenberger, Robert S. "General Dynamics Gets F–16 Job." *The Wall Street Journal,* November 3, 1986.

Hallion, Richard P. "A Synopsis of Flying Wing Development, 1908–1953." History Office, Air Force Flight Test Center, Edwards Air Force Base, CA, 1986.

Hotz, Robert. "New B–36 Performance Revealed at Probe." *Aviation Week*, August 22, 1949.

———. "Why B–36 Was Made USAF Top Bomber." *Aviation Week*, August 15, 1949.

———. "Symington and Defense Chiefs Exonerated." *Aviation Week*, September 5, 1949.

Jernell, Lloyd S. and C. Baptiste Quartero. "Design of a Large Span-Distributed Load Flying-Wing Cargo Airplane." By Vought Corporation for NASA, Hampton VI, April 22, 1977.

Jones, Thomas V. Chairman and Chief Executive Officer, Northrop Corporation. Interview with author, 1982.

———. "Future Bright, Demands on Performance Never Greater." *Northrop News*, December 18, 1987.

Kotz, Nick. *Wild Blue Yonder: Money, Politics, and the B-1 Bomber*. New York: Pantheon, 1988.

Kresa, Kent. President and Chief Operations Officer, Northrop Corporation. Remarks delivered at Drexel Burnham Security Analysts Meeting. New York, NY, 1986.

Larson, George. "Dinner with Ken." *Air & Space*, August/September 1987.

Larson, O.H. "USAF X–4 *Skylancer*"; "USAF XP–56 *Black Bullet*"; "JB1 *Bat Glider*." Unpublished papers. Southern California Historical Aviation Foundation, Hawthorne, CA, November 1985.

LeMay, Gen. Curtis. Ret. Former Strategic Air Command Chief. Telephone interview with author, 1988.

Lindbergh, Charles A. *The Spirit of St. Louis*. New York: Charles Scribner's Sons, 1953.

Lockard, Captain John A, USN. "Strike Fighter Mission and the F/A–18: A Giant Step Ahead." *Wings of Gold*, The Association of Naval Aviation, Fall 1984.

"Look Who's Heading for No. 1 in Defense: Northrop." *Business Week*, April 19, 1982.

Macdonnell, Grant. Former Northrop Vice President. Interview with author, 1985.

Maloney, Edward. "Record Breaker YB–49." *Tam News*. The Planes of Fame Museum, Chino CA, 10:2 (1986).

———. *Northrop Flying Wings*. Planes of Fame Museum. Chino, CA, 1975.

———. President, Planes of Fame Air Museum. Interview with author, 1987.

Manion, Jack. Former Northrop Vice President. Interviews with author, 1985–1987.

McNeil, Darrell. Former Northrop employee. Interview with author, 1987.

Middlekoff, Dr. Robert. Director Huntington Library. Interviews with author 1985–1986.

Mikesh, Robert C. "*Albatros D.Va. German Fighter of World War I*." Washington, DC: Smithsonian Institution Press, 1980.

Millar, Richard W. Former Northrop Chairman and Director. Interviews with author, 1980–1987.

Myers, John. Former Northrop Vice President and test pilot. Interviews with author, 1985–1987.

Nelson, James. United States Air Force historian, Edwards Air Force Base, Edwards, CA. Interview with author, 1988.

Nettleton, Gilbert. Former Northrop sales representative and pilot. Interview with author, 1987.

Niven, John, Courtlandt Canby, and Vernon Welsh, eds. *Dynamic America: A History of General Dynamics Corporation and its Predecessor Companies.* New York: General Dynamics Corporation and Doubleday & Company, 1959.

Northrop 40. Looking Back on Forty Eventful Years. Los Angeles, CA: Northrop Corporation, August 1979.

Northrop Aircraft, Inc. *Pilot's Handbook for Model YB-49 Airplane.* Hawthorne, CA. Reprinted Appleton, WI: Aviation Publishers, 1984.

"Northrop N-3PB and the Bismarck." Northrop Corporation. Unpublished memorandum. March 13, 1980.

"Northrop Goes Up-Scale in its Advertising of the *Tigershark*, But Will the Pentagon Bite?" *Defense Week*, May 19, 1980.

Northrop, John K. "The All-Wing Type Airplane." *Aviation*, March 29, 1930.

———. "The Development of All-Wing Aircraft." The 35th Wilbur Wright Memorial Lecture. The Royal Aeronautical Society, London, May 29, 1947. Reprinted courtesy of Aeronautical Library, California Institute of Technology.

———. Interviews with author, 1977–1980.

———. Unpublished, transcribed autobiography, 1973.

Phelan, Arthur. Former Chief Engineer, Northrop Turbodyne. Interview with author, 1982.

"Propulsion Performance for the Pratt & Whitney STF 686 Turbofan and STS 678 Single or Counter-rotating Turboprop Engines." For NASA, Hampton Roads, VI, February 28, 1984.

Rae, Dr. John. Professor and Aviation Historian, Harvey Mudd College, 1983. Interview with author, 1985.

Report of the Annual Meeting of Shareholders. Los Angeles: Northrop Corporation, May 27, 1986.

———. Los Angeles: Northrop Corporation, May 21, 1980.

Richardson, John. Northrop Vice President for Industrial Relations. Interview with author, 1987.

Ropelewski, Robert R. "F-5E Keyed to Agility for Combat." *Aviation Week & Space Technology*, July 12, 1971.

Sears, Dr, William. R. "Recollections of the Northrop Flying-Wing Program." Unpublished paper, n.d.

———. Interview with author, 1987.

Scarborough, Rowan. "The Selling of the F-20." *Defense Week*, May 19, 1986.

Schemmer, Benjamin F. "Financial Analysts Estimate Stealth Bomber Costs Within 4% of Each Other." *Armed Forces Journal International*, October 1987.

Stanley, Max. Former Northrop test pilot. Interviews with author, 1984–1987.

Sweetman, Bill: "What You Don't See is What You Get." *Washington Post*, May 18, 1986.

———. *Stealth Aircraft. Secrets of Future Airpower.* Osceola, WI: Motorbooks International, 1986.

Symington, Stuart. Former Secretary of the Air Force. Correspondence with author, 1987.

"T-38 *Talon* Completes Quarter Century With Air Force." Hawthorne, CA: *Northrop News*, Aircraft edition. August 28, 1987.

"Technical and Economic Assessment of Span-Loaded Cargo Aircraft Concepts." By McDonnell Douglas Corporation for NASA, Long Beach, CA, January 1976.

"Technical and Economic Assessment of Swept-Wing Span-Distributed Load Concepts for Civil and Military Air Cargo Transports." By Preliminary Design Department, Boeing Commercial Airplane Company for NASA, Seattle, WA, October 1977.

Ulsamer, Edgar. "Shaping the Force." *Air Force Magazine*, January 1987.

Vartabedian, Ralph. "Northrop—a Company in Turmoil." *Los Angeles Times*, December 20, 1987.

Wolford, Roy. Former Northrop company photographer. Interview with author, 1987.

Wood, Carlos. Former Douglas and Chance Vought Chief Engineer. Interview with author, 1987.

Woolridge, E.T. *Winged Wonders: The Story of the Flying Wings.* Washington, DC: Smithsonian Institution Press, 1983.

INDEX